WRITING WITH PRECISION

Jefferson D. Bates is a former Editorial Director of the U.S. Air Force's "Effective Writing Program," and a former chief speech writer for NASA during Projects Gemini, Apollo, and Skylab. He has more than forty years of experience in general and technical writing and editing, teaching, and lecturing. For almost a decade he served as President of Speak/Write Systems, Inc., a consulting firm that trained students and business people in writing and public speaking. The author of numerous books, including *Writing Out Loud*, *The Portable Office*, and *The Executive's Guide to Conferences, Meetings, and Audiovisual Presentations*, Bates has ghostwritten articles for such publications as *The New York Times*, *The Washington Post*, *The Saturday Evening Post*, and *National Geographic*. He lives in Reston, Virginia.

Writing with Precision

How to Write
So That You Cannot Possibly
Be Misunderstood

Jefferson D. Bates

P E N G U I N   B O O K S

PENGUIN BOOKS
Published by the Penguin Group
Penguin Putnam Inc., 375 Hudson Street,
New York, New York 10014, U.S.A.
Penguin Books Ltd, 27 Wrights Lane,
London W8 5TZ, England
Penguin Books Australia Ltd, Ringwood,
Victoria, Australia
Penguin Books Canada Ltd, 10 Alcorn Avenue,
Toronto, Ontario, Canada M4V 3B2
Penguin Books (N.Z.) Ltd, 182–190 Wairau Road,
Auckland 10, New Zealand

Penguin Books Ltd, Registered Offices:
Harmondsworth, Middlesex, England

First published in the United States of America
by Acropolis Books 1978
This new, expanded edition published in Penguin Books 2000

1 3 5 7 9 10 8 6 4 2

LIBRARY OF CONGRESS CATALOGING-IN-PUBLICATION DATA
Bates, Jefferson D., 1920–
Writing with precision : how to write so that you cannot
possibly be misunderstood / Jefferson D. Bates.—[Rev. ed.]
p. cm.
ISBN 0 14 02.8853 8
1. English language—Business English.   2. English language—
Rhetoric.   3. Business writing.   I. Title.
PE1479.B87B37   2000
808'.06665—dc21   99–046544

Printed in the United States of America
Set in ITC Garamond
Designed by Kate Nichols

To Mr. B. and Susie,
who first inspired my love for
the English language.

Credo

I BELIEVE that writers have responsibilities to their readers. The first of these responsibilities is never to waste the reader's most valuable commodity—time. The second, closely related and just as important, is to strive diligently to write clearly, concisely, and PRECISELY.

I BELIEVE that anyone in business or government who writes documents affecting the lives of the public has a special obligation to honor these responsibilities.

I BELIEVE that anyone willing to expend the effort can learn to write plain English that says what it means and means what it says.

That's what this book is all about.

Contents

Preface to the Penguin Edition

*We can lick gravity, but
sometimes the paperwork
is overwhelming!*
—Wernher von Braun (1912–1977)

Management expert Peter Drucker says that *the one basic skill
needed in industry is the ability to organize and express ideas in
writing and speaking.*

What's the most practical and effective way for people to learn
that skill? That's a problem Mr. Drucker doesn't address. I suppose
I should be glad. Otherwise I might not have spent the last 50
years wrestling with the realities of trying to teach myself and others how to write clearly and effectively.

Half a century ago, students were (at least) exposed to courses
in grammar, rhetoric, and composition. Today, many college grad-
uates, even the brightest ones, have never learned to write a de-
cent English sentence.

That's the problem *Writing with Precision* addresses.

Today's workers and job seekers need information they can
learn and apply quickly. Pressures pile up; there's no time to fool
around. Facts, not theory, must be the watchword. I've done my
best to give you a useful, down-to-earth, and practical approach.
This new edition of my book summarizes a lifetime of work. My
greatest hope is that it will help the generations that follow me to

express their thoughts clearly and precisely. I'm proud of it, but I constantly wish that it could be even better.

In preparing this update, I've agonized over how much I should change the many examples and references I've drawn from the 1970s and '80s. I eventually chose to follow the adage, "If it ain't broke, don't fix it."

Many of the persons to whom I owe the most, including my mentors, James R. Aswell and Mazie Worcester, and my long-time partner, Charles ("Chuck") Waterman, are now "long gone." It has often seemed too painful to change earlier text referring to these great people and dear friends as if they were still living. In my mind and heart, they are.

I'm now beginning my 80th year. I've managed to outlive many of the pioneers in this business. If I can just last long enough, maybe I'll get to be the dean of effective writing. Not!

Remember, this book's prime concern is with basic principles. But, as you improve your skills, you'll become more and more concerned with the finer points of writing and editing. That's why I recommend many books that you might want to seek out for further study. Don't overlook the bibliography.

You know as well as I do that many of the world's greatest problems stem from faulty communication. Someone writes something one way, and someone else reads and interprets that writing in a different (often an opposite) way. This happens all the time. I want to help you avoid the pitfalls. Don't fail me!

Preface

Less than a month after taking office, President Jimmy Carter issued an order; in future, all federal directives must be written in clear and straightforward language.

No instant miracles occurred.

Veteran bureaucrats smothered yawns. Then they went on grinding out ponderous prolixities and polysyllabic pomposities. On the surface, at least, nothing had changed.

Don't you believe it! For, as John Barrymore remarked when asked why he liked playing roles in which he kissed the ingenue's hand, "You have to start somewhere."

And President Carter had started something.

He had taken the first and most important of the four steps it will take to "straighten out the [writing] mess in Washington," if we may paraphrase President Eisenhower, The steps go like this:

1. An order must come down from the top.
2. All the high-ranking members of the administration must join in the battle.

3. Middle management must be convinced that communications can really be written in plain English without losing face.
4. Writers must be taught a few basic principles of clear writing, and trained editors must be spotted around at strategic positions to make sure these principles are applied.

Zero Base Gobbledygook

There have been starts before—starts that came to sad and untimely ends. But this time there's a good chance for things to be different. As I've said, we already have step one: the demand for clear writing came as an order from the top instead of as a wistful hope from the bottom. That's a real switch.

Step two is also under way. The then head of the Civil Aeronautics Board, Chairman Alfred Kahn, wrote a memo expressing his abhorrence of the artificial and hyperlegal language that is sometimes known as "bureaucratese or gobbledygook." His memo went on to spell out some specific abominations and some suggested remedies for stamping them out.

Cynical Washington newswriters quickly concluded that Chairman Kahn did not understand the ways of bureaucracy, but evidence piled up that they might have judged too quickly. Kahn was no tyro. He had earned his spurs fighting similar battles in New York State. The word is out that he's making good headway at CAB.

Next, *The Washington Post* reported (July 18, 1977) that Daniel O'Neal, then Chairman of the Interstate Commerce Commission, had set up an EO (Eschew Obfuscation) Committee—also known as the ZBG (Zero Base Gobbledygook) Committee—to see that ICC regulations were written in English. "They are now in Cro-Magnon, it is believed," said the *Post*. Chairman O'Neal wrote an excellent memo to his agency as a follow-up. I am grateful to him for permission to reprint portions of his memo in Chapter Nine.

Private Business Joins the Battle

Government in Washington gets most of the flak for poor writing, but private industry has always contributed its share. In recent months, there have been several examples of groups that have decided to clean up their own writing acts. The National Bank of Washington leaped on the bandwagon by rewriting many of their official documents in everyday language.

Public schools in the metropolitan area have programs to teach their students to write clear and logical compositions. In Montgomerey County, Maryland, the top brass of the school system declared war on "education-ese," a specialized jargon bearing absolutely no relationship to English.

The legal profession is also shaping up, largely at the urging of Jim Miner and his associates who teach seminars in legal writing for the American Bar Association.

For years some of my friends in the writing profession have been advocating a draconian solution, quoting Shakespeare's famous line: "First . . . let's kill all the lawyers." Now, if Jim Miner and his friends keep up their good work, we'll see the millennium yet.

Winning Over Middle Management

This step may not be easy, but again things are looking promising. A whole generation of middle managers has moaned piteously that they would write beautiful, crystal-clear prose—if only the top brass would let them do it. Very few of them ever showed me any actual samples, but I always wanted to believe them.

Many of them write the way they do because they think that's the way they're supposed to write. Honest to God. A young friend of mine wrote a nice clear letter a few months ago, and his supervisor sent it back and told him to "garbage it up a little," I quote.

Another young person I know wrote a memo that started "As we discussed by telephone. . . ."

Somebody sent it back. "We can't write that way around here. You must say telephonically." I swear I am not making this up.

Preaching the Gospel of Clear Writing

So it looks as if the time has come for some hardsell education. We must get the word out that administrative writing doesn't have to be gobbledygook. And we must remind administrators that they already know quite a lot about good writing if they will only think about it and put what they know into practice.

That's what this book is all about.

Acknowledgments

*The man is most original who can adapt
from the greatest number of sources.*

—Thomas Carlyle (1795–1881)

If Thomas Carlyle was correct, I must be a very original writer. This treatise owes a debt to "every book I've ever read and every person I ever knew." Even that statement is "borrowed"—straight from Bergen Evans's acknowledgments for his Dictionary of Quotations. Where better could one lift a quote?

English majors are always told that "borrowing from one book is plagiarism, while borrowing from many is scholarship." By this definition *Writing with Precision* is a scholarly work. For more than 40 years I've been collecting books on writing, style, composition, rhetoric, grammar, and related subjects. Over the years they have gradually mixed together in my mind like a rather untidy English pudding. Thus, when I began to track down the sources of many of the ideas in this book, it took considerable detective work. Any lack of success is not because of a corresponding lack of effort.

For the record, when borrowing well-known phrases from equally well-known writers—as I am occasionally wont to do—it seems a bit stuffy to use quotation marks. Clearly, all you highly literate readers will know that "a consummation devoutly to be wished," or "to the manner born," used nowhere in this book except right here, didn't originate with me!

Writing a book on writing presents special problems. You readers know, of course, that everyone (except you, of course) who reads such a book takes fiendish delight in shooting down the writer for any malfeasance. This book should give joy to many a heart, in ways this writer shall discover when it is too late.

But no—what I refer to here is the problem of who gets the credit line when a term must be defined—for example, noun, pronoun, etc. Most of us first encounter these terms in grade school. If any single individual deserves a tip of the hat here, it is probably the late Frank Colby. About 30-odd years ago he used to write a scholarly and witty column on usage that I admired, read religiously, and learned a lot from. I have not knowingly stolen any of his definitions, but I have certainly been inspired by his approach. He was deeply concerned with defining in plain, nontechnical terms. So am I.

Thanks to Books and Authors . . .

The debt this writer owes to the works of Rudolph Flesch, Robert Gunning, H. W. Fowler, Walter B. Pitkin, and Bergen Evans should be obvious. Less obvious, perhaps, is the influence of some others, including Jack Woodford, Theodore Bernstein, Wilson Follett, Robert Graves, Alan Hodge, Roy Copperud, Dr. Isaac Asimov, and Dr. James Boren.

Thanks for Permission . . .

Thanks and appreciation for the use of copyrighted material to Bill Gold and *The Washington Post* for permission to use excerpts from "The District Line" column; to William and Mary Morris and Harper and Row, Publishers, Inc., for permission to use excerpts from *The Harper Dictionary of Contemporary Usage*; to John Kidner and Acropolis Books Limited for permission to use quotations from *The Kidner Report*; and to Colman McCarthy and Acropolis Books Limited for permission to use quotations from *Inner Companions*.

Some of the material (contained in Part Two of this edition) was published in article form in *The Editorial Eye*, a newsletter for professional writers and editors produced by EEI (formerly Editorial Experts, Inc.).

For earlier editions, special thanks to former Chairman A. Daniel O'Neal and his staff at the Interstate Commerce Commission for permission to reprint portions of the memo, "English—let's use it at the ICC," and for giving me the idea for the subtitle, "Zero Base Gobbledygook," used in earlier editions of this book.

Thanks to Mentors . . .

With all respect to those listed above, much of what this book preaches does not come out of other books. It stems in large measure from the teachings of a few mentors. First on this list must come James R. Aswell and Mazie (Rodgers) Worcester, whom I told you about in the preface. I did not think to mention the next three "master teachers" in the first three editions, but in retrospect I should have. They were all very important influences in my life. So, belatedly, my thanks to:

Miss Martha Shea, who taught English Comp I at my alma mater, Southeast Missouri State College (now Southeast Missouri State University), Cape Girardeau, Missouri. Miss Shea was a phenomenon—an emeritus member of the faculty, well into her seventies (almost as old as I am now!) when I took her course. Her influence probably explains why I use more commas than people do nowadays. (Of course, I use more parentheses and dashes than most, too. That's not Martha Shea's fault. She used to give me hell for it—in a most ladylike way.)

Dr. H. O. Grauel, who required his students at Cape to write daily compositions on cards of his own design, well-known on campus as "Grauel Cards." He taught us how important it was—and is—to be concise, even when we used both sides of a card. His influence doubtless explains why I've used index cards as one of my major writing tools for more than 40 years.

Miss Helen Cleaver, an inspiring teacher of French and Spanish who gave me valuable insights into the Romance roots of English.

Thanks to Colleagues . . .

We can learn from our peers. I owe the most to my friend and colleague who used to sit at the desk next to mine at NASA—Virgil Carrington "Pat" Jones. It was largely at his urging that this book was written. He has blue-penciled the manuscript at several stages—probably not harshly enough, because he is one of the last true gentlemen of this world. I accepted many of the changes he recommended, and if I had good sense I would probably have taken the rest.

Special Thanks are Due Also to . . .

My wife, Poggy, for help with the manuscript, library research, and (at least most of the time) a tolerant attitude.

Louis J. Hampton and Charles E. ("Chuck") Waterman, who prepared many of the additional exercises in Part Four of this book.

John McJennett, editor-writer and information specialist, Department of State and NASA (where we shared an office as fellow speechwriters for a couple of years).

Linda McJ. Micheli, Ph.D., poet and instructor in writing.

Lillian Levy, NASA's Senior Science Writer, who first encouraged me to teach seminars in effective writing.

Ralph Gibson, Randolph Hawthorne, and Miles Waggoner, all of NASA's Office of Public Affairs, and all former colleagues.

Carl Sieg, management specialist and seminar leader.

About this Book . . . Who Needs It?

Professional Writers?

If you write for a living, this book is probably not for you. The approach may appear overly simplistic. Perhaps it is.

On the other hand, it just might remind you of some of the basic principles you've known for years, but probably haven't thought about much since your school days. A bit of review now and then seldom hurts anyone.

Business Managers, Industrialists, Professionals . . .

If you belong to any of these categories, it is almost certain that you're not a professional writer. But chances are you're in a job that calls either for writing or for editing the work of others. This book is designed to help you do both. Welcome!

Scientists, Engineers, Mathematicians . . .

You have probably come this far without ever having been exposed to more than the barest minimum of English Comp courses.

Furthermore, you probably didn't like them very much. Still, your job almost undoubtedly calls for some writing, and you'd like to be as precise and workmanlike as you are in your technical specialty. This book gives you a down-to-earth and practical course in how-to-do-it.

Government Workers, Members of the Armed Forces ...

Many of you are the civil service or military equivalents of the various management and professional positions mentioned earlier. You are aware, as I always was during my years as a government employee, that you have a reputation for writing gobbledygook. Make sure it's not deserved. Clear writing that says what it means is needed both in and out of government. This book recognizes the special problems you face.

Students ...

From what you've seen so far, you may think that this book is written solely for those already on the job. You may feel that it can't work for you. Don't believe it. When readers are asked to remember what they've learned about English in school, you have a head start. This will more than make up for your lack of on-the-job experience. Studying this book, which is oriented toward the problems of the real world, will help prepare you for the kind of writing you must do when you get out of school and into the job market.

Readers Whose Native Language is not English ...

In recent years I have done my best to learn how to help nonnative readers learn how to handle some of the problems inherent in so-called "American English," and furnished some explanatory comments on a few idiomatic expressions and related subjects. Admittedly, these notes are only a beginning. But as I say more than once in this book, "You have to start somewhere."

Teachers . . .

Teachers, you too can profit. Some of the worst gobbledygook in the world is the variety called "education-ese." Here's a chance to fight back!

The Approach

This book grew out of material I put together as instructional material for courses in Effective Writing that I originally taught under the auspices of Georgetown University's Continuing Management Education Program. But, since you may be reading it on your own, I've designed it to double as a "self-teaching" instruction book and handbook.

You may be temporarily confused when you discover that *Writing with Precision* starts with *editing*—not *writing*.

Does this seem to be putting the cart before the horse? Well, it really isn't. Writing is a devilishly hard job, at best. It takes even the best writers many years to learn their skills, and they must keep learning always—at least if they're concerned about writing well. My seminar students and readers have often taught me new tricks, and I've been at the trade for a long time.

But what we all want and need is information we can learn and apply quickly. The work keeps on going; we don't have time to fool around. Facts, not theory, must be the watchword.

So, in this book I try to practice what I preach, and follow Axiom Number Three: Get straight to the point. You will immediately begin to learn some tricks of the trade you can put to work right away—not next year, not next month, but today. To do this, you will start with some basic editing skills.

The very first editing principle you learn will cut your average sentence length by at least 25 percent. You don't need to be told that most administrative writing is far too long. That's one reason we are all suffocating under mountains of paperwork. So what could be a better way to start?

The rest of the Ten Principles are not so spectacular, but each one will increase readability and effectiveness. All are simple and easy to understand. Each one tackles a frequently encountered problem in administrative writing. Many things you worried about in high school or college composition classes won't even be mentioned here—mostly because they simply don't occur in administrative writing. In 40 years, I've hardly ever seen a run-on sentence, for example. So the only time you'll find that problem mentioned in this whole book is right here.

The principles you will learn are not the be-all and end-all, but experience shows they can eliminate about 75 percent of the worst problems found in everyday correspondence. Ladies and gentlemen, that's a damned good start!

Part 1

Writing with Precision

1

Introduction

The most dangerous illusion that a good writing course will try to shatter is that creative writing is teachable. Writing is; creating isn't. The most a writing course can do is expose the future writer to rules, techniques, habits, styles, and ideas that make it easier to be taught by oneself, not by another, how to create.

—Colman McCarthy, *Inner Companions*[1]

Can Good Writing be Taught?

That depends on what kind of writing you mean.

If you're talking about "creative" writing, whatever that is, the answer is an emphatic NO. (And that is the kind of writing Colman McCarthy is talking about in the paragraph quoted above.) Admired literary figures such as James Joyce, Willa Cather, Ernest Hemingway, and John Steinbeck did not learn to write the way they did by listening to learned professors or participating in classroom discussions. Their kind of writing (for simplicity, let's call it "creative" writing) does not come out of academic exercises or textbooks on composition and rhetoric.

First of all, a creative writer must have talent: that is the basic in-

[1] For all you readers who care about such things, this inscription at the head of each chapter is called an *epigraph*. For many years I have used this device at the beginning of each chapter I write, because the chosen words help set my theme for the chapter very quickly. Also, and perhaps even more important, these epigraphs offer me an easy way of saying wise, witty, or humorous things that I wouldn't have been able to think of by myself.

gredient. Undoubtedly, even a born literary genius can and does polish and improve that basic gift, but no creative writer is worthy of being called by that name unless the talent is there to start with.[2]

BUT if you are talking about writing as a craft rather than writing as an art, that's another story. If you are concerned with what we might describe as "practical" or "useful" writing—clear, precise, well-organized writing that's easy to read and understand—the answer to your question is YES.

The skills and crafts of useful, practical writing can be taught—and learned. Rest assured, however, that acquiring those skills takes plenty of hard work and continuing application. Writing—any kind of writing—isn't easy. And writing that communicates clearly and precisely is hard work indeed. It requires turning on the brain,[3] and few of us enjoy doing that.

Well-crafted writing, whether literary or useful, can be beautiful. Some lucky individuals can write what my friend Miles Waggoner would call a "singing line." (Miles knows because he can write that kind of line himself.) Others may work hard for a lifetime and never achieve it, or if they upon occasion do, it is only by accident.

But many of the rest of us, by diligent study and practice, can learn to put together a respectable English sentence. That in itself is no mean feat.

This book is concerned with "useful" writing only: communicating ideas as clearly and crisply—as precisely, if you will—as possible. Doing that is a never-ending and often thankless task. It requires our continuing attention; we get lazy and fall

---

[2]Some writers today continue to hold on to the long outmoded belief that one should never end a sentence with a preposition. Most of the experts whose opinions I value will tell you this idea is totally wrong. For a detailed discussion, look up "*Prepositions—ending a sentence with*" in the Handbook section.

[3]A variation on an ancient joke (before the days of automatic transmissions) that compares the process of "turning on the brain" to the necessity for engaging the clutch before shifting gears. I had no particular reason for using it here except that I like the sound of it.

into slovenly habits if we don't keep our minds constantly on the job.

What Is Good "Useful" Writing?

Writing is a subjective study in many ways. You and I may not admire or appreciate the same kinds of writing—chances are we often don't—yet we both may be confident our own opinions are best. Quality in anything, after all, is intangible. A writer whose talent I admire—Robert M. Pirsig—filled page after page in an effort to define "Quality." He generated many thought-provoking ideas, but didn't succeed in defining "Quality"—certainly not to his own satisfaction. (Read his *Zen and the Art of Motorcycle Maintenance* anyway. It's an astonishing book.)

How, then, are we going to decide what good writing is, let alone, how are we going to achieve it?

Happily, the decision is not so difficult as it might at first appear. Sample the comments of some of the recognized experts and you'll find more of a consensus[4] than you might expect.

Surprising?

Not at all. What is perhaps more surprising is that you, the readers of this book, already have a sound conception of what constitutes clear, useful writing even though you've not given the matter much thought since you were in school.

What makes me think so? For more than 30 years I've been asking office workers, students, editors, professional writers—even the ubiquitous "average citizen"—the same questions:

"What are some of the basic elements you believe are important to good, clear, useful writing? What makes such writing different from poor or imprecise writing that is hard (or impossible) to understand? Can you give me some 'rules'?"

---

[4]This word is frequently misspelled, through confusion with the word "census." I have spelled it properly here. While we're on the subject, many editors will tell you that to say "consensus of opinion" is redundant. I have willingly gone along with that belief. (Just for the record, though, I'll tell you that many dictionaries and style books say there's nothing wrong with the expression.)

I'm no longer surprised to find that people almost always come up with essentially the same answers. Those answers, not arranged here in any particular order of importance,[5] invariably go something like this:

- Be concise. Keep sentences and paragraphs short.
- State your purpose clearly.
- Get straight to the point.
- Be specific; avoid abstractions.
- Know your audience.
- Write to be understood, not to impress.
- Prefer the active voice. Put action in your verbs.
- Weed out unnecessary words, phrases, and ideas.

And so on. Before you go on reading, try this experiment. Ask some of your friends and associates to give you some "rules for clear writing." I'll wager they respond with essentially the same kind of list, with more variations in form than in content.

But, you might ask, if people already know all this, why don't they practice what they preach? (You don't have to look beyond the correspondence on your own desk to discover that they—and you—don't.) Why don't they? And why don't you? Two very good questions. Most of the rest of this book will be devoted to answering them.

---

[5]I originally made up this list "off the top of my head" (an idiomatic expression meaning "offhand"). I wrote it down at a time when this book was still just a nebulous idea existing only in my mind. I had not even started to put my "rules" in their logical order. If you prefer a list that goes in order of importance, see the "Ten Principles" set forth in Chapter Two. (As an aside, you may be interested to know that the first "rule" in Strunk and White's highly respected *Elements of Style* is concerned with when writers should use an "apostrophe s" in forming a possessive. My comment: It is certainly not the most important "rule" in the book, but they had a perfect right to put it wherever they wanted to. Ironically, hardly any working writer I know pays any attention to that particular "rule" these days, although, perhaps out of deference, I always follow it myself. For example, I prefer writing "Bates's" to "Bates' " and always write it that way.

Why the Confusion About "Good Usage"?

Is there such a thing as "good usage" or "correct usage" any more?[6] If you've done much reading on the subject, you may wonder.

This is in spite of the fact that the experts in conventional or traditional grammar[7] agree almost unanimously. What seems to be the problem?

Well, traditional or conventional grammar has been under a concerted attack for some time—from the influential group of scholars known as structural linguists. When you or I hear or read statements made by members of this important branch of linguistic science, we must listen with respect—even when we bump into theories that seem "far out" to us. For example, "A native speaker of a language cannot make a mistake." That statement is one I've heard frequently; possibly you've heard it too.

No wonder we're confused. Either the statement is ridiculous, or there's no such thing as "correct usage" any more. Right?

Wrong. On the one hand,[8] we can't afford to dismiss the opin-

---

[6]Some writers would prefer "anymore" to "any more." My trusty old *Merriam-Webster's Second* shows only the two-word version. The much newer *Oxford Complete Wordfinder* shows one word. For further discussion of this subject, see Chapter 19 in Part Two of this book.

[7]Again, I suppose I'm showing my age. As a child of my times, I grew up learning what was then the only kind of grammar there was. Noam Chomsky and his colleagues had not yet invented "structural linguistics" and "transformation grammar." I willingly admit that the scholarship of structural linguists has added much to our understanding of the way language works. In view of my admitted crotchets, it's not easy for me to say this!

[8]Some years ago, an editor who read an earlier version of this manuscript called me on the carpet for using the expression "on the other hand," without having first used "on the one hand." In all my years of writing and editing, I had never before encountered any such "rule," and I had read—and studied—literally hundreds of books on English usage and style.

Eventually I found one reference, *Modern American Usage*, by Wilson Follett, that backed my critic's assertion. "On the other hand," (now I'm playing games!) I have found dozens of examples by writers whose work I admire that pay no attention to this obscure "rule." (Even so, that critic battered my ego and weakened my self-assurance—I am now scrupulously careful about using both parts of the pair. Mind you, I'm not holding you to the same limitation. I'm perfectly willing for my readers to let their own consciences guide them.)

ions of the erudite scholars who preach the gospel[9] of structural linguistics. On the other hand, plenty of hard evidence shows traditional grammar is not yet totally out the window;[10] it still deeply concerns many persons, including most professional writers and editors.

In trying to sort things out, we must first be aware of one thing—the structural linguists, in making their statements about native speakers of a language, are referring almost entirely to the *spoken* language. (Many of them, apparently, believe that's the only language worth caring about. That's what raises my blood pressure!)

I can assure them—and you—that a great many people care very much about style and usage in the *written* language. And despite all the potshots taken at traditional grammarians, one fact is clear: the language of business, the language of government, the language in which our country's vital communications are conducted—all these are concerned with the supposedly "old-fashioned" or "outmoded" rules of traditional grammar and usage.

Still, the prime concern of this handbook is not with formal grammar. Plenty of excellent textbooks on that subject already exist. No. The aim here is to help you, the reader, learn to look at the writing and editing processes in a new and systematic way. As you learn, you'll begin to apply easy and logical principles that will immediately sharpen your writing. *Writing with Precision* is more than the name of this book—it's a goal you can shoot for every time you have to write.

Why Bother to Write Better?

Most business and government executives, when cornered, will tell you that writing is probably the most important single skill an ambitious young person can have. The ability to write well is rare; a person who develops the skill is likely to rise rapidly, so long as the talent doesn't threaten the boss and other powers that be.[11]

---

[9]A biblical reference used as an idiomatic way of saying "expounding on a principle one advocates."
[10]Idiomatic expression meaning "no longer in use."
[11]Idiomatic expression meaning "those in authority."

People who hate to write, or are afraid to try, often attempt to get by with talk instead. Sometimes this works. Other times (more often than not) it stirs up extra problems and wastes time, money, and energy. Why? Because without the discipline of writing, their spoken efforts often come out half-baked[12]—ill-conceived and ill-expressed.

Writing helps you think.

Communication breakdowns—or worse yet, total lack of communication—are probably the greatest causes of problems in both government and business.

The moral is simple: learn to write as crisply and clearly and effectively as you possibly can. Learn to say what you mean and mean what you say.

The Economics of Clear Writing

There are many other good reasons for learning to write better. One of the most important is simple economics.

Do you have any idea what it costs the average organization or agency to turn out a single one-page letter or memo? Take a guess.

If you guessed anything under $14.00, you're living in the past.

The latest figures available to me indicate that the cost per typewritten[13] page usually runs between $14.00 and $24.00, depending on various factors including the amount of research involved, and the number of management levels that have to "sign off" on the correspondence.

The computation includes (a) the time it takes an executive to figure out the problem, do any necessary research, and dictate the letter or write a rough draft; (b) the time necessary for the secretary or typist to transcribe, type, and proof. And that's the short, simple version.

---

[12]Idiomatic expression meaning "incompletely considered or planned."

[13]Since the original version of *WWP* was published, the old-fashioned "typewriter" has virtually disappeared from the scene. I've kept my original language here because it is still meaningful, at least to me. But nowadays, writers usually use the terms "word processors" and "keyboarding." Seldom has a new technology become established so fast.

In many organizations that would be only the beginning. The letter or memo was probably written by an underling for someone at a higher level to sign. Add the time of an executive in the next echelon—and perhaps of another one a notch higher than that—and so on, ad infinitum.[14] Now suppose that all of these worthies manage to insert a few editorial changes of their own. I'll bet you know plenty who would feel they aren't earning their pay if they don't mark things up enough to advertise their own expertise. Of course, even a minor change calls for a fresh keyboarding. The overall[15] cost can accelerate like a rocket. Even though most offices today are equipped with word processing equipment, the time saved in multiple retypings is not nearly so much as you probably imagine. The main advantage of such equipment is fewer errors—mind you, I'm not knocking that—and quicker revisions. (But then don't forget to add the monthly cost of your fancy machines to the overhead.[16])

All right, does it sound hopeless? How are we going to cut down the costs per letter before we all (government and industry) go broke.[17]

What if you could reduce the average length of each memo or letter your office turns out—by, say, about 25 percent. Think about it.

What if, simultaneously, you could reduce the time required to write each memo or letter by about that same percentage—or more? Think about that, too.

Because. . . if you follow the principles outlined in this handbook, you're going to achieve those results—time after time, day after day, from here on out to the golden days of retirement.

That's still only the beginning. There's more, lots more.

---

[14]Some editors would italicize "ad infinitum." I prefer not to, since the word appears in most dictionaries, and is today an accepted part of the English vocabulary.
[15]During most of my working life, I was careful to distinguish between "over-all" (an adjective), and "overall(s)" (a noun meaning "a kind of garment"). I have now given up; the distinction has totally disappeared in recent years.
[16]A term frequently used in business to mean "*basic* or *fixed* or *running* operating costs."
[17]Colloquial expression meaning "having no money."

How much time will your readers save if they can understand the communication the first time they read it instead of the second or the third or the tenth try? What if you are writing a regulation or an order that must be read by hundreds or thousands or millions of readers instead of just one? Think about all the potential savings in their work hours. Finally, consider how great it would be if each one of those umpteen[18] readers would no longer find it necessary to write you letters of inquiry (each of which is also costing somebody from $14.00 to $24.00) to ask what in the world you really meant. Maybe your company would have enough money left over to give you a big Christmas bonus. Or maybe the government could cut a few taxes.

Okay, maybe we're all dreamers. Still, it could happen.

I hope the point is clear. Writing that does not communicate effectively, concisely, and precisely is costly to both your own organization and to any person(s) or organization(s) doing business with you.

The Life You Save . . .

So far, everything I've said on this subject involves dollar economics—an important factor indeed, but not the most important. Over the years, many of my seminar students have been involved with writing rules and regulations. Some of these can quite literally mean life or death. Poor, ineffective, or ambiguous writing can kill people. We'd better do our best to remedy that situation, pronto.[19]

My own concern with precision came first with the editing of technical reports on complex military weapons; later, that concern intensified when I began trying to translate difficult Air Force regulations and instructions into language that even high school dropouts could read and understand. That was more than 40 years ago, and I've been concerned with precision ever since.

I realize, of course, that many of you readers will not be con-

---

[18]Informal or jocular term meaning "indefinitely many" or "a lot of."
[19]Colloquial adjective borrowed from the Spanish language, meaning "quickly" or "promptly."

cerned with matters of life and death. Even so, a bit of precision won't hurt a thing. The same care in writing that saves lives in one instance might save time or money in another. And that ain't bad either.[20]

Getting Down to Brass Tacks[21]

You can't build a house (a brick house, that is) without bricks. Words and sentences are the bricks—the building blocks—of the writing trade. So those basic items of words and sentences are going to be our first concerns. In the chapters that follow, you're going to work with those building blocks and learn how to sharpen your skills. What's more, you're going to concentrate at first on the *editing* process, not the *writing* process. Good editing is far from easy, but you can learn it much quicker than you can learn the far more complex processes of writing.

Equally important, as you train your editing eye, you'll find yourself gaining new insights into the problems and processes of writing and organizing. These latter tasks will become increasingly easy as you work through later units. This system has been verified by thousands of students who attended my seminars in Effective Administrative Writing at Georgetown University's Continuing Education Program and in other seminars sponsored by both government and industry.

Exercise: Brief Autobiography

At this point, take time out and write a brief autobiography—one or two handwritten pages. Write something about yourself, your job, your education, your interests, your family, your hobbies. What do you enjoy reading for pleasure? Have you published anything? If so, what?

---

[20]All my life I've heard the old saw, "There ain't no such word as *ain't*." I use the term here in what I intend to be a humorous cliché that was good enough for the great Mark Twain and a number of other writers who are not only my betters, but like him, objects of my admiration.

[21]Idiomatic expression meaning to get down to basic details.

Don't be self-conscious. This exercise is intended to give some idea of your present writing style. It may disclose some of the problems you'll need to work on later. Even if you are using this book independently, as a self-teaching device, please go ahead and write. You'll find you can analyze it yourself, later, after you've worked through Part One of this book.

Suggestion: You might have more fun doing this exercise if you stretch your imagination a bit. Consider trying an unusual approach or point of view, such as a third-person feature article, or an interview with yourself. Or here's another possibility that wouldn't have occurred to me a few years ago—writing one's own obituary could be an interesting enterprise. In my own case, this could be a good way—maybe the *only* way—of getting a favorable review.

Copyreading Marks

In the next chapter you will learn some of the skills of the copy-reader and editor. Illustrated below are some of the markings and symbols that professionals use. Study and learn them if you haven't already. It takes much less time to indicate by a hiero-glyphic what is to be done—use these marks and you won't have to spend nearly so much time spelling out instructions in detail.

Indent for paragraph	L or $\P$
Insert letter	...to furnish accomodations...
Delete and bridge over deletion	...to ~~better~~ make provision...
Spell out	...the (Pres.) notified Congress...
Abbreviate	..(General) Jones asserted...
Set in numerals	...a draft call of (seventy-nine) men was issued...
Spell out	(500) persons attended...
Transpose letters	...the f(ri)st to make the leap...
Transpose words	...was ⌐recently¬ awarded the prize...
Capitalize	...on Wilson st...
Make lower case	...J.D. Mine, Professor of Sociology...
Delete letter	...it benefitted millions...
Emphasize quotation marks edited in	...he said, "I won't go."
Emphasize commas edited in	...said he'd never, never go.
Emphasize apostrophes edited in	...said, "I'm not going."
Center, as by-line or subheads	]By James Williams[
Emphasize periods edited in	...to be at the ~~Coliseum.~~ field house®

2

The Craft of the Editor

No Passion on Earth
No Love or Hate
Is Equal to the Passion to Change
Someone Else's Draft.
—H. G. Wells (1866–1946)

Introduction

In this chapter, you'll learn some basics about the mysterious things an editor is supposed to do. Even more important—you'll also learn what an editor is NOT supposed to do. Next come a few tips on revising or self-editing. And finally, some useful checklists to make your editing process more thorough and systematic. With practice, you'll learn to perform these steps almost automatically.

Remember—walk before you run. The editing skills you learn now will mesh quickly with the writing skills that follow.

Duties and Responsibilities of the Writer: A Preview

You won't encounter exercises in the actual writing process until later in this book. Still, we should clear up one thing right now—where to draw the line on the division of responsibilities between writer and editor. Sometimes you'll be called upon to work on one side of the line, sometimes on the other. If you don't know where that invisible but highly important line is, you're doomed to failure in either case.

Always keep in mind that, first of all, *the writer is responsible for the technical content of a piece of writing.* The writer—not the editor—is supposed to be the expert on the subject matter. There are, of course, exceptions. If you happen to be the writer's boss, for example, that puts a different complexion on the relationship. You may assign a project to a subordinate who has less technical knowledge than you do. If so, you have good reason—as well as the privilege of rank—to question the facts presented as well as the manner of presentation.

Next recognize that *the writer is responsible for identifying the purpose of the writing.* The writer must decide what needs to be said, remembering always that to waste the reader's time is a cardinal sin. The editor should be free to second-guess[1] the writer by suggesting that more—or less—material should be used to convey the message clearly. The editor may also suggest ways of reorganizing the material to improve clarity or readability.

The writer must identify the audience and determine the best way of communicating the intended purpose directly and effectively to that audience. Here again, the editor may second-guess, and should feel free to suggest changes that should show clear-cut improvement.

The writer must learn (as you are learning now) *to employ editing skills, developing the ability to look with a cold eye at all those golden words, and to revise, revise, and revise again.* Later in this chapter, we'll discuss how you, as a writer, can edit your own work effectively.

Finally, as Allan Lefcowitz of the Writer's Center reminds me, *the writer must learn to have a professional attitude toward constructive criticism from the editor.* That isn't always easy. You'd be amazed at how much practice I've had at this over the years without ever learning to enjoy it. Apparently, some of my editors simply don't recognize the prerogatives of genius.

---

[1]Colloquial expression meaning "judge or criticize with the benefit of hindsight."

Okay, the lines of demarcation have been drawn. Let's get back to the nuts and bolts[2] of the editorial process.

Duties and Responsibilities of the Editor: A Preview

As an editor, your job is to improve the clarity, accuracy, and effectiveness—the *precision*, if you will—of any manuscript lacking any of these qualities. *It is emphatically NOT your responsibility to make changes for the sake of changes, or because of your own personal preferences (or prejudices).*

Furthermore, you must NOT change the original language so that it ends up saying something the writer didn't intend. Any time you alter the intended meaning, you overstep the bounds.

Still, the coin has two sides: suppose you discover that the writer has said something you have reason to believe is not what was intended. That's quite possible—indeed, it happens far oftener than it should. As an editor, you have a duty to point out the error—as tactfully as you can, but firmly enough to get the message across.

CAUTION: Any time you hear someone say "Do anything you like with this copy—I have no pride of authorship," watch out![3] What the writer is really saying is that there will be a knock-down-and-drag-out[4] fight over every single word you change. Everyone has pride of authorship, admitted or not. Writers simply will not sit idly by and let you carve up their brainchildren.

Take confidence from the fact that almost any editor worthy of the name can improve the work of almost any writer, however talented. The reason? A "cold eye." That is especially true when the original writer has drawn information from source material of dubious quality—badly organized, poorly written, or not factual.

---

[2]Idiomatic expression meaning "basic details."
[3]For a more detailed discussion of the relationship between writers and editors, see Chapter 25.
[4]"Colloquial expression meaning a "fight to the finish."

Some of these faults almost invariably rub off, a second writer or editor taking a fresh look has the immediate advantage of being one step further removed from the original garbage.

TEAMWORK is the key to a good relationship between writer and editor. Avoid the adversary attitude; even if you use all the tact at your disposal, there still may be times when you find yourself involved in a shouting match. Be aware that you'll win a few and lose a few. The more editing skills you learn, the more battles you'll win.

Here's a checklist of things a good editor should strive to do in going over a manuscript. We'll discuss these items—or at least most of them—separately as we progress through the handbook and exercises. Right now, you should find it helpful to see the items all at once.

Checklist of Editorial DOs and DON'Ts

DO—

- Make sure the reader is given all necessary information (Who-What-Where-When-Why-How)—in the clearest, most logical and orderly arrangement possible.
- Guard against factual errors; even though you're not the expert, you may know something the writer doesn't know. If you find mistakes and you know they are mistakes, correct them. If you're not sure, call the writer's attention to the problem with a FLAG. (See handbook section.)
- Correct all errors in grammar, punctuation, and spelling. Pay special attention to names, addresses, and figures. Check definitions and quotations.
- Make sure that all writing conforms to the accepted practices of your organization. (Check with the organization's style book, correspondence manual, or other published authority.)
- Watch out for double or ambiguous meanings and unconscious humor. (A touch of humor in itself is great, but not if it's accidental. Sometimes reading aloud will help you detect problems in this area.)

- Put yourself in the intended reader's place—watch the *tone* as well as the meaning. Guard against bad taste, officiousness, or other offensiveness. Read for the *connotation* (emotional overtone) as well as the *denotation* (definition) of words.
- Edit first for clarity and precision of meaning, then for conciseness of expression. But remember that conciseness can be an extremely valuable tool in obtaining the clarity you seek.
- Pay close attention to format. Help the reader get a handle by using appropriate typographical devices; headings, subheadings, bullets, numbered or lettered listings, italicized words, and indented paragraphs.
- Check "breakdowns" against "summaries." Add all figures to ensure that arithmetic is correct and consistent.

Now for the DON'Ts—

- DON'T make changes for the sake of changes.
- DON'T introduce errors of fact under the guise of making the writing easier to read and understand. Easy reading isn't much help if it gives incorrect information.
- DON'T take anything on faith. Be curious—and suspicious. Check out anything that sounds even remotely doubtful.
- DON'T permit overuse of technical jargon,[5] abbreviations, acronyms, or other technical shoptalk or shorthand. Remember, although they can save time and space when properly used, they may not be familiar to all readers. If there's a chance some readers won't understand them, urge the writer to spell out the terms (or define them in lay language) the first time they are used.
- DON'T be afraid of showing your ignorance if you're not sure about something. You'll find out the hard way that it's

[5]For a more detailed discussion of technical jargon, see Chapter 22.

much more embarrassing to let something get by that is wrong. Your readers will inform you of the error of your ways very quickly, and not always gently. So—play it safe. Ask an expert on the subject, particularly if you're working in an unfamiliar area.

You can't expect to remember all these items at first. Don't give up. With practice, they will soon become almost second nature. For the time being, just refer to this checklist and use it systematically, one step at a time. Before long you won't need the list.

The "Rules" of Editing

Nearly 40 years ago, I worked in the pioneering "Effective Writing Program" of the U.S. Air Force. It was a very educational experience. Our task was to rewrite Air Force regulations, manuals, and other official publications as clearly and precisely as we possibly could.

The writers I was supposed to be directing had their own opinions and ideas about how the job should be done. Diversity and originality are great, but we were getting more variety than the Chief of Staff really wanted. So we began to hold staff meetings to pull together the best ideas into a uniform approach. Those meetings evolved into my effective writing seminars—and after many years, this book.

As I have said, we were concerned with accuracy and precision above all else. Our First Commandment was to make official Air Force publications easier to read and understand without changing their meanings. The legal staff was constantly looking over our shoulders to make sure we didn't.

We mutually agreed that neither writing nor law can ever be an exact science. But we also agreed that you have to hang in there and try. As we compared notes, we began to detect patterns. We read the works of the pioneers of the field—Rudolph Flesch, Robert Gunning, Walter Pitkin, and others. We "borrowed" or adapted ideas that worked, and added ideas of our own. Eventually came the happy discovery that a few relatively simple "rules" would solve the great majority of the common difficulties.

The "rules" were, of course, not actually rules at all. There is nothing "official" about them. They haven't been handed down on tablets of stone. You may find that sometimes by breaking one or all of them, you may actually improve a given piece of writing.

Because we are concerned with using the right word instead of the almost right word, let's replace "rules" with "principles." That is what they really are. But whatever you call them, please learn them and apply them before you decide to break them!

I have revised and reorganized the list many times over the years, on the basis of continuing experience. This is the most recent version. I am listing them in summary form here; in later chapters, I'll elaborate and explain each one in detail.

Ten Principles for Improving Clarity and Precision of Written Documents

---

1. Prefer the active voice.
2. Don't make nouns out of good, strong "working verbs."
3. Be concise. Cut out all excess baggage. Keep your average sentence length under 20 words.
4. Be specific. Use concrete terms instead of generalizations.
5. Keep related sentence elements together; keep unrelated elements apart. Place modifiers as close as possible to the words they are intended to modify.
6. Avoid unnecessary shifts of number, tense, subject, voice, or point of view.
7. Prefer the simple word to the far-fetched, and the right word to the almost right.
8. Don't repeat words, phrases, or ideas needlessly. But don't hesitate to repeat when the repetition will increase clarity.
9. Use parallelism whenever it is appropriate—that is, when you are expressing similar thoughts, make sure you write

your sentences so that the elements are in similar or parallel form. But do not use parallel structure when expressing thoughts that are not truly similar.

10. Arrange your material logically. Always begin with ideas the reader can readily understand. If you must present difficult material, go one step at a time. Do not skip any steps. Arrange your format to give the reader every possible "handle" on the material.

Study and use these ten principles until they become second nature. Even if—Heaven forbid—you learn nothing else about grammar or style, these simple principles alone will eliminate most of the common errors of business writing.[6]

Editing Your Own Copy— Hardest Editorial Task of All

Why is it so hard to edit your own copy?

Mostly because you're so familiar with the ideas you are expressing that you may think you've stated them quite clearly when actually you have not. That's why a "cooling off" period is so important any time you aren't facing a tight deadline.

If possible, put your manuscript away when you finish it; work on a totally unrelated project. Keep your golden words in your hold basket or a bottom drawer for at least three days. By then they won't look quite so golden. You'll be able to spot problems you otherwise would have missed. And remember—even a brief cooling off is better than none.

The next suggestion may seem far out—particularly if you don't intend to become a professional writer or editor. On the other hand, many of my seminar students have told me they have learned to enjoy this little game.

Here's a simple tip: practice reading *everything* you come across—every bit of correspondence, every memo or report, even

[6](**NOTE**: Some of the grammatical or technical terms used in this chapter may not be familiar to you. You'll find definitions of these terms in the handbook section.)

your daily newspaper—with a stern and critical editorial eye. Does that sound dull? Not really. It can be fun. Almost every day you'll find choice little items such as this one—a caption that appeared beneath a picture on the sports page of the *Washington Star-News*,[7] 12 June 1976:

> Pele, the star of Team America, soothes the ankle he sprained in a scrimmage with an ice pack.

Editorial comment: You had better watch out for those fierce ice packs.

Or how about this one? Turnabout is fair play, so we'll quote a few lines from *The Washington Post*. Here's the first sentence of a movie review that appeared on 13 June 1976. Please note that the whole paragraph is just one sentence:

> The film-making husband-and-wife team of Volker Schlondorff and Margarethe von Trotta won quite a few admirers with "A Free Woman," but they should add quite a few thousand more with this compelling and thought-provoking adaptation of Nobel Prizewinner Heinrich Böll's 1974 novel about the grimly ironic repercussions of a case of character assassination by newspaper, inspired by the writer's own clashes with the peculiarly virulent and vindictive right-wing yellow press of West Germany.

Get the idea? Once you start looking, you can turn up gems such as these almost every day. In the process, you'll become more alert to the differences between good and bad, clear and unclear writing. Learning to recognize the differences will speed you along in the difficult process of becoming a better editor.

With practice, you'll soon learn the basic editing steps most professionals use. At first you'll proceed one step at a time, very sys-

---

[7]Sad to say, this excellent newspaper went out of business a few years after *WWP* was first published. I still miss it.

tematically. Later, as your skills improve, you'll combine several or all steps in a single pass.

Here is a brief checklist you can use as a reminder when editing your own copy:

Checklist of Steps in Revising or Self-Editing

---

1. Read all the way through your manuscript—or a unit of it, such as a section or a chapter—before you begin to make any editorial changes. Make sure you get the total picture. Ask the questions a newspaper reporter would ask: Who-What-When-Where-Why-How (and sometimes How Much), not necessarily in that exact order. Then carefully check to make sure you haven't omitted any of these essential facts.

2. Read through again; now begin to apply the principles described earlier in this chapter. If you find it easier to do so, take one principle at a time. That may seem slow at first, but as you get the hang of it, the process will go much faster. Pay special attention to getting rid of passive constructions and smothered verbs. You'll be surprised how this will sharpen and strengthen your writing.

3. Boil down sentences by making one word replace several words or a phrase. Cut the deadwood and redundancy. Keep the average sentence length under 20 words if you can. Remember, fewer words than that will usually be even better.

4. Re-read your manuscript one more time, aloud. The ear can detect flaws the eye misses. Check for logic and completeness; search for "wrong words" that are inappropriately used or have undesirable connotations. Put yourself in the reader's shoes and see if the writing tells the things he wants and needs to know. If necessary, add an example, a definition, or an analogy.

3

Editing for Strength

*The chief aim of the writer
is to be understood.*
—John Dryden (1631–1700)

Introduction

Administrative writing is loaded with passive[1] constructions, and I do mean loaded. Why?

Habit, mostly. Nobody has ever pinpointed where or when it happened, but the evidence is clear: somebody who had the power to do so must have laid down the law—administrative writing must be impersonal and indirect. Since that evil day, the style has caught on better than hula hoops or skateboards ever did. Passive constructions have multiplied faster than bunny rabbits.

But perhaps I'm getting ahead of myself. Let's begin at the beginning, which I should have done in the first place. You, the reader, have every right to be asking, "What in the world is a passive construction, anyway?" Some of you undoubtedly do re-

---

[1] I am appalled at how many supposedly educated people, including some world-famous television commentators, don't know the term "passive voice." Within a matter of days, when a lot of politicians were going around saying, "Mistakes were made," (one of the favorite applications of the passive voice), I heard three different commentators referring to "passive tense." The term *passive* has nothing to do with *tense*.

member the distinction between active and passive voice. Others probably haven't thought much about formal grammar or definitions for a long time—perhaps not since grade school or high school days. So I hope the rememberers[2] will forgive me for refreshing the memories of the forgetters.

Definitions of *Active* and *Passive Voice*

When a sentence is written in the *active voice,* the subject performs the action. When a sentence is written in the *passive voice,* the subject is acted upon. For example, *I rang the bell,* is in the active voice. *The bell was rung by me* is in the passive voice. Again, *This office completed the action,* is in the active voice; *The action was completed by this office* is in the passive voice. As you can see by these examples, the *active voice* gives writing a sense of strength, energy, vitality, and motion. The *passive voice* slows things down. Look hard at the memos and letters crossing your desk and see how many passive constructions you can spot. You'll probably be surprised. In government and business writing, one fault stands out: *overuse of the passive voice is by far the biggest single offense.*[3]

Most of the "experts"—Strunk and White, Gunning, Flesch, and all the rest—warn us against passives. But they put this particular "rule" well down the list. In my book (that's a pun, son) it comes up as Rule Number One. Nothing else you can learn will do so much, so quickly, to improve conciseness, readability, and precision.

Try it for yourself. Go through a piece of writing looking for passives; then rewrite the sentences using active constructions. Not only will the revised version be stronger and straighter, but it will be 20 to 30 percent shorter as well.

[2]I just made up this word, which can't be found in any dictionary that I know of. But I don't think readers will have the slightest trouble understanding exactly what I mean.
[3]All of you alert readers will notice that I have stated this offense in the passive voice. I didn't do it accidentally. On page 29, you'll find an explanation of the (rare) occasions when the passive is preferable.

This phenomenon, incidentally, is the strongest argument you have for convincing management that it's time for a change. Obviously, any device that can cut average sentence length by roughly a third—and that's what changing passives to actives can do—is worth using.

Make Every Word Count

We have said earlier, and now shamelessly repeat, that clear writing is concise. That doesn't mean quite the same thing as short; to be concise means, in a nutshell, that you make every word count, and eliminate all extraneous material.

Structural linguists (see, I quote them joyfully when what they say suits my purpose!) have found that in general writing, about 75 percent of all sentences follow the basic subject-verb-object (S-V-O) pattern. But, they tell us, in official writings—both government and industry—about 75 percent or more of the sentences are written indirectly. That is, the word that should be the *object* becomes the *subject*.

An Unwritten Rule?

I know that you're getting weary of hearing it. I'm weary of saying it, but it must be said: *There seems to be an unwritten rule that everything must be stated in the passive voice.* And that's what it is—an unwritten rule. Nowhere has any management ever spelled out any such rule. So, for Heaven's sake, let's wipe it out here and now. It's a bummer.

Passive constructions are bad enough any time, but they're worst of all when used in directives, instructions, or regulations. Suppose an organization posts a rule for its employees: *A copy of each sales letter originated in Division A will be submitted to the vice president in charge of sales.*

That sounds simple enough. But—is it likely to get the job done? Will the copies be submitted as ordered?

Perhaps they will. But then again, perhaps they won't. Who is actually responsible for carrying out the order? The trouble with this kind of passive construction is that it leaves out the key point—who is supposed to do the work?

Wouldn't it be better to say: *The sales manager for Division A must send the vice president in charge of sales a copy of each sales letter originated in the division.* (We know that the sales manager's secretary will probably do the actual sending, but we also know that the responsibility for the job has now been nailed down.)

Let's consider another example. Suppose we write something like: *This regulation will be explained to each new employee.* Who's supposed to do the explaining? The reader has to guess. Let's write, instead, *The branch chief will explain this regulation to each new employee.*

Perhaps I should mention that technical editing offers some slightly different problems. You've probably noticed that many experienced tech editors use passives constantly. Their reason for using the passive in such writing makes a bit more sense—namely, to keep the personal element out of the writing.

Here's a typical example:

> After the frammis is unscrewed from the doohickey, it should be thoroughly washed in solvent and inspected for cracks in the surface; then the threads should be checked before it is reinserted in the doohickey.

Still, wouldn't it be clearer to write:

> (a) Unscrew the frammis from the doohickey; (b) wash the frammis thoroughly in solvent; (c) inspect it for cracks in the surface; (d) make sure the threads are clean and not stripped; and (e) reinsert the frammis in the doohickey.

Most readers can follow this kind of instruction quite easily. The results will usually be much better than those achieved in following a straight narrative version of the same information. So, think twice before you buy the old "technical writing" excuse for using passives. Sometimes, maybe. All the time? No way.

When Should You Use a Passive Construction?

Does all this mean that the active voice is preferable to the passive voice every time?

Not at all. The passive exists for a reason. Sometimes you may be very glad it's available. It can be quite useful upon occasion.

For example, you should use a passive construction when the performer of the action is unknown or irrelevant. You can use passives to advantage, also, when the emphasis is (a) on the receiver of the action, (b) on the verb, or (c) even on the modifier.

Here's the rule of thumb I use in my own writing to ascertain whether an active or a passive construction would be preferable:

If the person or thing receiving the action is more important than the person or thing doing the action, use the passive.

If the person or thing doing the action is unknown or unimportant, use the passive.

For example, it would probably be better to use the passive in a sentence like this one: *The Senator was struck by a golf ball.*

The active-voice version, *A golf ball struck the Senator,* is actually a weaker construction in this instance. The key is that, after all, the Senator (or at least, we hope *most* Senators) can be considered to be more important than most golf balls.

All this lengthy dissertation has been leading up to what I consider to be the most important single principle for improving most administrative writing. Here it is in its own box:

Principle One: Prefer the active voice.

By now you should understand not only why this principle is important but you should also understand why we use the word "prefer." Remember that there are indeed some cases when the passive voice may be preferable.

What you need now is some actual practice in spotting passives and changing them to actives. Below, you'll find a preliminary exercise that starts simply, but gets a bit harder as you go along.

Preliminary Exercise: Passive Constructions

Change the passives to actives in the following sentences. Make other minor editorial changes you believe will improve strength or clarity, if you so desire.

1. The letter was written by the manager.
2. The accounts were balanced by a CPA.
3. A duplicate sales slip was furnished by the clerk.
4. A commotion was caused by the children in the front row.
5. An argument was prevented by the referee.
6. The papers were filed by the attorney for the defense.
7. It is requested that this report be submitted by 30 June.
8. A motion was made by John Smith to table the action until Tuesday.
9. The pistol was dropped by the burglar as he fled from the store.
10. The storeroom had been carelessly left unlocked by someone.

Did you have any trouble with any of these sentences? You probably did not, but if there are some you aren't sure about, you may find the following suggested rewrites helpful. (In this, as in most of the exercises in this book, you'll find there are seldom any absolutely right or absolutely wrong answers. Sometimes several different answers will be almost equally good or equally poor, with various gradations in between. You will have to learn to develop confidence in your own editorial judgment.)

On the next page, you'll find some suggestions for rewrites. Please don't look at these until you've done the exercise!

Suggested Rewrites for Preliminary Exercise:

Passive Constructions

1. The manager wrote the letter.
2. A CPA balanced the accounts.
3. The clerk furnished a duplicate sales slip.
4. The children in the front row caused a commotion.
5. The referee prevented an argument.
6. The attorney for the defense filed the papers. (*OR, perhaps you decided to make the sentence more concise by changing it to read,* "The defense attorney filed the papers." *If you did, that's great. You're already ahead of the game.*)
7. Please submit this report by 30 June. (*Note that this sentence, and others like it, can be restated crisply and clearly by using what we call, in the language of grammar, the imperative mood. The imperative expresses commands, such as* "Do your work; finish your assignment," *etc. We'll discuss the imperative further in later chapters. Note also that we keep the concept of a request rather than a command by using the word* "please.")
8. John Smith made a motion to table the action until Tuesday. (*OR, perhaps you improved the sentence even more by writing,* "John Smith moved to table the action . . .")
9. The burglar dropped the pistol as he fled from the store.
10. Someone had carelessly left the storeroom unlocked. (**NOTE:** *The* "had left"—*which is the past perfect form of the verb—is important. You should not have changed it to the straight past tense* "left." *Remember that you, as an editor, must preserve the same shade of meaning that the original writer intended. The past perfect tense indicates that an action or condition was begun in the past and completed in the past, before the other past action or condition.*)

Exercise: Passive Constructions

You will find a somewhat more difficult exercise in Part Three, at the back of this book, I hope you won't skip it. It is carefully designed to increase your understanding of the passive voice, how to recognize it, how to change it to the active voice, and, on rare occasions, how to use the passive voice effectively when it is preferable to the active voice.

Smothered Verbs

When I was studying English Comp I[4] back in the dark ages, one of my professors liked to talk about "controverted verbs"—an academic term for verbs that have been changed or transformed into nouns. Your teacher may call these *smothered verbs,* instead. This term means the same thing, and is a much neater appellation.

The main trouble with smothered verbs is this: any time you change a working verb to a noun, you must add another verb to complete the sentence. (To get back to basics, think of the definition of a sentence that you probably had to memorize back in the third grade: *A sentence is a group of words containing a subject and a predicate and expressing a complete thought.*) Obviously, then, when you smother a working verb, turning it into a noun, you will have to replace it with another verb in order to make a complete sentence. Usually, the word that replaces the working verb will be some form of *to be,* and there won't be any action.

Principle Two: Don't make nouns out of good, strong "working verbs."

What is a *working verb?* One that expresses action. Strong, working verbs are the backbone of English sentence structure.

---

[4]That's what we used to call the basic course in Freshman English that most colleges offered 50 years ago. The term "dark ages" is supposed to be humorous. Again, my advanced age and general decrepitude may be showing, but I think students learned more about writing English in those days than most of them do today. That's one of the main reasons I have kept trying to improve this book.

They are the engines that make sentences move; they put action into writing.

Why, then, should anyone want to change useful, hardworking verbs into long-winded nouns, by adding endings such as *-ance, -tion, -ization,* and so on? Frankly, I don't know, but it's a very popular custom in most administrative writing.

Let's consider an example or two:

SMOTHERED: Authorization for the absence was given by the leader.
IMPROVED: The leader authorized the absence.

You can see from this example that smothered verbs and passive constructions frequently go together. In fact, they are almost inseparable. If you can unsmother a verb and, at the same time, change a passive to an active construction, you'll cut sentence length by a third.

SMOTHERED: My new assistant is negligent in the details of his work.
IMPROVED: My new assistant neglects the details of his work.

It is also possible to derive adjectives from verbs. You can probably think of many words that have both a noun and a verb form, or an adjective and a verb form. Think hard and you may come up with some that have all three forms—*verb, adjective,* and *noun.* Sometimes a word may have exactly the same form as a noun and as a verb—for example, *answer, end, estimate, index,* and *reply.* Be aware of this, but don't worry about it. All you need to remember is that many problems that plague administrative writers stem from overuse of smothered verbs with endings such as *-ion, -tion, -ment, -ance, -ancy,* and *-ization.*

A simple preliminary exercise to use as a warm-up follows:

Preliminary Exercise: Smothered Verbs

Write the root verbs of the following:

1.	authorization	9.	documentation
2.	performance	10.	negotiation
3.	illustration	11.	concession
4.	implementation	12.	quotation
5.	advancement	13.	employment
6.	realization	14.	determination
7.	transmittal	15.	relation
8.	confrontation	16.	administration

You shouldn't have had any trouble with the preceding exercise, but if you have any doubts, you'll find the answers below. I hope you don't really need to look them up.

I devoutly trust you didn't lull yourself into saying "confrontate" or "documentate" or "administrate," which aren't legitimate words.[5] But if that happened, cheer up. You're not the first.

Answers for Preliminary Exercise: Smothered Verbs

(1)	authorize	(9)	document
(2)	perform	(10)	negotiate
(3)	illustrate	(11)	concede
(4)	implement	(12)	quote
(5)	advance	(13)	employ
(6)	realize	(14)	determine
(7)	transmit	(15)	relate
(8)	confront	(16)	administer

[5]Of course, if enough people keep using words incorrectly, eventually the bad will drive out the good. Sorry about that. Let's all do our best to hold the line.

4

Editing for Conciseness and Clarity

If it is possible to cut a word out, always cut it out.

—George Orwell (1903–1950)

Introduction

Most administrative writing contains a high percentage of unnecessary words and phrases. A skillful editor can often cut a manuscript by half, simply through pruning the deadwood.[1]

Here's a typical example:

BEFORE: This is in reference to your letter of 28 April, in which you requested further information about the status of your application and also queried as to whether or not it will be necessary for you to furnish additional references and supporting documents.

AFTER: We can finish processing your application as soon as you send us a certified copy of your military discharge certificate. That's all we need.

Note that the "Before" version contains 43 words, and hasn't even started. The reader is being told things already known, and

[1]Colloquial expression meaning "one or more useless people or things."

the answers to the questions will require still more words. The "After" version contains 24 words, answers both of the reader's questions, and requires no preliminaries.

The situation is somewhat different if you are answering, say,[2] an inquiry from a Senator, whose office turns out dozens or even hundreds of letters every day. You will help the Senator's staff (let's be realistic) figure out which letter (and which constituent) is involved by referring to the date and subject. But that's a different ball game.[3] In most letters to the general public, it is totally unnecessary to repeat what has been said in a letter to which you are responding. (The private individual doesn't write all that many letters.) Just be sure to phrase your answers in a way that will help recall the questions without the need for repeating them.

Why Is Conciseness So Important?

Numerous scientific and psychological studies show that long sentences are harder to understand than short ones. (Like many other scientific truths, this one seems much too obvious for all the bother about it.) You can easily check this out for yourself. Turn back to page 23 and read the one-sentence paragraph there. Time yourself. Now see how much of it you can remember. Fair enough?

When you have finished, try reading this mildly edited version the same way:

> The film-making husband-and-wife team of Volker Schlondorff and Margarethe von Trotta won quite a few admirers with "A Free Woman." They should, however, add quite a few thousand more with this compelling and thought-provoking adaptation of Nobel Prizewinner Heinrich Böll's 1974 novel. The book concerns the grimly ironic repercussions of a case of character

---

[2]"Say" is a word that has literally hundreds of uses and meanings. As I have used it here, it means "for example."

[3]Colloquial expression meaning "a particular affair or concern."

assassination by newspaper; it was inspired by the writer's own clashes with the peculiarly virulent and vindictive right-wing yellow press of West Germany.

By dividing this passage up into bite-sized ideas, this very simple editing makes life much easier for the reader. One of my early idols, the late Walter Pitkin, once wrote that a sentence ". . . grows worse by the square of the number of words it contains, to put it very roughly. A poorly built sentence of twenty[4] words is about four times as hard to attend to and to understand as an equally poor sentence of ten words." (*The Art of Useful Writing*, pp. 51–52.)

Pitkin's excellent advice about using short sentences has been strongly reinforced by the works of such "readability experts" as Rudolph Flesch and Robert Gunning. They (and many others) advise readers to keep their sentences short and sweet if they want to be read and understood. For a more detailed treatment of this subject, see **readability formulas**, listed alphabetically in the handbook section of this book.

You can follow their advice without having to write primer-like prose. Heaven forbid. A long succession of sentences, structured always in the simple declarative, is guaranteed to drive adult readers straight up the wall.[5] You know the kind I mean: *I see the cat. The cat is black. He is a nice cat.* I suspect that these sentences don't thrill children all that much either. No wonder they have such a rough time learning to read.

What can the writer do about this? Simple—just balance short sentences with longer ones. Keep the *average* sentence length under 20 words—and fewer words are even better, most of the time and for most readers.

Proper punctuation helps readers understand long sentences. (And keep in mind that long sentences are okay—once in a

---

[4]Because this is a direct quotation, I have not changed any of the words. If this were *my* sentence, I would have followed the style of the GPO Manual and written the numbers as "20" and "10."

[5]Colloquial expression meaning "to irritate or annoy severely."

while.) Good, workmanlike[6] constructions with clearly defined relationships and carefully placed modifiers can make such sentences easy to follow. But—beginners beware. George Bernard Shaw could fashion marvelously balanced sentences of 100 words or more. That doesn't mean the rest of us should rush out and try it.

Break some of the really long thoughts into shorter segments. Later, when you are doing readability tests or fog counts, remember that for such purposes you don't always have to consider the period as the only "full stop."[7] If you break up sentences with *semicolons, dashes, question marks,* and other punctuation marks that indicate a strong pause, that's okay. You don't have to rely on periods every time.

> **Principle Three:** Be concise. Cut out all excess baggage.[8] Keep your average sentence length under 20 words.

As we have seen, long and complicated sentences can make life very difficult for the average reader. Let's look briefly now at some of the underlying problems. Time and space permitting, we could spend many pages on this one subject, but we'll just try for the high points. Here are a few common difficulties to watch out for:

---

[6]Feminists conceivably might say that I shouldn't have used the word "workmanlike." Frankly, I anticipated criticism, and thought hard about whether I should use it here. After due deliberation, I concluded that it is exactly the right word to convey the intended meaning. I do NOT believe it is sexist.

[7]A predominantly British usage for the punctuation mark we call the "period." As an American, I gladly borrow this and other such usages when they seem particularly apt for expressing an idea. Some of my British colleagues might not agree with me that semicolons, dashes, and question marks can be considered as "full stops." I ask not that they agree, but that they keep an open mind.

[8]A term borrowed from the airline industry, meaning "baggage or luggage exceeding a weight allowance and liable to extra charge." By extension, the term has come to mean "something unnecessary and burdensome."

Redundancy

In the space program, "redundant" was a good word. In writing, it's a bad one. Space engineers borrowed the term, but in their parlance, a redundant component is a back-up to another used for the same purpose. It's designed to build in extra safety, and we can't fault that.

In space, it isn't so easy to go back for a spare part.

In writing, on the other hand, you almost never need a backup. Say a thing one time, clearly, and that should be ample. The reader, at least figuratively, can go back—re-reading, even several times, if necessary. So you, the writer, needn't waste words.

There are, as always, a few exceptions. In a long piece of writing, put a summary at the end, reiterating important points. This ensures that your reader will remember them, and saves time in the process.

To be concise, don't repeat words or ideas unnecessarily. Also, don't give both the positive and negative of an idea if one of them alone would suffice for understanding.

Suppose, for example, we have a statement to this effect:

It would appear that proper planning, coordination, and execution of the project, if achieved, will permit the building to be finished on time and within budget.

Now, continuing, this positive statement is followed by a negative:

However, we recognize that any failure during one or more of these important preliminary steps will undoubtedly result in a failure to meet the completion schedule and/or the likelihood of bringing in the project at higher costs than had been initially envisioned.

Why state this both ways? To save words, use one statement or the other, not both. And preferably, as Johnny Mercer[9] put it, "Accentuate the positive."

[9] A gifted American songwriter and lyricist, now deceased.

Wordiness

"Wordiness" is not the same thing as redundancy, but it's a first cousin. Wordy writing is caused by using more words than you need to express an idea. Watch out particularly for needless repetitions of the same word or words in a sentence or paragraph. For example:

WORDY: Company health records are further subdivided into two sections which are medical treatment records and dental treatment records. Medical treatment records will be contained in Form 20-A. Dental treatment records will be contained in Form 20-B.

Here's a suggested rewrite:

> Company health records are further subdivided into Medical Treatment Records (Form 20-A) and Dental Treatment Records (Form 20-B).

Conceivably, we could have cut another "records" or two, but perhaps at the loss of some clarity. So, don't repeat words unnecessarily, but don't be afraid to repeat if you think the reader will understand more clearly. Okay?

Sometimes the difference between redundancy and wordiness is not so clear. The following example to some extent illustrates a combination of the two:

> This regulation prescribes uniform policies and procedures by which servicing from the Department of the Air Force to the Department of the Navy may be effected in support of Military Air Transportation System (MATS) aircraft and personnel assigned by the Department of the Navy, and from the Department of the Navy to the Department of the Air Force in support of MATS aircraft and personnel assigned by the Department of the Air Force. This regulation applies to Air Force and Navy installations and activities in the Zone of the Interior and overseas.

Try your hand at rewriting. Then you can compare your version with the way we rewrote the paragraph in the Air Force "Effective Writing Program" more than 30 years ago. Maybe your version will be better.

> This regulation tells how the Department of the Air Force and the Department of the Navy can give reciprocal service to Military Air Transportation System (MATS) aircraft and personnel assigned by the other Department. This regulation applies to all Air Force and Navy installations and activities world wide.

Words With Overlapping Meanings

Another common fault in administrative writing stems from a bad habit that afflicts many of us. The words of certain trite phrases seem locked together in our minds; we carelessly use these words in the same combinations time after time. What's worse, we often pile up several of these offenders in the same sentence. One such expression leads to another, unless we stay constantly alert. Here are some typical examples. Keep a sharp lookout for them:

DON'T SAY	SAY
absolutely complete	complete
advance planning	planning
ask the question	ask
assembled together	assembled
continue on	continue
cooperate together	cooperate
consensus of opinion	consensus
each and every	each **or** every (not both)
enclosed herewith	enclosed
exactly identical	identical
expired and terminated	expired **or** terminated (not both)
repeat again	repeat
same identical	same
still remains	remains
the reason is because	because

Roundabout Prepositional Phrases

We have said that unnecessary words in a sentence stand between you and your reader. Some of the worst offenders are long-winded prepositional phrases. Many times you can cut down on them sharply by referring to the list below:

LONG-WINDED	STRAIGHTFORWARD
along the lines of	like
as of this date	today
as to	about (or leave out entirely)
at the present time	now
by means of	with, by
for the purpose of	for
for the reason that	since, because
from the point of view of	for
inasmuch as	for, as
in order to	to
in a position to	has, have
in the possession of	has, have
in a satisfactory manner	satisfactorily
in the case of	if
in view of	because, since
in the nature of	like
in the event of	if
in connection with	of, in, on
in relation to	toward, to
in the amount of	for
in a number of cases	some
on the basis of	by
on the grounds that	since, because
owing to the fact that	since, because
on the part of	by, among, for
on behalf of	for
on a few occasions	occasionally
prior to	before
subsequent to	after

with a view to	to
with reference to	about (or leave out)
with regard to	about (or leave out)
with the result that	so that

By all this I don't mean to imply that you should never use *any* of the phrases listed in the left column. Sometimes they can be useful. Make a considered judgment; if you then decide that by using such a phrase or phrases, you can add needed emphasis, or give your sentence a better cadence, go ahead. But keep on guard. Don't use any of them habitually.

Preliminary Exercise: Conciseness

Strike out all the wasted or unnecessary words in the following sentences. Feel free to rewrite the sentences completely if you believe that further changes will clarify meaning.

1. They all arrived at a consensus of opinion in regard to the basic principle that the continuing utilization of the worn-out methodology of the electoral college is antiquated, outdated, and generally inefficient.

2. In very few cases, if any, do members of politically liberal types of groups have any degree of approval concerning the free and totally unrestricted widespread proliferation of unlicensed handguns, pistols, automatics, revolvers, and sidearms.

3. During the time period that the two elderly old gentlemen were patiently waiting for the governor to make his arrival upon the scene, they whiled away the idle hours by participating in the ancient and fascinating game known the world over as chess.

4. During the entire chronological time frame of reference that Abner Jones was a participating member of the naval portion of America's armed forces, he had the opportunity to participate in only one sea voyage.

5. Because of the unfortunate fact that it happened to be raining at that particularly point in time, we came to the conclusion that we would refrain from going to the outdoor concert.

6. By approximately 10:05 o'clock A.M., on the morning at the following day, a rather slight but steady drizzle of rainfall had muddied the surface of the ground to a considerable extent, and this fortuitous but fortunate occurrence made the tracks of the fugitive readily visible to the unaided eye of the sheriff.

7. The new high-rise motel building is constructed of steel, with very large glass window areas from bottom to top. It has a large and very conspicuous neon sign displayed somewhat flamboyantly upon the roof. You can thus identify the building quite plainly even when you are viewing it from quite a considerable distance away.

8. It so happens that there turned out to be a grand total of five persons among the onlookers and spectators who were equipped with flashlights as a part of their emergency paraphernalia.

On the next page you'll find some suggested answers. But remember, there is no single "right" or "wrong" way to edit any of these sentences. Your own version might be better.

Suggested Answers to Preliminary Exercise: Conciseness

1. All agreed that the electoral college is outdated and inefficient. *(Perhaps you used "They" instead of "All." Not bad, but you lost the idea of unanimity implied by the "all" in the original version. We could argue about it, but let's not.)*

2. Liberals seldom approve of unlicensed handguns.

3. Patiently awaiting the governor's arrival, the two old men played chess.

4. While Abner Jones was in the U.S. Navy, he made only one sea voyage. *(Perhaps you left out the word "sea." Okay, but don't forget that during the Apollo Program, an all-Navy crew made a "space voyage" to the Moon.)*

5. Because it was raining, we decided not to go to the outdoor concert.

6. By about ten o'clock the next morning, a slight but steady drizzle had muddied the ground enough to make the fugi-

tive's tracks easily visible to the sheriff. (*Or maybe you said* "... easy for the sheriff to see the fugitive's tracks.")

7. The new steel-and-glass high-rise motel, with its large and conspicuous neon sign on the roof, can be plainly seen from afar.
8. Five of the spectators had flashlights.

Okay, now you should be ready to try a harder exercise, based on a real document.

Exercise: Conciseness

This is a very difficult exercise. Consider it a challenge! I did not make it up—the paragraph below is an excerpt from a real document. "Only the names have been changed to protect the innocent." Read it through carefully. See if you can understand it on first reading. If you can, you're a better reader than most people.

Take a few moments to analyze why this material is so difficult to understand. Then see if you can rewrite it more clearly. I'll give you a few hints when you are ready to begin.

USE OF FIREARMS BY AGENCY PERSONNEL. In addition to the requirements set forth by the Department concerning the use of firearms, agency personnel covered by this order shall resort to the use of firearms only when there is a clear and present danger of serious injury to/or loss of life of the law enforcement officer or security guard or innocent bystander resulting from a display of deadly force on the part of another individual, and then only to that extent which is necessary to render the individual responsible for the threat incapable of continuing the activity which prompted the law enforcement officer, security officer, or contract guard to use a firearm.

All right, let's look at this together. Note that readers must decipher a sentence more than 100 words long. By any readability scale ever devised, this sentence is monstrous. Still, it's truly no worse than many others I've encountered.

Before we begin to analyze the writing itself, let's ask an important question: "Who is supposed to read this regulation and understand it—and, more important,[10] comply with it?" (Are the individuals being addressed likely to have more than a high school education?)

Next question: "Is it important that the reader understand every detail?" (You'd better believe it. This regulation carries a great responsibility—to spell out specifically when to draw and, if necessary, fire a deadly weapon. Human lives are at stake.)

Next question: "How many different ideas are packed within that one sentence?" Here's a quick summary for you: (a) other (Department) requirements; (b) who is covered by the regulation; (c) what the personnel concerned are supposed to do; (d) when they are supposed to do it, and under what circumstances; (e) what other persons are involved; and (f) when the use of firearms is supposed to stop.

Suggestion: Take special care to ensure that your rewrite covers all these points. The clearest way to do this would be to discuss each point in a separate sentence, or at least a separate clause.

Probably neither you nor I could come up with a perfect rewrite, even with more information than we're given here. The first step in real life would be to confer with a member of the legal staff. For example, what does "resort to the use of firearms" mean? Does that mean placing a hand on the weapon? Unbuckling the holster strap? Drawing the weapon? Firing it? Frankly, I don't know. I've had police officers tell me they've been instructed not to draw a weapon unless they intend to fire, and not to fire unless they are shooting to kill—UNLESS the intended target is fleeing. The "Code of the West" says it's a sin to shoot people in the back. If all this confuses you, it confuses me, too. But you will undoubtedly run across problems at least this difficult in real life. When that time comes, be sure to do your homework.

Another question: what if there is a "clear and present danger of serious injury to/or loss of life of" another criminal, rather than an

[10]Many writers would say "more importantly" here. They would be wrong.

"innocent bystander"? Should a firearm then be used? (I would think probably not, but it's a question to consider. A conscientious editor should not fail to check out such contingencies.)

And so on. Remember, this is just an exercise; here you're more concerned with word choice and sentence structure than with legal technicalities. The latter are beyond the scope of this book. All I can say is: Check and double-check.

Too Much of A Good Thing?

Is it possible to be too concise?

Indeed it is. Cutting too much can be even worse than cutting too little. If you strip your writing to the barest statement of fact, eliminating every shred of supporting detail, you'll inevitably reduce clarity. What's worse, you'll risk losing the reader's interest as well.

Avoid also any tendency to copy foibles of newspaper style—particularly the recent tendency to omit the articles, *a*, *the*, and *an*. That would be okay for saving words in a telegram—in the olden days, we used to have to fit messages into ten words—but who writes telegrams any more? Still the telegraphic style lingers. I suggest we retire the "telegraphese" as well as the telegraph itself.

Too much conciseness can also be construed as bad manners or, at best, a lack of concern. If someone has written you a lengthy letter or report—one that clearly reflects thought and effort—you need to respond with more than a simple "okay" penciled on the routing slip. If you've studied anything about Transactional Analysis, you know that a bit of "stroking" is in order. Even though the answer you have given is a positive one, that in itself is not enough. Take the time to write at least a few lines, even though you could convey the message in fewer words. Again, common sense and common courtesy—neither being all that common—should be the guiding principles.

5

The Quest for Clarity

I keep six honest serving men
(They taught me all I knew):—
Their names are What and Why and When
And How and Where and Who.

—Rudyard Kipling (1886–1946)

Introduction

How many times have you taken a photograph that might have won a prize if only it had been in focus? Such experiences have probably happened to all of us.

But photographs are not the only things that can be out of focus. Writing can be out of focus, too—and unfortunately often is.

What can we do to ensure that our writing stays in sharp focus? Well, it's never easy, but this checklist should help:

Checklist: How to Keep Writing "In Focus"

1. Aim directly, with a specific purpose, at a central subject. (The analogy to picture-taking is clear.)
2. Omit all extraneous material.
3. Emphasize the important attributes of the subject. If necessary, give examples.
4. Play down the less important material. If you keep the really important items in sharp focus, you can permit the lesser ones to get a bit "softer." Just be sure they don't get "fuzzy" instead.

The trick is to take the time to think before you write, just as you might "frame" a picture in your mind before you actually shoot it.

Clarity Is Everything

In football coach George Allen's game, winning is everything. In our game, clarity is everything. Strive for the crisp, sharp focus we have been talking about. Strive always and unremittingly. Remember, our goal is to avoid any possibility of MISunderstanding. Admittedly, that's an impossible goal. Writing, like law, is far from being an exact science. The best efforts we can manage will still be none too good. But if Robert Browning will forgive me, "A person's reach should exceed a person's grasp, or what's a Heaven for?"

If you keep trying hard to apply the principles learned so far, you will at least be headed in the right direction. Remember, simply cutting excess verbiage will help your readers. But brevity isn't everything. It doesn't help to boil down so much that you omit vital details. Good writing, in the final analysis, is simply clear thinking on paper.

Few writers succeed at this all the time. Some never even come close. But one thing is sure: none of us will ever fight our way down to anywhere near the goal line if we're not in there trying all the time.

Think every problem through. Then explain it in the most logical way you can conjure up.[1] Try using the trick many professional writers rely on: think hard about the subject, then relax and let your subconscious mind take over. You'd be surprised how well this works. And that's why I chose the words "conjure up." They are more apt here than you might have thought.

Once you've put some ideas down on paper, ask yourself a series of questions, based on Kipling's six honest serving men:

---

[1]This expression is a good example of a case where it is absolutely necessary to end the sentence with a preposition!

- Does it tell who is responsible for doing whatever is required?
- Does it explain clearly what is supposed to be done?
- Does it tell when? where? how? why? And finally,
- Does all this really say what I intended to say?

Those are the questions a good reporter would ask. Make sure you have answered every one of them. Leave nothing to your reader's imagination.

Principle Four: Be specific. Use concrete terms instead of generalizations.

Don't Sacrifice Clarity in Your Quest for Speed

At various places throughout this handbook, I have advised you to proceed "with all possible dispatch" once you start writing. That's extremely good advice, but I must add a warning here: *never*—repeat—*never* sacrifice clarity in your quest for speed. Remember that clarity must always remain your primary goal. Speed will be no help if you run your reader off the road.

To be clear, you must (excuse my blunt language) know what you are talking about. On top of that, you must know exactly what you want to say about your subject. Even then, you must also have mastered the tricks of the writing trade to the point that you can employ each word with understanding of its individual *denotation* (meaning) and *connotation* (emotional overtones). And finally, you will have to learn to string those individual words together with proper regard for the grammar, rhetoric, and usage of American English.

Abstraction—the Enemy of Clarity

The term *gobbledygook* was coined by the late Maury Maverick. You probably already know what it means, but—just in case—

one definition is "the language of circumlocution, jargon, and pomposity."

Here's one of my favorite examples, courtesy of an entertaining little book entitled *Gobbledygook Has Got to Go*. (Formerly available from the Superintendent of Documents, U.S. Government Printing Office.)[2] It tells about a memo issued early in World War II to instruct federal workers on what to do in case of an air raid. The memo went like this:

> "Such preparation shall be made as will completely obscure all Federal buildings and non-Federal buildings occupied by the Federal Government during an air raid for any period of time from visibility by reason of internal or external illumination. Such obscuration may be obtained by blackout construction or by termination of the illumination."

Here's how F.D.R. dignified the memo by giving it simplicity:

> "Tell them," President Roosevelt wrote, "that in buildings where they will have to keep the work going to put something over the windows; and in buildings where they can let the work stop for a while, turn out the lights."

If this kind of unpompous, simple writing means a loss of dignity, then we know a lot of readers who wish a lot of writers would lose a bit of "dignity" writing this way. F.D.R. did it all the time. Once, when Frances Perkins was getting a speech ready for him, she wrote this line: "We are endeavoring to construct a more inclusive society." That night when F.D.R. read the line on the radio, it came out this way: "We are going to make a country in which no one is left out."

---

[2]Sad to say, this delightful little book is no longer in print. When I called (April 1990) to check on its availability and price, the clerk that answered the phone hadn't even heard of it. What a pity.

Use the Right Name for Things

To write precisely, you must constantly guard against using *abstract words* that other persons can interpret in different ways. Never use an abstract word when you can use a more precise, easily pictured, and harder-to-misunderstand concrete word.

Words are symbols. The celebrated grammarian Otto Jespersen once said, "A word is a human habit." Language relates to the real world much the way a road map relates to the territory it depicts. A road map is a system of conventions and symbols. Map readers must know and understand the symbols, or they are just as lost as if they didn't have a map at all.

Words, then, like maps, can have degrees of abstraction. The word *machine*, for example, covers a wide variety of devices—different in purpose, size, shape, and an almost endless list of other things. Nevertheless, the word *machine* undoubtedly brings a picture or a concept to your mind. The picture it evokes for me may be quite different. Still somehow there are enough common elements that we can communicate, however vaguely.

Mind you, I am not knocking abstraction—we couldn't do without it. Indeed, the ability to abstract probably lies at the root of human knowledge, and certainly at the root of human language. Without abstractions, we wouldn't be able to communicate. What's more, we probably wouldn't have anything worth communicating.

The Ladder of Abstraction

Early in life we learn that many English words have several different meanings. A child learns to define those words—and those various meanings—as an individual, through experience. Consequently, if I try to define *my* terms for you, the reader, I can't be sure you'll accept my definitions. You've had experiences of your own, and you're quite likely to prefer your own definitions. Frankly, I don't blame you.

Our best hope of reaching a common ground is to use concrete, specific words as often as we can—words that narrow and control the mental images produced. Words having a sensory base are more likely to communicate what we intend. That is to say, words representing objects the reader can see, hear, touch, taste, or smell.

Structural linguists and semanticists have a ball with this subject, and (would you believe I am saying this) their findings make a lot of sense. They have given us a method of coding different meanings of the same word, but that's a bit complex to go into here. They have given us another concept—both simpler and more useful—that I'll pass on to you.

Look at the illustration below. The lower rungs of the ladder represent the concrete terms the reader can easily identify in terms of physical senses. Ascending the ladder, you'll find each word becomes more abstract than the one just below it. At the same time, each reference grows more general, more vague, and—accordingly—more open to different interpretations.

As mentioned earlier, abstract words are invaluable. We can't

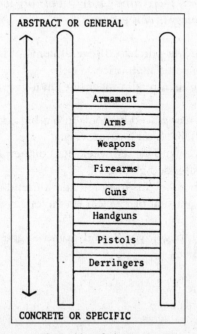

The Ladder of Abstraction

get along without them; I certainly don't want to purge them from your vocabulary. But I would suggest that, in your writing, you link your abstractions to specific experiences by using *examples, analogies,* and *illustrations.* Even better, replace the abstractions with concrete, sensory-style words as often as you can. The more abstract words you use, the harder your copy is to understand. Concrete words make the writing more readable and the meaning more specific.

Now let's try an easy exercise in levels of abstraction:

Preliminary Exercise: Abstract vs. Concrete Words

In the following sentences, change the abstract words into more concrete or specific terms. Please don't look at the suggestions for rewrites until you have completed your own versions. And remember that, as usual, there aren't any "right" or "wrong" ways to do any of the sentences in this exercise.

1. The housewife purchased several items of food for which she had to pay a high price.
2. The young man read a magazine until very late yesterday evening.
3. The workman placed his tools into a big container.
4. We had a talk about a controversial issue.
5. We went downtown last week, had dinner at a restaurant, and later attended a concert.
6. My pet ran away this morning and a friend of mine found him in an unusual place clear on the other side of the city.

On the next page, you'll find some suggestions about the rewrites. Don't peek.

Suggested Rewrites for Preliminary Exercise:

Abstract vs. Concrete Words

1. Mrs. Trudy Brown purchased bread, meat, and potatoes, and her bill was $57.80. (*Maybe you were even more specific than that: what kind of bread, what kind of meat, what kind of potatoes, etc. And maybe you put in an additional clue to the reader about the prices being high. You might have said something like "*. . . and her bill was exorbitant—$57.80." *Get the idea?*)
2. Teenager Bill Jones read *Newsweek* until ten o'clock yesterday evening. (*Maybe you mentioned a specific day.*)
3. The plumber placed two monkey wrenches, a blowtorch, and a pipe threader into a large steel toolbox.
4. Albert Kincaid and I had an argument last night about the pros and cons of enforced busing.
5. My cousin Engelbert and I went to downtown Washington last week, had dinner at the Rive Gauche, and later attended a piano recital at the Kennedy Center Concert Hall. (*You can tell I made that one up. We really had dinner at McDonald's and heard a free concert by the U.S. Army Band on the Capitol steps.*)
6. My pet alligator Hubert ran away and my friend Alfonso found him sunning on a fire escape at the Singles Towers condominium at Beltsville Road.

Exercise: Concrete vs. Abstract

That ought to do it for now. For more practice, try Exercise Four in Part Four.

6

The Quest for Precision

Of all the faults found in writing, the wrong placing of words is one of the most common, and perhaps it leads to the greatest number of misconceptions.

—William Cobbett (1762–1835)

Introduction

Frankly, all I know about William Cobbett is that he was an English writer who used the nom de plume[1] "Peter Porcupine." That has a nice ring to it. Also, whatever else he knew or didn't know about good writing, he was absolutely right about the improper placing of words.

Word order is far more important in the English language than in any other language I know of.[2] Most other European languages are *inflected;* that is, a word changes its form according to the part that word is playing in a sentence. The inflection usually involves adding a prefix or a suffix to a "root" word. From these inflections,

---

[1]Some writers would italicize this word because it is a French expression. I choose not to, because it is an expression so commonly used in English that it can be considered a proper part of the language. It means "pen name, or an assumed name under which a person writes."

[2]Please notice that there is a distinction between "know" and "know of." I "know" only a few languages, but I "know of" (recognize the existence of) a great many more. Also, I can take advantage of this construction to point out, yet again, that sometimes it's necessary to end a sentence with a preposition.

or special beginnings or endings, the reader can readily tell if a word is the subject of a sentence, a direct object, a possessive, and so on.

From second-year Latin, I recall the first line of *Caesar's Gallic Wars* (just about the only thing I recall from second-year Latin). The line goes: *Gallia est omnis divisa in partes tres.* The translation, for you of today's generation, is *All Gaul is divided into three parts.* But I am told that old Julius had a lot of options open to him. He could just as easily have written *Omnis Gallia in tres partes divisa est* and his intended meaning would have remained unchanged. Neat.

As you undoubtedly know, English used to be inflected, too, back in the "olden days." (My kids think I was there.) If you've ever had to study Chaucer's *Canterbury Tales*, you discovered that you had to expend almost the same effort as if you were learning a new and foreign language. Yet Chaucer's language is much more closely akin to our present English than was the "Old English" or "Anglo-Saxon" of yet earlier times. If you've read any of *Beowulf,* you remember that the language of that epic poem was really more closely related to some of the Germanic languages than it is to our modern English.

But the English language has from its beginnings always been growing and changing. Some of the more extreme changes came after the Norman invasion of 1066. Since then, the language of the British Isles received an infusion of Romance-root words to take their places beside Anglo-Saxon words. What we now call Modern English became gloriously enriched in the process. We now have at least two words, and usually more, for just about everything. But, as the language grew in vocabulary, it also began to change in other ways at an increasingly rapid rate.

The Importance of Word Order in the English Language

By Shakespeare's time, many inflections had begun to disappear. And how much more the language has changed since then. Today, when modern readers attempt *Hamlet,* or *Romeo and Juliet,* they must make a special study of the archaic language of The Bard[3] before they can understand it fully.

Yes, the grammatical construction of English today is in many ways much simpler than it used to be. But we have paid a price for losing the language's inflections; now we must pay more and more attention to arranging words in their proper order. If today's writers deviate from the so-called "natural" word order of subject-verb-object, or subject-verb-complement, they run a strong risk of being misunderstood.

In my youth I was a dedicated fan of the "Gashouse Gang."[4] So I am still faintly embarrassed at quoting one of their old archrivals from the Brooklyn Bums,[5] "the Brat." But Stanky had a saying he often used that demonstrates what I'm talking about, so here goes: *It ain't the size of the dog in the fight, it's the size of the fight in the dog.*

Note that essentially the same words are used in both halves of the sentence—but they mean very different things. Word order is the key.

For good measure, here's another example: *The dogcatcher chased the dog. The dog chased the dogcatcher.*

Same words in each sentence. Totally different meaning.[6]

---

[3]This expression is short for "The Bard of Avon," and refers to William Shakespeare, who was born at Stratford-on-Avon. I have capitalized the "T" in "the," because I think that using the capital letter makes it easier for readers to recognize the usage. I am aware that many careful writers would prefer to use a lower case "t." If and when they do so, I promise not to object.

[4]An affectionate nickname for the St. Louis Cardinals of the late 1930s. As a boy growing up in rural Missouri, I idolized such rough-and-tumble players as Dizzy Dean and Pepper Martin. On one of the hottest days ever recorded in St. Louis (and summer in St. Louis is HOT), that zany pair built a bonfire in the outfield and danced around it wearing Indian blankets.

[5]A term that Brooklyn Dodger fans used to call their own team. Brooklyn fans didn't take it kindly, however, when they heard non-Brooklyn-ites using it. Apropos of nothing in particular, during the last U.S. presidential campaign, Bob Dole was ridiculed for referring to the (now) San Francisco Dodgers as the "Brooklyn Dodgers." As a contemporary of Mr. Dole, I understand his problem. I also have a hard time associating the Dodgers with anyplace but Brooklyn.

[6]Many purists would object to these two sentences, which are not "complete." That is to say, they have no verbs, and hence don't comply with the rule that *a sentence must have a subject and predicate and express a complete thought.* All I can say is that many excellent and otherwise careful writers use this device whenever they want to, and I long to be in that number. (Those last few words, incidentally, are quoted from a line in the old Dixieland jazz warhorse, "When the Saints Go Marching In.") If you know the rule, you probably know enough to be able to figure out when it is okay to break it.

Ambiguity

Murphy's Law[7] is true in spades[8] when it comes to interpreting ambiguous statements. If a sentence can possibly be misunderstood, it will be. And improper word order is probably the greatest cause of double (and triple) meanings. An adjective will do its utmost to attach itself to the nearest noun; an adverb will do the same to the nearest verb, adjective, adverb, or sometimes even the nearest clause.

Remember—if you put any modifier near a word or phrase that might be considered "eligible" for modification, but isn't the real one to be modified, you will inevitably mislead the reader.

> **Principle Five:** Keep related sentence elements together; keep unrelated elements apart. Place modifiers as close as possible to the words they are intended to modify.

Observe that the problem often does not lie with the modifiers themselves; they may be perfectly all right. It's the company they keep.

Misplaced Modifiers

Watch out especially for *misplaced modifiers*—that is to say, modifying words or phrases that appear to modify one word in a sentence, but actually are intended to modify another. Consider the difference, for example, between "We *almost* lost our entire investment," and "We lost *almost* our entire investment." Version one means that the entire investment was almost lost, but was not. Version two means that the greater part of the entire investment was indeed lost.

---

[7]A jocular maxim that states, among other things, that "Anything that *can* possibly go wrong *will* go wrong."
[8]Idiomatic expression meaning "to a high degree; with great force."

Here's one with a misplaced phrase instead of a single word. Compare "He polished the beautiful Mercedes-Benz his father had given to him with tender care," and "He polished with tender care the beautiful Mercedes-Benz his father had given to him." See the difference?

Look Out for "Only"

The word "only" is one of the trickiest in the English language. Some years ago I ran across an interesting sentence. By changing the position of the single word *only* you could change the shade of meaning of the entire sentence. Sometimes the meaning changed a little—other times quite drastically. When I was updating an earlier edition of *WWP*, editor Barbara Hart introduced me to a new version that I like much better than the one I started out with. Credit goes to Maxwell Numberg. So, with appropriate thanks to both of them, I offer this new version, with a few remarks of my own:

1. *Only* John said that he loved Mary. (This means that no one else—only John—said . . .)
2. John *only* said that he loved Mary. (This is what English teachers call a "squinting" construction. The *only* could modify either *John* or *said*. We often use this kind of word order in speech and are seldom misunderstood. In writing, however, we must be more careful; strive for a more precise placement. It isn't really all that much trouble.)
3. John said *only* that he loved Mary. (This means that John made the simple statement and didn't say anything else.)
4. John said that *only* he loved Mary. (Poor Mary. I hope that her parents and siblings at least like her!)
5. John said that he *only* loved Mary. (Another "squinting construction," but with different interpretations from the second example.)
6. John said that he loved only Mary. (Lucky Mary—assuming that her feelings for John were reciprocal!)
7. John said that he loved Mary only. (Means much the same

as sentence 6, but with increased emphasis on the only, since it is the final word in the sentence.)

In fairness, I must tell you that I may be nit-picking[9] on this. Some of the most respected American authorities on usage are not nearly this fussy about the placement of the word "only." They believe that in colloquial English it is perfectly all right to say, for example, "He only spent a dollar," rather than "He spent only a dollar." I respectfully disagree—at least in the context of the intent of this book. If we are truly concerned with accuracy, and with avoiding ambiguity, we had better watch where we put this slippery word.

Another constantly misused phrase is "not all." You've seen a jillion[10] television commercials in which the statement is made that "All toothpastes (or mouthwashes, or dog foods, or whatever) are not alike." Wrong! (The correct structure for that kind of sentence is "Not all toothpastes are alike.")

Dangling Modifiers

There are several different kinds of dangling constructions, but the faults are similar in all of them. For those of you who remember your formal English grammar, they can be dangling *gerund phrases*, participial phrases, or infinitive phrases. Actually, you can get along quite well in life without knowing these things. A *gerund* and a *participle* look exactly alike; both have *"-ing"* endings. The first is used as a *noun*, the second as an *adjective*, just in case you've forgotten the distinction. You very likely do remember that an *infinitive* is a form of the verb preceded by the *sign of the infinitive*, the preposition *to*. (*To go, to talk, to walk*, etc.)

Phrases are said to dangle when they do not clearly and logically refer to the appropriate noun or pronoun.

Here is a dangling gerund phrase. *After climbing the mountain, the view was beautiful.* The view didn't climb the mountain.

9Colloquial expression meaning "petty faultfinding."
10Colloquial expression meaning "a very large indefinite number."

Change this to something like *After climbing the mountain, we saw a beautiful view*. In other words, add a noun or pronoun for the dangling phrase to modify. Or, if you desire, you can change the phrase to a clause or an absolute construction. Say something like *After we climbed the mountain, we saw a beautiful view*. (The trick is to give the clause its own subject.)

Here's a dangling participial phrase: *Moving to Arizona, his rheumatism quickly improved*. (The rheumatism didn't move to Arizona—or at least, not as a separate entity.) Change this one to read: *After moving to Arizona, he found that his rheumatism quickly improved*. Or: *After his move [or moving] to Arizona, his rheumatism quickly improved*.

Here's a dangling infinitive phrase: *To save money, the thermostat must be turned down to 68 degrees*. Change that to something like *To save money, you must turn the thermostat down to 68 degrees*.

Squinting Modifiers

A modifier is said to "squint" when it can be interpreted as modifying either of two (or more) sentence elements. The reader will be confused, or perhaps totally unable to decipher which meaning the writer intends. Usually it's a matter of not being able to tell whether to look *forward* (that is, toward the end of the sentence) or *backward* (toward the beginning). Look at this example:

Dr. Jones instructed the patient while in the hospital to watch his diet very carefully. Think about this one. Did the doctor do the instructing while the patient was hospitalized? Or did the doctor instruct the patient to watch his diet during the period that he was going to be in the hospital? Either interpretation is possible.

You could rewrite this by saying something such as *Dr. Jones instructed the patient to watch his diet very carefully during the time he was in the hospital*. Or, another interpretation: *While visiting the patient in the hospital, Dr. Jones instructed him to watch his diet very carefully*.

Exercises

You will find exercises on Misplaced Modifiers and Dangling Modifiers in Part Four.

Consistency

Clarity and precision in writing require consistency. Your reader will have a much easier time comprehending quickly what you have written if you are consistent in your approach. (Keeping this in mind will also help you to organize your points.) Try to stick to one point of view, one subject, until there is a definite need to change it. When a change is needed, start a new paragraph.

Principle Six: Avoid unnecessary shifts of number, tense, subject, voice, or point of view.

Many different kinds of shifts are lumped under this one heading, for—although they are all different—in many ways they are all very much alike. The basic principle is simple: don't throw your reader any curves.[11] If you start out down a particular path, don't constantly twist and turn. Keep going straight ahead, and if you *must* turn, give the reader as much warning as you can.

Watch out particularly for:

Shift of Number

Careless writers have always been inclined to write such things as "Everyone should save *their* money." As you can see, the subject, *everyone*, is a singular noun. Harking back to the rules of grammar you learned in grade school days, you know that a pronoun is supposed to agree with its antecedent in number. The word *their* is obviously plural, and hence does not agree with the singular subject. Why, then, do so many writers constantly use this kind of construction?

[11]Baseball idiom related to the spin a pitcher puts on the ball to change its flight path.

Probably we can ascribe this in part, at least, to the advent of the women's movement. Writers don't want to appear sexist, so they use the plural form *their*, which has no connotation of sex, even though they are aware that the construction is incorrect. They don't want to have to say his, which would be grammatically correct, but sexist. They feel that *his/her* looks and sounds awkward. (I agree.) So they choose *their*. Thus, they avoid sexism, but in the process they break the rules of grammar. Granted, it's a dilemma.

Most of the time, though, there's an easy way out. All you have to do is use a *plural* form of the word up front, as the subject. Then you can legitimately use *their* as the pronoun. Thus, instead of writing "Everyone should save *his* money," or worse, "Everyone should save *his/her* money,"[12] why not try something like: "People should save *their* money."

Of course, this device doesn't always work—after all, nothing's perfect. But, in the few cases when it won't work, there are other ways. We won't go into them here, but for some other possible solutions, refer to the **he/she dilemma** in the handbook section.

Shift of Tense

This mistake, while also a very common one, usually stems more from carelessness than from ignorance. A writer will be going merrily along, and will suddenly and inconsistently change tenses, for no good reason. "When he heard about the accident, he screams and cries like a baby." This kind of error is very easy to correct. Simply put all verbs in the same tense: "When he heard about the accident, he screamed and cried like a baby."

Shift of Subject

"Abraham Lincoln was born in Kentucky, but Illinois was his home in later years." To correct this, make the subject of one verb the subject of both verbs: "Abraham Lincoln was born in Kentucky,

[12]In regulatory or legal documents, sometimes "his/her" is acceptable, to ensure precise meaning.

but lived in Illinois in later years." (Or, if you really want to have the states as subjects, you could say something like this: "Kentucky was the birthplace of Abraham Lincoln, but Illinois was his home in later years.")

A few explanations and cautions are probably in order here. Do not let this "rule" hog-tie[13] or inhibit you. Actually, it is really very flexible, and is often broken by even the best and most careful writers. Most problems come when the subject is changed within a compound sentence. It's okay to change the subject in a complex sentence, and it often would be difficult not to. Don't worry about it.

One other thing. Don't let this rule inhibit you when you change, for example, the direct object of one sentence to be the subject of the next. This construction has a long and honorable history. Remember one of the first Mother Goose rhymes you learned as a child: "The farmer takes a wife. The wife takes the child. The child takes the dog. The dog takes the cat. The cat takes the rat." And so on. There is nothing wrong with this, and, indeed, it is frequently a useful way of keeping the reader on track.

Shift of Voice

This, too, is a common error. It's no great crime, but it doesn't contribute to clarity and reader understanding. Let's consider a typical example: "If a coach wishes to win the respect of his team, a firm discipline must be maintained." (Notice that the sentence begins in the active voice, then shifts to the passive halfway through.) Simply put both verbs in the active voice: "If a coach wishes to win the respect of his team, he must maintain a firm discipline." (Of course, both the original sentence and the rewrite are sexist, so let's try one more time: "If coaches wish to win the respect of their teams, they must maintain a firm discipline.")

[13]To impede or disrupt in movement or action. I thought this was a colloquial expression (or possibly just farmer or cowboy slang) until I looked it up. My trusty *Webster's Second* shows it as a standard verb, customarily hyphenated, as I wrote it, but occasionally written as one word.

Shift in Point of View

"When you look through a microscope, the cell divides to form two organisms." Even the logic is faulty in this one, since the cell is going to divide whether you are watching it or not. To correct the sentence (and the logic) give both clauses the same subject: "When you look through the microscope, you can see the cell divide to form two organisms."

Exercise

You will find an exercise on Unnecessary Shifts in Part Four.

7

The Right Word

The difference between the right word and the almost right word is really a large matter—'tis the difference between the lightning and the lightning bug.

—Mark Twain (1835–1910)

Introduction

The right word is usually the simple word. H. W. Fowler, one of my heroes, put it like this: "Prefer the familiar word to the far-fetched. Prefer the short word to the long. Prefer the Saxon word to the Romance." (*The King's English*, p. 11.)

Fowler went on to explain that the principles he listed were "roughly in order of merit," and that "the last is also the least." By all means read his full explanation; you'll enjoy it. Suffice it to say here that Fowler wasn't exhibiting a prejudice against Latin-based words. As he himself pointed out, the Romance word may well be the "right word" in many instances. Indeed, the French language has exactly the right words for "exactly the right word"—the word writers and editors are supposed to be constantly looking for, but can't always find. The French call it "le mot juste."

Fowler's main point is that Saxon-root words are usually shorter. Latin-root words, frequently incorporating prefixes and suffices, are much more likely to be polysyllabic. (Several words in the previous sentence demonstrate the point admirably.)

Choosing the "Right Word"

How does a writer choose the right word? Sometimes the process is arduous. Obviously, a person with a good vocabulary has a much better chance of finding an appropriate word than does another person having fewer words to choose from.

If, as many psychologists believe, vocabulary is one indication of intelligence, making a conscious effort to improve one's vocabulary is probably not a bad idea. *Reader's Digest* has had a monthly feature on this subject for many years. And while it's long been a popular sport among the literary intelligentsia to put down the *Digest*, I'll unhesitatingly take the other side. If you want to find examples of clear, tightly edited prose, you'll look a long way to hunt down anything better than you can encounter in any issue of the much maligned *Reader's Digest*.

Good English Is Appropriate English

As everyone knows, people talk and write at different "levels," according to the situation. If you're talking with friends at a party or a picnic, for example, you'll use one level. If you make a presentation to the Board of Directors, you'll use another. And there are other levels in-between.

Is one level "better English" than another? Linguistic scholars don't believe so, and they are probably right. English is not "good" if it is out of place; using Board-of-Directors language at the corner bar might get someone a horselaugh, or maybe even a punch in the nose.

The point is that good English, so-called, is language that is appropriate to the situation. The language spoken at Joe's Bar is what the late H. L. Mencken called "vulgate" English (from the Latin word for popular or common). Mencken chose that term because none of the other descriptive words in use at the time filled the bill. Some scholars were calling such English "vulgar," but to many persons that word carries a connotation different from the one intended. The term "illiterate," once in vogue, wasn't much better—it implies "unable to read or write." And the terms "popular" or "folk" make such English appear more acceptable than it usually is when it is employed in the world of business, industry, or government.

One notch above "vulgate" comes informal English. (Structural linguists might say one type of language is not "above" another. Nevertheless, the word "level" implies "higher" and "lower" to most people, probably including the scholars themselves.) Informal English, the level most people use in conversation, can be carried over to some extent in our everyday writing. Obviously, some levels overlap considerably, particularly in the subgroups of language called slang, jargon,[1] and shoptalk. The last two terms describe the vocabulary—often consisting of a sort of verbal shorthand—used by persons in the same occupation.

At the top of the ladder comes "formal" English. More often written than spoken, it is used primarily by highly educated persons addressing their peers. Some element of snobbery is probably involved, but let's not make any educational or social judgments. Suffice it to say that *formal writing* has its place. But business writing—intended to communicate with, and be understood by, the general public—is not that place. For those concerned more with communication than with elegance, formal writing may seem overly confining. That's bad enough, but to readers it is even more restrictive; it interferes with their natural right to comprehend.

Business writing should consist of good informal English.[2] That is, it should be much like informal speech, but with tighter sentence structure and more precise expression.

Principle Seven: Prefer the simple word to the far-fetched, and the right word to the almost right.

[1]For a detailed discussion on the subject of slang and technical jargon, see Chapter 22.

[2]This simple statement and the sentence that follows it together comprise one of the most important ideas that form the foundation stone for *WWP: How to write so that you cannot possibly be misunderstood*.

The Evils of Elegant Variation

"Elegant variation" is a term coined by H. W. Fowler to describe a device writers sometimes use to avoid repeating a word—usually they set an arbitrary limit, such as within the same sentence, within 20 words, or within a paragraph. They do this because, somewhere along the way, they've been brainwashed into believing that there is a "rule" *never* to use the same word twice in the same sentence.

Used sensibly, the "rule" isn't a bad one. Unfortunately, many writers don't use it sensibly. Listen to a broadcast of sports scores any evening, and you'll probably hear at some time one of the following elegant variations: *The Redskins emerged victorious; the Colts romped to victory; the Cowboys slaughtered the opposition; the Dolphins clobbered their opponents;* and so on, ad nauseam. Up to a certain point it can be amusing. That point is quickly reached; after that, the entire technique becomes at best boring—at worst, ridiculous.

Leave it to elegant writers to use elegant variations. In *useful* writing, such variations often mislead the reader. Suppose, for example, that the same individual is both the president and the treasurer of an organization. A writer striving for elegant variation might write something like this: *The president announced that the company had completed a very successful year. Treasurer Jones said there had been a profit of $3.25 a share.*

In useful writing, don't let yourself be handcuffed by this so-called rule against elegant variation. You're the boss. Here's the principle you should follow:

> **Principle Eight:** Don't repeat a word or words unnecessarily. But don't hesitate to repeat when the repetition will increase clarity.

Exercises:

Exercises involving problems of Unnecessary Repetition and Elegant Variation can be found in Part Four.

Reference Works

Dictionaries and Related References

If you can't find "le mot juste" in your working vocabulary, what's the next step? Some writers will turn immediately to such references as *Roget's Thesaurus, Webster's Dictionary of Synonyms*, or *Rodale's Word Finder.* We'll discuss such works later. Right now, let's begin with the book most writers reach for first—the dictionary.

A generation ago, "the dictionary" meant just one thing: the *Merriam-Webster New Second International Dictionary*, or its desk-sized junior partner, *Webster's Collegiate*. True, there were other dictionaries—good ones—but the *Second* was considered by most American writers and scholars to be the final authority on American English.

Unfortunately, few of today's writers are willing to say the same thing about its present-day successor, the *Third International.* Even though the *Third* is a work of towering linguistic scholarship, it would appear to be written more for linguistic scholars than for the rest of us—that is to say, the vast majority of the human race.

Since it's unlikely most of you can locate a copy of the *Second*, or would be willing to lay out that much money if you do happen to find one, what's your alternative?

Well, you have several. Let's mention a few of the new dictionaries that are very good indeed. In my opinion, your best buy is probably the paperback edition of *The American Heritage Dictionary.* If you use it as much as I do, however, you'll quickly wear it out. So you want to spend a bit more and get the hardback edition. (No, they aren't paying me a commission.)

Another good candidate is *The Random House Dictionary of the English Language.* Many writers swear by it. Both *Random House* and *American Heritage* are described as "unabridged," but actually are not. They would have to contain many more words—or, in dictionary talk, "entries,"—to qualify for that description.

So if you really feel the need for an unabridged dictionary, get the *Oxford English Dictionary.* There's no risk in saying the *Oxford* is far and away the greatest English language dictionary in the world. The full-sized edition comes in multiple volumes and is a masterpiece of scholarship and completeness. But even it has its drawbacks; it is bulky, very expensive, and very "British." You can get around the first two drawbacks by buying the "MICRO" version; it contains the same information, but reduced in type size to fit into two volumes. The print is minuscule[3] in the true sense of that word, but the publishers thoughtfully furnished a powerful reading glass to go with it. (No, they don't pay me a commission either.)

One other comment about dictionaries before we move on.

If you love language, you probably also love dictionaries. You're in the habit of looking words up, and that's good. It helps ensure knowing not only what you think a word means, but also—far more important—what the word is likely to mean to others. What we need is to get an insight into the difference between *denotation*—the way a word is defined—and *connotation*—the emotional overtones that often accompany the word. Many words that appear acceptable to readers if interpreted according to strict definition might actually be considered discourteous or offensive to many because of the underlying connotation. Writers, beware.

We must always be aware of dictionary meanings, of course. Look words up if you have any doubt about them. But learn to look past the formal definition. Using a word with bad connotations can evoke strong emotion you'd sooner leave unstirred. For shades of meaning and connotation, you'll find some other books are even more useful than a regular dictionary.

References on Usage, Shades of Meaning, and Connotations of Words

One of the most helpful references on this subject was published in 1976. It is the *Harper Dictionary of Contemporary Usage*, edited by William and Mary Morris.

What makes this book valuable is that the Morrises are con-

---

[3]This word is frequently misspelled "miniscule." My spelling of "minuscule" is correct.

cerned with the English used by writers, editors, teachers, and others who care about precision. They accordingly chose a panel of more than 130 experts—novelists, poets, scholars, and even a Supreme Court Justice noted for writing more clearly than most of his distinguished but verbose colleagues.

To find out what these experts think about word usages, the Morrises began sending them questionnaires, starting back in 1971. They carefully chose words about which opinions often differed strongly; then they asked the experts to comment. The panelists voted as to whether they would use a particular word in speech or in writing; often they commented as well.

The book makes fascinating reading. Some of the comments are pungent, some enlightening, and some funny. For example:

Is there a distinction between "flaunt" and "flout"—used interchangeably by two court justices—worth preserving?

Michael J. Arlen, writer: "I should damn well hope so." Ben Lucien Burman, novelist: "No wonder Roosevelt wanted to fire the Supreme Court!" Stanley Kunitz, poet: "I flout those who flaunt their ignorance." (Comment: Beautiful!)

May "author" be a verb?

Saul Bellow, author: "No, nor the word 'crafted.' Abominable!"

Herman Wouk, novelist: "No, no, no, no, no, no, no, no! NO!"

Berton Roueché, writer, voting no: "Why should error be approved?" (My comment: Amen.)

How about "giving input" to the President?

Lewis Mumford, author: "Input has a legitimate use in computerdom. Otherwise it should be shunned. It is the equivalent of y'know for those who don't know the right word." Berton Roueché, author: "I accept 'output', but—I don't know why—input turns my stomach. Maybe it's the people who use such words." Pierre Berton, author: "I do not mingle socially with people who talk that way and would not expect my readers to stick with me if I used it." Peter

DeVries, author: ". . . The thought of putting information into a President is a little grotesque." Red Smith: "This usage brings a violent output of nausea here. Couldn't the President have access to advice instead?"

Well, that's enough to give you the flavor of the book.

Other Reference Works and Software

If there is one reference work other than the dictionary that word-conscious writers refer to constantly, it is probably *Roget's Thesaurus*. This useful work is available in many sizes and shapes. The version I use most of the time is called *The New Roget's Thesaurus in Dictionary Form*, edited by Norman Lewis. If you don't have some kind of thesaurus, you should remedy that situation right away.

If you use a word processor, as many writers do, you might want to get the software for a built-in thesaurus program and spelling checker. (The spelling checkers are often called "Dictionaries," but they don't define words—they just tell you how to spell them. I happen to be a very good speller, but I use such a program constantly, because it spots typos so quickly and efficiently. I have a couple of thesaurus programs also, but use them very little. Most of the time they don't list the words I need synonyms for. Maybe you'll have better luck than I do.)

Another good word reference is *Webster's Dictionary of Synonyms*. I suspect it has even more words than *Roget's*.

A slightly different approach can be found in a series of works published some years ago by the late J. I. Rodale. A self-educated man and noted health food enthusiast, Rodale was fascinated with words: he commissioned a group of scholars to help him put together *The Word-Finder*, *The Adjective-Finder*, and *The Adverb-Finder*. Some or all of these are probably out of print now, but perhaps might be found secondhand. They are worth looking for. One of the good things about *The Word-Finder* is that it suggests combinations of words—adverbs and adjectives to go with particular nouns, for example.

Let me close this discussion by telling you about another very helpful reference that I discovered the year this book was first published. Suppose you know the definition of a word you want, but can't think of the word itself—has this happened to you? Welcome to the group. Well, Theodore Bernstein came up with the answer to our problem: an innovative book called *The Reverse Dictionary*. (It may be out of print now, and available only in secondhand bookstores.) Over the years, I've found it to be extremely helpful. It gives you a handle on all those words you know you know, but can't think of when you need them. In recent years I find the list growing ever larger. Bernstein's book is often my salvation.

Other Valuable Reference Works

A Dictionary of Contemporary American Usage, by Bergen and Cornelia Evans.

Writer's Guide and Index to English, by Porter Perrin.

Modern American Usage, by Wilson Follett, edited and completed by Jacques Barzun.

Modern English Usage, by H. W. Fowler (or the American English version by Margaret Nicholson).

The Merriam-Webster Pocket Dictionary of Proper Names, compiled by Geoffrey Payton.

Last, but definitely not least, is a superb book that I find increasingly useful. The better I become acquainted with it, the better I like it. (Maybe that's because I find myself agreeing with almost everything it says.) It's called *Success With Words: A Guide to the American Language*, and it was first published by *Reader's Digest* in 1983.

8

How to Make Order
Out of Chaos

*In whatever paragraphs or essays you write, verify the sequence
of ideas and take out or transpose everything that interrupts the
march of thought and feeling.*

—Jacques Barzun, *Simple and Direct*

Introduction

There are many stylistic and grammatical devices available to improve and clarify the communication process—the process of transferring thoughts from the mind of the writer to the mind of the reader. Among the most useful of these devices is the one teachers of English call "parallelism," or "parallel construction."

Parallelism

Parallelism is neither complicated nor difficult. All you need to know is that you can show the similarity of certain thoughts or ideas by using similar grammatical constructions in a number of successive units—whether those units be words, phrases, clauses, sentences, paragraphs, or even longer units.

Let's illustrate the virtues of parallelism by listing them in a parallel construction, thus:

Parallelism is a useful device that can:

- tidy up thoughts or ideas;
- clarify relations;
- straighten out mixed-up phrases, clauses, or sentences;
- convert entire paragraphs, pages, sections, or chapters from chaos to order; and
- unify entire documents or books.

Parallelism has a strong appeal to the reader's sense of order. To a person educated in the proper usage of language, hardly anything sounds quite so disorganized in writing as structure that is not made parallel when it should be. Compare these two sentences:

NOT PARALLEL: Briefly, the functions of the executive staff are to advise the president, transmit his instructions, and the supervision of the execution of his decisions.

PARALLEL: Briefly, the functions of the executive staff are to advise the president, transmit his instructions, and supervise the execution of his decisions.

As you can see, parallelism makes for an economical use of words at the same time it is helping to clarify meaning and relationships. In the process it also produces an aesthetic symmetry that pleases the reader's eye. That effect is pure *lagniappe*, a French expression that means something thrown in as a bonus. The slang term in English would be "freebie." It is better not to use foreign words like this, but if you do, explain them, just as I have done here.

Many inexperienced writers think of parallelism only in terms of sentences and paragraphs. That's fine, but why stop there? It's wasteful to ignore the potential benefits that can emerge when the reader can look at the big picture. Parallelism can be enormously useful in putting together an outline, a table of contents, or even a system of headings and subheadings for a long piece of writing. Again, the system helps the reader figure out relative values of items, and how everything fits together.

Principle Nine. **Make sentence elements that are parallel in thought parallel in form. But do not use parallelism to express thoughts that are not parallel.**

To express parallel thoughts, match words with words, phrases with phrases, clauses with clauses, or topics with topics. Do NOT match an element with a larger or structurally different element.

NOT PARALLEL: She began walking back and forth and to frown worriedly. (Notice the shift from the participle "walking" to the infinitive "to frown.")

PARALLEL: She began to walk back and forth and (to) frown worriedly. (Change both to infinitives.) OR She began walking back and forth and frowning worriedly. (Both participles.)

Here is another type of nonparallel construction that seems to be particularly common in administrative writing:

The duties of the Secretary of the Women's Association are—
(a) to take minutes of all the meetings; (infinitive phrase)
(b) the secretary answers all the correspondence; and (clause)
(c) writing of the monthly reports. (gerund phrase)

Change this by using all infinitive phrases, thus:

The duties of the Secretary of the Women's Association are—

(a) to take minutes of all the meetings;
(b) to answer all the correspondence; and
(c) to write the monthly reports.

Or change it by using all gerund phrases, thus:

The duties of the Secretary of the Women's Association are—
(a) taking minutes of all the meetings;
(b) answering all the correspondence; and
(c) writing the monthly reports.

Or (I like this version the least—it sounds terrible to my ear) using all clauses:

Here is a list of the secretary's duties:
(a) she takes minutes of all the meetings;
(b) she answers all the correspondence; and
(c) she writes the monthly reports.

Notice that in addition to the obvious changes involved in using all phrases or all clauses, there is a less obvious one of inserting a "the" in item (c). To make your parallelism clearer and more effective, you'll find it helpful to repeat articles, such as was done in this case, or prepositions, or pronouns, or helping verbs, or signs of the infinitive.

Parallelism is a handy tool for organizing, but it can't do everything. Some other principles—mostly related—are useful in organizing material for maximum reader interest and understanding.

The trick is to take advantage of the human mind's natural capacity for order. How? Simple—if one thing is similar to another, point out the similarity. If it is different, emphasize the difference. And if the two items are related, point out the relationship.

Making Logical Arrangements

Remember that no writer can ever tell the whole story about *anything*. James Joyce's famous work *Ulysses* takes 783 pages to describe the events of a single day in the lives of a limited number of characters. Even then, masterly as the work is, it gives only a hint of Joyce's admittedly impossible intent. A detailed account of a single hour in the life of a single character could take a conscientious novelist six months or a year to write—perhaps even longer. And the sad part is, it wouldn't begin to do the job.

So the writer must decide early on what to put in, and—more important—what to leave out. This is a difficult decision. What can be omitted without harming the reader's understanding?

The guidelines are: (a) stick to the essential facts, and *only* the facts; and (b) excise all extraneous material.

Strive constantly to put everything in logical order. Start with basics all readers will understand. Then progress one step at a time until perhaps the reader can arrive eventually at more difficult concepts that were beyond comprehension at the beginning.

> **Principle Ten:** Arrange your material logically. Always begin with ideas the reader can readily understand. If you must present difficult material, *go one step at a time*. Do not skip any steps. Arrange your format to give the reader every possible "handle" on the material.

Let's delve a bit deeper into what makes one arrangement of presentation easier to follow than another. For simplicity, let's consider a one-page document. Later we'll work up to larger projects.

To begin with, let's use one of the abilities that seems to make the human mind unique—the ability to categorize. Many psychologists have written that the ability to sort things out is one of the most important tools we have in learning and remembering. Indeed, much of our human knowledge appears to be derived from these skills.

For those of my readers who are as unorganized as I am, this illustration may sound familiar. My wife often asks me to stop by the supermarket on my way home from work. She has her own way of making out a grocery list, putting items down as they come to her mind—maybe a quart or milk, a loaf of bread, a head of lettuce, a can of tomatoes, some paper towels, and various other items in no particular order.

Anyone with what Jim Aswell would call "bat sense" would rearrange the list, putting similar things together. Then it would be easy to pick up every item located in a particular department, move on to the next, and so on. Simple logic.

Well, I never remember to do that; once in the supermarket I take many an extra step, wandering back and forth from one department to another. I rationalize that all the extra walking gives me some much needed exercise. But in writing, that's exercise you don't need!

The General-to-Specific Method of Development

Probably the best single way of arranging most material for easy understanding is what we call the general-to-specific order. This means that you start with a general statement; then follow up with additional facts that elaborate or explain the statement. This makes it extremely easy for your readers to follow all the way.

For example, the opening statement, "We need to buy a new word processor," might be supported by the following facts: (a) our old machine no longer does acceptable work; (b) it is impossible to get replacement parts; and (c) a new machine will quickly pay for itself in time saved and increased quality of work.

The Chronological Method of Development

This method of development, also extremely useful, is a simple one: all you have to do is to discuss events in the same time sequence that they actually occur; start with the first event and proceed chronologically, one event at a time, until the last. The chronological method is almost always the best way to write a history or a biography. It is also frequently used for news stories. And it is almost essential for explaining a process in which time relationships play an important role.

Sometimes, however, the chronological approach is inappropriate. In such cases, it may confuse both writer and reader. We become so used to thinking about almost everything in terms of chronology that we can be trapped into using that approach even when it may keep us from expressing our thoughts clearly.

Suppose, for example, that you're writing a test report on a new aircraft. For heaven's sake, don't start with what happened when the Wright Brothers were at Kitty Hawk. (And don't think I'm exaggerating—some report writers I know would probably start there!) Don't even begin with what happened last year or last month. Remember the important thing is to get straight to the point.

Other Methods of Arrangement

In a college English Composition course, you would learn many other systems of arrangement. What I have described as "general-to-specific" would probably be called "deductive order." Its opposite number, "specific-to-general" is known as "inductive order." You'd also hear about analytical order, spatial order, and perhaps cause-and-effect order. All of these are good to know, but for practical purposes we're going to skip them here. Chances are, you'll never even miss them in your everyday writing projects.

Whatever method you decide is appropriate for a particular project, the following points will be important:

Checklist: Logical Arrangement

1. **Start with something the reader is familiar with, and interested in**. Then move on, one step at a time. Don't skip any steps. Lead the reader at a comfortable rate from the known to the unknown, or from the general to the specific.
2. **Use analogies, comparisons, contrasts, examples, or illustrations** to help explain any difficult ideas or concepts.
3. **Use the same system all the way through**. This means if you're using measurements, for example, you'll stick to the same kind. Don't use "feet" or "miles" in one section and "meters" or "kilometers" in another. If for some reason you need to use both systems, ordinarily you should give the familiar one first, then use parentheses to convert the figures into the other system. Don't make your reader do the math!

    NOTE: If you are working for an organization that's trying to do missionary work by converting readers to the metric system, go ahead and put the metric numbers first; then follow with the conventional U.S. system in parentheses. Ordinarily, this wouldn't be a good arrangement, but circumstances alter cases.

4. **Choose a logic that will be quickly clear to the reader**. For example, if you are discussing four animals—a cat, a dog, a horse, and an elephant—what would be a logical arrangement? Well, according to my logic, at least, the order I just used would be the best one, although you might argue for other ways. My logic here is that people usually think in terms of going from the small to the large, and might be confused if you started at the other end of the size scale. (The converse would be true if you were discussing items in the microscopic or submicroscopic range.) Also, the first animals listed would be more familiar to most readers.

Another way might be to organize the individual items into related groups: *cats, lions,* and *tigers; coyotes, dogs,* and *wolves; burros, horses,* and *mules;* and so on.

Don't underestimate the power and usefulness of **a-b-c**'s and **1-2-3**'s. Children learn these from *Sesame Street* before they even start to school, and grow up being comfortable with alphabetical and numerical arrangements. These will often work when no other logic is readily apparent.

5. **Work out a suitable layout and format to help the reader**. If you are discussing just three or four items, a narrative paragraph will probably work fine. But if you are dealing with a longer list, you might want to consider tabular form, or numbered or lettered items, so that the differences and similarities can readily be contrasted and compared by the reader.

6. **Use tables, graphs, and pictures whenever they seem appropriate**. Many readers will find material much easier to understand in pictorial form. Don't hesitate to augment narrative descriptions with tables, charts, graphs, or other illustrations. Some critics might consider this approach wasteful of space and paper; don't believe them. Some readers are word minded; others are oriented more toward mathematics, engineering, and visual displays. Help both groups, not just one.

7. **Make important items stand out**. Use freely all the typograph-

ical devices that are available to you. Employ logic and imagination—the basic aim is to put in any kind of device that might help the reader locate important information and relate it to other items for comparison and contrast. That means you can use, at a minimum, all the devices available on a word processor keyboard: *underscore, capital letters, asterisks, bullets,* and so forth. You can also use different fonts and sizes to great advantage. Whatever the system, you should plan to make maximum use of major and minor headings and subheadings. Also use plenty of "white space," which can help the reader as much or more than many other devices.

Exercise: Orderly Arrangement

You should now be ready to tackle Exercise Ten(A), which you'll find in Part Four.

9

How to Write Letters and Memos

There are only two tests for telling whether a letter is too long. One is whether it says more than need be said. The other is whether it takes too many words to say it.

—Mona Sheppard, *Plain Letters*

Introduction

The first axiom for writing letters and memos—indeed, for writing *anything*—is this:

Axiom One: Do not write without good reason.

We're all being smothered in blizzards of paperwork. Some of it is necessary; unfortunately, much more of it is not. Make sure *your* writing doesn't fall into the second category.

Your priorities should go this way:

- If you can **talk** your message in person, do it.
- If you can't talk it in person, **telephone**.
- If telephoning won't get the job done, then, and only then, **write**.

Talking in person is quickest, least expensive, and least likely to lead to misunderstandings.

Talking by telephone is almost as quick, usually only slightly more expensive, and still gives the advantages of instant feedback.[1]

Writing is by far the slowest method; it is also by far the most expensive. As we have said earlier, the average letter or memo these days costs at least $14.00, and often much more. So, if you must write, keep it short. Write as concisely and effectively as you can. Turn on the old "*gray matter*"; organize your thoughts. By spending a little extra time in the planning stage, you'll save much time later—for both you and your reader.

Plain Letters

Let me introduce you to a classic text on letter writing, *Plain Letters*, by Mona Sheppard. (Available from the Superintendent of Documents, U.S. Government Printing Office, Washington, DC (Federal Stock Number 7610-205-1091.) When I first ran across this small masterpiece back in 1956 it cost 35 cents. The last time I checked with GPO, they told me the title had been changed to *Managing Correspondence: Plain Letters*, and the price is $5.00. So much for progress. The little book could still be one of your better investments.

Ms. Sheppard says "A good plain letter merits this 4-S badge of honor: Shortness, Simplicity, Strength, and Sincerity."

For SHORTNESS, Mona Sheppard says:

- Don't make a habit of repeating what is said in a letter in your answer.
- Avoid needless words and needless information.
- Beware of roundabout prepositional phrases, such as "with regards to" and "in reference to."
- Don't qualify your statements with irrelevant "ifs."

---

[1]"Feedback" has been an acceptable word in a number of different scientific disciplines for many years. Today, it has become quite acceptable in everyday English usage, meaning "response."

For SIMPLICITY, she says:

- Know your subject so well that you can discuss it naturally and confidently.
- Use short words, short sentences, and short paragraphs.
- Be compact. Don't separate related parts of sentences.
- Tie thoughts together so your reader can follow you from one to another without getting lost.

For STRENGTH, her "rules" are:

- Use specific, concrete words.
- Use more active verbs.
- Don't explain your answer before giving it. Give answers straightaway; then explain if necessary.
- Don't hedge. Avoid negative words.

Finally, for SINCERITY, Ms. Sheppard recommends:

- Be human. Use words that stand for human beings, like the names of persons and the personal pronouns *you, he, she, we* and so on.
- Admit mistakes. Don't hide behind meaningless words.
- Don't overwhelm your reader with intensives and emphatics.
- Don't be obsequious or arrogant. Strive to express yourself in a friendly way and with simple dignity befitting the United States Government. (Or your business, company, corporation, etc.)

Applying the 4-S Formula

None of Ms. Sheppard's suggestions for clear letter writing should come as a shock if you carefully study the rest of this book. Most of the principles she suggests have been discussed in some detail; what you have in the *Plain Letters* approach is a useful—and memorable—way of putting it all together.

Here are a few more of her suggestions for brevity and natural-ness:

- Avoid stilted openings as "Reference is made to your let-ter," "This is in reply to your letter," and "We are in receipt of your letter."
- Refer to the inquiry by its date only, as "Thank you for your letter of June 10," or mention the subject of the in-quiry in just enough words to let the reader know you un-derstand what he had to say."
- Refer to the inquiry indirectly with a subordinate clause, as "*The Craftsmanship of Lettering*, which you asked for in your letter of May 23, is out of print."
- Don't describe an incoming letter as recent, particularly when the description doesn't fit. If you are embarrassed by the age of the inquiry, apologize for the delay in an-swering. For example, begin by saying, "We are sorry for the delay in answering your letter."

There are a few minor exceptions to this generally excellent ad-vice. Let me mention a couple of them here:

If you are answering a Congressional inquiry, you'd probably better identify the original correspondence by both title and date in your opening paragraph. Many organizations and agencies re-quire this, and it makes good sense, even though it appears to waste words.

Simply put, the reason is this: Senators and Congressmen (or, in actuality, their Administrative Aides) write literally scores, or even hundreds, of letters every day and every week. They can't be ex-pected to keep track of this correspondence or to remember it the way an individual would. You and I, for example, ordinarily write only a few letters and we know very well what we said in them.

So, if you can neatly apply Ms. Sheppard's advice to Congres-sional responses without breaking your organization's rules, fine. By all means do so. But take special care to make sure the corre-spondence you are answering can be readily identified.

Another important exception involves letters forwarded to you from another organization. When I was at NASA during the Apollo program, for example, letters written to the President were forwarded to us for answers. For a time we received hundreds or even thousands of letters every week.

In such cases, the rule is simply this: explain that the letter—identified by subject and date—has been referred to you for answer. State this politely and simply. Then get straight to the answer.

More Advice on Letter Writing

Daniel O'Neal, former Chairman of the Interstate Commerce Commission (ICC) is one of the best friends of clear writing that I know. We need many more like him. In 1977, he issued a memo to the agency's Managing Director and to heads of ICC bureaus and offices. The title: "English—let's use it at the ICC."

The advice in the memo is so good that I'd like to pass some of it along to you. With Mr. O'Neal's permission, here are some cogent excerpts:

English is a remarkably clear, flexible, and useful language. We should use it in all of our communications.

Commission correspondence is an important part of the face we turn to the world. Each letter we write creates a distinct impression of this agency in the mind of the reader. It also conveys, or fails to convey, information. Letters should be both informational and understandable.

Although there has been general improvement in the quality of correspondence, I think it is worthwhile to lay a few ground rules for writing letters.

First, a few thoughts on style and tone.

Too often government writers fall back on the black sheep of the English family—Bureaucratese.

ICC communications should be written in plain English, with a simple vocabulary. One of the greatest writers of English, Winston Churchill, recommended the use of "short, simple words" and that remains good advice today.

Convey your thoughts clearly. Use short, clear, declarative sentences. Use a noun, a verb, and an object of the verb when necessary. Use adjectives and adverbs only when they are essential to clear meaning.

Don't get wrapped up in legal jargon that makes sense only to lawyers. Look at it from the reader's point of view. Take into account his probable understanding of the Commission and government in general. Ask yourself, "If I had written this letter . . . what sort of response would I want?"

Above all, don't sound bureaucratic. Don't go through linguistic contortions to convey a simple thought . . .

Just speak normally. Be sure to avoid legalistic words or phrases such as *caveat, estopped,* or *viz.* Plain English will get the point across more effectively. And don't let the letter get bogged down with unnecessary details. Stick to the point. Irrelevant statements may indicate an extensive knowledge of the issue, but will probably confuse the reader.

The most common errors in the correspondence I have seen are dangling participles, split infinitives, and most of all, incorrect use of the plural pronoun. For example, the Southern Railroad is "it," not "them" or "they."

If the correspondent wants to know the status of a pending case, develop a reasonable estimated date of decision and give that date . . . Make sure the case meets the deadline . . .

Avoid defensive, self-serving, self-congratulatory statements . . . The correspondent will judge how well we do.

Also, in addition to making the letter understandable, try to make it personal. Let the reader know that a human is on the other end. Convey a warm tone.

Don't be afraid to break up a complex explanation of an issue with an occasional personal comment, just to remind the reader that a human is behind all those facts and figures. "I know this is a difficult situation . . . ," for example, might do in some cases where things look bad. "It's good to hear from you . . ." is appropriate when the correspondent has been helpful.

Letters needn't be puffy or flippant to be personal. They should simply let the reader know that somewhere in Washington, DC, a human, not a computer, wrote that letter.

Avoid passing the buck. An individual should be referred to another federal agency only when absolutely necessary. We should refer the letter ourselves and tell the correspondent that we have done so. If we cannot provide the information, we should at least give a reason why.

Also, let's be willing to admit it when we make a mistake. We're not perfect . . .

One final point: The letters we write are for the benefit of the recipient, not the writer. Keep in mind that someone out there is waiting for the letter you are writing. Someone will have to make sense out of it. If it is hard to understand or if it wallows in a complex, bureaucratic double-talk, that individual's confidence in the government will drop a little bit more.

Remember that the person on the receiving end of a letter is our employer and we are explaining something about how the government—the citizens' tax money—is operating. It's not enough for a letter to be understood among ourselves.

A government letter writer should put himself in the shoes of the recipient and wonder whether somebody in Peoria or Spokane would really understand and be satisfied with a letter that starts, "Pursuant to Public Law 94-210 . . ."

Language is a mirror of thought. If our letters are rambling, twisted, and confusing, it's a pretty good bet that the thought behind them is that way too. And that is exactly how they are perceived by readers.

Let's show the American people that [fill in the name of your own organization here] speaks and writes plain English.

(signed) O'Neal

To the above remarks, a heartfelt "Amen." (signed) Bates.

What Mr. O'Neal wrote so eloquently does not apply just to the ICC, or even just to the government. Writers in private industry are advised to take a leaf from his book as well. The advice is excellent, and can be applied straight across the board.

The Importance of Tone

Every letter you write should have two purposes. The first is to accomplish an immediate objective, such as to convey information, to make a sale, or to ask for information. But your second purpose, although not so obvious, is also important: to build goodwill for yourself and your organization.

If you write in a way that angers or frustrates your reader, you will probably fail in *both* purposes. The effectiveness of your writing will be nil.

In general, tone in written communication is a lot like tact in personal relations—the more effective you are at it, the less likely it is to be noticed at all. If your technique becomes even slightly visible or conspicuous, chances are you had better go back and try again.

Guard against these common mistakes:

- Don't write in a way that angers or frustrates your reader.
- Don't insult the reader's intelligence.
- Don't say anything that might be construed as a put-down.
- Don't preach or pontificate; keep off the soapbox and out of the pulpit.
- Don't talk down to the reader.
- Don't write over the head of the reader.
- Don't use unsuitable humor or backslapping familiarity.
- Don't use sarcasm, exaggeration, or attempts at satire. The odds are almost totally against you. You will almost inevitably be misunderstood or misconstrued by most of your readers.
- Don't make dogmatic, highly opinionated, aggressive, or smart-alecky pronouncements.
- Don't "argue" with the reader—that is, don't blatantly accuse the reader of being wrong, of having misunderstood, or of not being clear.

- Don't sound off at the reader.
- Don't write when you are angry; or if you do, don't mail it for a few days until you've had a chance to cool off. Chances are that by that time you'll tear it up and re-write it.
- Don't pass the buck; if you have made a mistake, admit it.

Don't be Obsequious or Phony

Remember that you can lose points by going too far in the other direction. Being overly obsequious, or buttering up the reader in an obvious way can be irritating, to say the least. Tact, courtesy, and sincerity—those are all good words, and good things to strive for. But be alert to how easy it is to step over the line toward submissiveness or insincerity.

Your letter represents not just you, but your organization or agency as well. You are responsible for doing your part to preserve its dignity. Don't whine, grovel, or get carried away with flowery words and honeyed phrases. And, don't make promises that cannot be kept.

The "You" Attitude

Many government or corporate writers seem to believe they are justified in taking a cold, haughty, or detached approach toward members of the public. Not so. The writer is there to serve the public, not to hand down pronouncements from on high.

There is no reason not to use words that convey warmth, graciousness, and friendliness. Sometimes, though, you may feel you have a particularly difficult problem because of a boss's attitude. I've worked for people, and you probably have also, who put out orders against using the personal pronouns "I" and "we." (The prohibition against the "I" might pass muster. In many organizations, nobody but the top person is supposed to say "I." But the prohibition against "we" is misguided, in my opinion. Still, you'll just have to live with it. Neither you nor I is likely to change the world—let alone the organization or the boss.)

Fortunately, there is a solution, and it's not so difficult as it may seem. Try the "you" approach. Instead of saying "We are . . ." and going into your sentence, simply recast it so that it starts with "you." Most of the time you'll find this works extremely well.

A few cautions are in order. There is danger in overusing "you." It is possible to overdo even a good thing. If your letter begins to sound phony, or appears to the reader to be overly altruistic—that is, if it creates a suspicion that you are trying to put something over—it won't *work*. Suppose, for example, you are writing a letter of application. Your concern is for yourself, not your reader. In such cases, the "you" approach would be patently phony.

Here's a timeworn, but still apt, illustration of the point: "I've talked enough about my marvelous and incredible accomplishments. Now let's talk about *you*. What do *you* think about my marvelous and incredible accomplishments?"

Using "Word Softeners"

Avoid any inclination to use hard-nosed expressions when something less offensive to the reader will get the message across just as well. Why say something such as "I have received your rotten letter in which you complained that . . ." when it is just as easy (and much more effective) to say, "I have received your letter concerning . . ."

You'll never find a better place to employ the golden rule. Put yourself in the reader's shoes. Sympathize. How would you like it if someone wrote to *you* that way?

Is Tone Always Important?

It's true that tone is usually a factor in written communications, just as its counterpart, tone of voice, is important in oral communications. There are differences, however. If you are simply communicating run-of-the-mill information to persons you don't even know, or with whom your relationships are not close or delicate, you need not waste any extra attention on tone. Be polite and courteous, and that will be ample. To create the effect you desire, slant your material to your reader. That means you must determine what relationship exists, or what relationship you desire to achieve. You must appraise both the reader and the situation you are writing about. With these things in mind, it should be relatively simple for you to choose appropriate words. The reader will "hear" them as you intend, without misunderstandings or hurt feelings.

Exercise: Faulty Tone

Sometimes my seminar students get carried away. The following exercise comes from real life. A student, trying to follow the principles of being concise and getting straight to the point, wrote this memo to his boss. The next day he brought it to class, a look of bewilderment on his face. Why was the boss so upset over a simple little memo?

Read what the student wrote and see if you can figure out what he did wrong. Then rewrite, with a more appropriate tone.

Memo To: John Joseph McBoss
From: Alexander Q. Subordinate

I must have your sign off immediately on the enclosed Personnel Handbook, which we have received from Bob Otherguy for review before forwarding to Mr. Headman for final approval.

I intend to take no further action until I hear from you.

Suggested Rewrite:

Bob Otherguy has sent us the enclosed Personnel Handbook for review. If it meets your approval, please initial okay and send it back to me *(or maybe you wrote* return it *instead of* send it back*)* so I can forward it to Mr. Headman for final approval.

10

Know Your Audience

Let us treat men and women well;
Treat them as if they were real;
Perhaps they are.

—Ralph Waldo Emerson (1803–1882)

Introduction

To communicate, you must aim your message directly at your audience. To do this, you must (a) know as much as possible about the make-up of your audience; and (b) know as much as possible about the interests of that audience.

Regardless of what your message may be, you can't expect to deliver it successfully if you always use the same approach, paying no attention to the differences in background of your various readers. What works extremely well for communicating with one group may not work at all for another. To make the problem more difficult, the reasons for the differences may not be at all obvious.

I have used the term "audience" here advisedly. It's true that the word is usually reserved for listeners attending oral presentations. But that's narrowing the term unduly; as used here, it's intended to be a synonym for readers, not simply listeners. And since readers—unlike listeners—do not give you instant feedback, it becomes all the more important that you size up your audience in advance.

Axiom Two: Slant your presentation for your audience.

An audience is comprised of individuals with different backgrounds and personalities, and each of those members is likely to hear or read your message in a different way. Don't be taken in by the fact that the word "audience" is a collective noun that takes a singular form of the verb. That's just a quirk of grammar. An audience can be construed as being either singular or plural, and you can be quite sure that an audience of more than one person will seldom if ever react as a single entity. You can transmit a message you believe to be unmistakably clear, and yet various members of the audience will "hear" very different things—perhaps some of them will come up with diametrically opposite interpretations.

Why is this so? Simple—each individual represents the sum total of a lifetime of "perceived reality," and that "perceived reality" can never be the same for any two persons. Thus, one individual shares a message with another to a limited extent only—namely, the congruent area of "perceived reality" that the two individuals have in common.

When a writer uses words or ideas alien to the reader's knowledge and experience, there are inevitably some gaps in the communication. And the harder the writer may try to bridge the gaps, the more likely that for some of the audience the message may become distorted or bent totally out of shape.

Checklist for Audience Analysis

Fortunately, there are many things you can usually find out in advance, and if you take the composite results, you are much more likely to send a "receivable" message.

The following checklist items are not necessarily in order of importance, but you will want to get answers to as many of them as you can. Here's what you need to find out about your audience:

- Age (or range of ages)
- Sex (or percentage of each)

- Occupations represented
- Educational background (average years of schooling completed, types of studies, majors, etc.)
- Levels of experience

NOTE: Even though the concern here is *written* communication, I have used the same audience analysis checklist most speechwriters use. Much of what I've learned about analyzing audiences comes from speech writing—the best training, and the toughest school, for learning how different audiences respond. If a speech gets off on the wrong foot[1] you find out very quickly—the hard way. Feedback from the audience may take many different forms. If you're lucky you'll get off with scowls or sullen expressions. If you're not so lucky, it can be anything from heckling and jeers to the launching of overripe fruit.

Age

This is usually fairly easy to find out. For purposes of simplicity, let's stick to the speech writing analogy, even though most of your writing will probably be directed to readers rather than to listeners. In either event, you are probably going to know whether you are writing for, say, grade school, high school, or college age people; or perhaps, members of the Junior Chamber of Commerce (relatively young), the Rotary Club (probably somewhat older), or the Association of Retired Employees (senior citizens, to use the current euphemism).

Sex

You can probably find out whether you are writing for an all-male audience, an all-female audience, or a mixture of both. Some years ago I wrote a speech intended for an audience of electronics engineers. Then, at just about the last possible second, I discovered that the occasion was to be a dinner meeting, and that the engineers' wives would be there too. In the revised version, done in

---

[1]Colloquial way of saying "get off to a bad start."

total panic on an airplane en route[2] to Chicago, many of the points of the speech remained essentially the same, but the overall approach had to be changed drastically.

Occupation

Obviously you would write quite differently for a group of electronics engineers than you would for a group of sociologists or an association of retail merchants. There's no need to labor this point.

Educational Background

Remember that education and occupation are the items that separate otherwise similar persons into what sociologists call "subcultures." People with major differences in those two important areas are often likely to have little in common; they may find it difficult to communicate with one another at an abstract level. In writing for disparate groups, keep in mind the importance of concrete words that have meaning in terms of the senses: seeing, hearing, smelling, touching, and tasting. Other, more abstract words may mean one thing to members of one subculture, and something entirely different to members of a different subculture. Look out especially when you use slang terms. Slang changes so fast that by the time one group newly discovers it, the group that originated it has probably already discarded it. As a member of the older generation, I went through a period when I had trouble understanding the language of my teenage children—until fortunately, either they or I, or perhaps all of us, grew out of it.

Levels of Experience

Once more you must be analytical. You must try to deduce what your audience already knows or understands about your subject.

---

[2]Although this is originally a French phrase, meaning "on the way," it has long since found its way into standard English. I see no need to italicize here (as one would ordinarily do with a foreign phrase).

Anticipate as well as you can what additional information the readers will need or want to have.

Analyzing Your Reader(s)

Okay, let's stop talking about speech writing and turn to written communications such as letters and memos. Let's take a hypothetical case in which someone has written you a letter, and you are responding.

Your first clues—indeed, virtually the only ones—will undoubtedly come from the letter you've received. Read it carefully, looking for every clue you can find.

What kind of paper is it written on? Embossed stationery? A piece of lined paper torn from a tablet? A business letterhead? If the latter, does it indicate the person's organization, business, or other affiliation? Is the writer's title indicated?

Is the letter handwritten or typewritten? How well are the ideas expressed? How about the vocabulary? The spelling? All these items can help add up to an overall impression.

The "age" question may or may not be answered, but you can probably tell whether a letter has been written by a young student on the one hand, or by an adult, on the other. The "sex" question can usually, but not always, be answered by the person's name and title, or there may be other indications.

The occupation or profession is often self-evident, or at least easy to figure out: business executive? farmer? physician? and so on.

Suppose some or all of these questions remain unanswered even after your best analytical detective work. What do you do then?

Writing for the "Average" Reader

Is there such a thing as an "average" reader? Probably not, but many times you'll have to write as if there is. Essentially, what you must do is write for the "least common denominator."

That doesn't mean you must "write down" or condescend.

Heaven forbid. It does mean you must choose your words and thoughts so they will have appeal to beginners *and* old hands, tyros and experts, young and old, and all the other possible permutations.

Picture an imaginary reader in your mind—a reader who is reasonably intelligent, but not necessarily schooled; a reader who has good common sense but probably doesn't have a specialized background in the subject you are discussing. The clearer that mental picture, the better you will write.

Okay, take it from there. This means you'll use simple words, weeding out technical shoptalk and jargon[3]—or you'll explain such language if you feel you must use it for accuracy of expression. You will start on common ground, choosing as a beginning something that your reader probably knows about. You will progress one step at a time to the more difficult material. You will be as logical and clear as you possibly can. And you will strive to "slant" the material so it will be as interesting and understandable as you can make it.

Al Lefcowitz, in his excellent *Writer's Handbook*, puts it this way:

". . . shape the expression to fit the thought. That is, the audience should not have to struggle through language more complex than the situation requires."

[3]For a detailed discussion of technical shoptalk and jargon, see Section Three, Chapter 22.

11

Getting and Holding the Reader's Attention

"Hell," said the Duchess, "Let go my leg!"
—Traditional "Narrative Hook"

Introduction

Effective writing must be something more than just well-conceived ideas clearly expressed. Important as these qualities are, they aren't the be-all and end-all.[1] There is another necessary ingredient: the writer must win the reader's attention and interest, or there is no real meeting of the minds.[2]

A generation ago, students of the short story were constantly drilled to employ the device known to the trade[3] as the "narrative hook." The example at the top of this page is a humorous demonstration of how to do it. As an attention-getter, that famous line is supposed to combine a number of things of great interest to the average reader: *excitement,* portrayed by the mildly profane "Hell,"

[1]Colloquial expression meaning "the whole being or essence."
[2]Agreement or shared understanding.
[3]Colloquial expression meaning that "persons engaged in the specific trade—in this case, writing—are familiar with the technical term—in this case, "narrative hook." I haven't heard anybody use the term "narrative hook" in years. When I was a beginning writer, many years ago, all writers talked about it a lot, and in general agreed that if a writer didn't have an opening that instantly grabbed the reader's attention, the story just didn't "cut it." (Nobody says that any more either!)

chosen instead of other Anglo-Saxon monosyllables that would have been more shocking to the average reader in those euphemistic days of my youth; *royalty,* personified by the Duchess; and *sex, violence, and action*—summed up neatly in the "Let go my leg!"

Today we most often encounter the short story, slightly disguised but recognizable, in prime time television "action" shows. Watch a few of them as they come on; later that night you can compare their openings with those of the late, late shows— movies filmed in the 1930s[4] and 1940s. You'll quickly see an object lesson.

The show always starts right out with the most exciting action sequence that can be plucked out of the entire hour. The opening grabber will undoubtedly be some very different actions from one week to the next: one time it may be someone being punched in the nose; in the next episode, a victim may be thrown off Brooklyn Bridge. But whatever it is, you can lay odds that it will be the most exciting and dramatic moment the writers can dredge up from anywhere in the full-hour script.

Most writers don't call this technique the "narrative hook" any more. More likely they'll call it a *teaser* or a *grabber.* But whatever they call it, it has but one purpose—to grab the viewer's attention, instantly. That is the moment when the network shows are all changing at once; viewers are reaching for their remote controls to zap quickly through each program until they find something that interests them. The sponsors don't intend for those potential view-

---

[4]Several critics have taken me severely to task for using this particular form of simply adding the letter "s" to the year. What's truly strange about their complaints is that none of them agreed on how I should fix it. All good editors—and some bad ones—have crotchets. Wouldn't it be nice if they could all get together? Let me give you an example: one critic wanted me to write 1930's, with an apostrophe. (Some style manuals say that's the way to do it. I say, let's apply a bit of logic.) What's the apostrophe supposed to do? In this case, using it would imply that a letter had been left out. Did that happen? No way. Suppose I had written "the '30s." Then there would be an excuse for an apostrophe. Granted that various style books show various ways of doing this, my personal crotchet is that I truly believe I have chosen the best way after looking over all the rest. Once again, you readers have a perfect right to disagree.

ers to be put off by seeing a long list of titles and credits; they know that's the best way to force the viewers to keep surfing.[5]

Chances are, they will make sure to hook you, and all other potential viewers, by not "rolling the credits" until perhaps as long as five or six minutes into the action.

Compare this approach with that of a movie coming on the late, late show—one that was not originally filmed for television. You'll observe that the opening credits are likely to keep rolling for several minutes or more.

The pace is leisurely; you'll see the name of the producer, then perhaps the logo or trademark of the studio. Observe how long MGM's Leo keeps yawning (hope this mental image isn't contagious), before they even get around to letting you know the name of the picture. Notice the elapsed time as they scroll down the credits; the producer, the directors, all the stars, great and small—some of the really big ones listed as "Mr." or "Miss"—followed by the supporting players, the bit players, the camera and sound men, the script girls, the grips, and so on ad infinitum. Perhaps, in very small print, they'll eventually even show you the name of the writer. Or, in bigger print, the name of the producer's brother-in-law who was given all the credit.

The audiences those movies were made for had traveled—perhaps for miles—to get to the theater. What's more important, they had bought tickets at the box office and paid their way in. They were definitely a captive group. There wasn't any danger they'd change channels for a more exciting show.

Well, there's a great deal more competition for the viewer's attention these days. That's why everyone goes to so much trouble to introduce some interest and excitement right up front.

Notice what they do next. Once they've captured that attention, they can start going back, picking up earlier details, filling in the background, explaining what has gone before and how it all fits together.

---

[5]The word "surfing" in this sense is almost brand new, but I think it has already found a permanent place in the language. I can't imagine any modern reader not knowing this, but it's what we used to call "channel hopping."

That's not a bad trick for all writers to remember, all the time. We live in a media-dominated age. Audiences aren't nearly so patient as they used to be. If we intend to capture their attention, we'd better do our best to get to our point quickly, without any fooling around.

How many letters have crossed your desk in recent weeks that you had to read several times before you could even begin to figure out what the writer was driving at? Chances are, quite a few.

Did you have to fight your way through rambling introductions, extraneous material, and unnecessary background information before the writer actually got down to the main business?

If those letters were TV shows, you undoubtedly would have tuned them out. Since they were probably important to you, you fought your way through them, wasting your valuable time and perhaps never finding out exactly what you wanted to know.

Engrave this in big, bold letters on the tablets of your memory: The reader has a right to know, as early on as possible, what a communication is about. Write so that your reader can get the message quickly—on the very first reading.

Here's a step-by-step analysis of how to do it:

Axiom Three: Get straight to the point.

1. Formulate a simple, one-sentence statement of what the writing is all about. Do this before you actually begin to write.
2. Write down your statement of purpose. Phrase it so it will make the reader interested in continuing to read. The best way to do this is to put yourself in the reader's shoes, and figure out what would be important to you in such a case. In the process, ask yourself the following questions:
   a. What is the real reason I am writing this?
   b. What is the main idea I want to convey?
   c. What response do I desire to elicit from the reader?
3. Set forth the points more interesting or important to the reader at the very beginning. (These may not be the same points as

those of most interest to you. Don't think of your own preferences at all; put the reader first.)

4. **Put the conclusion, or its equivalent, near the beginning**—perhaps not in the very first paragraph, but certainly as close to it as you can manage. Remember that you're not writing a detective story in which you hold things back from the reader. Do just the opposite of that: give the answers the reader needs without trying for a build-up of suspense.

5. **Use the "flashback" technique to fill in the details.** Make your reader have full understanding by furnishing the background, the ancient history, or whatever it takes to explain and support your case.

Here's a good example of a memo that's straight to the point, with no "flashback" needed. The sender and receiver were both thoroughly familiar with the problem under discussion.

THE WHITE HOUSE

> To: John Dean
> From: Charles Colson
> Now what the hell do I do?

Exercise: Getting Straight to the Point

This is an actual announcement, copied from an original posted on the company bulletin board. "Only the names have been changed, to protect the innocent." Please read this announcement carefully several times before you answer the questions that follow it.

ANNOUNCEMENT

SUBJECT: Meeting on "Management by Objective," December 10–12.

1. On December 10–12 the Corporation will host a conference on Management by Objective which will be held in the Building Six Auditorium.
2. Approximately 300 conference participants are expected, which will cause crowding at some of the Corporation's

facilities. The Building Six Parking Lot will be reserved for conference attendees. Employees who normally park there should make an effort to use other lots. Also, between 11:30 A.M. and 12:30 P.M., the Administrative Building Cafeteria No. 3 will be occupied by conference attendees. Corporation employees should plan accordingly.

3. As always your cooperation in these matters is greatly appreciated.

To help you in your rewrite, I suggest you now answer these questions:

1. Does the subject line really tell the reader what the announcement is all about?
2. If you were a corporation employee reading the announcement on the company bulletin board, would you—after reading paragraph 1—get the impression that you were being invited to attend the conference?
3. After careful reading, what do believe are the two *real* messages the announcement is intended to convey?

When you've answered these three questions, rewrite the announcement, reorganizing and restructuring it. Put first things first. Start with the subject line itself. (Hint: Do you need a "To" line? That is, should this announcement be addressed to all corporation employees? Or is it really addressed to just a portion of those employees? Think about it.)

Please don't look at the suggested rewrite on the next page until you have completed your own version. There's a good chance yours might be better.

Suggested Rewrite for Exercise: Getting Straight to the Point

---

ANNOUNCEMENT

TO: All Employees Who Park on the Building Six Parking Lot, and All Employees Who Eat in Cafeteria No. 3

SUBJECT: Parking Restrictions on Building Six Parking Lot on December 10, 11, and 12. Eating Restrictions in Cafeteria No. 3 from 11:30 A.M. to 12:30 P.M., same dates.

1. Please use other parking lot and cafeteria facilities during the time periods indicated in the subject line.
2. We ask you to cooperate in observing these restrictions because the Corporation is hosting a conference on "Management by Objective," December 10, 11, and 12, in the Building Six Auditorium. We expect to accommodate about 300 conference participants from other organizations. As hosts, we must reserve facilities for them.
3. We're sorry about the inconvenience, but your cooperation will help us make the conference run smoothly. We appreciate it very much.

Exceptions to the Rule

Are there ever cases when it would be better *not* to get straight to the point? Well, there are exceptions to just about everything, and this one is no exception.

Suppose you have to tell the reader some bad news, or turn down a request. In that case you will want to break it gently; cushion the blow, as it were. If you can, start with some kind of good news first, or at least seek a common ground with the reader. Be human, and humane.

But the bad news is still there, and you can't avoid it indefinitely. So, cushion the blow—but then, get to the point. Express regret or sympathy if you can, but don't apologize. Remember that you do no kindness by keeping the reader in suspense unnecessarily. And you do an actual unkindness if you hold out hopes that you might change your mind. (This subject is discussed in more detail in the chapter on letter writing.)

12

How to Do "How-to-do-its"

When all else fails, read the instructions.
—*Ancient adage*

In case of fire, stand in the hall and shout "Fire!"
—John Kidner, *The Kidner Report*

Introduction

Instructions should be simple, direct, concise, clear, and precise. All these virtues are important enough in any kind of writing, but in doing "how-to-do-its" they are absolutely essential.

This chapter is chiefly about techniques for writing instructions, but most of the information given here can be carried over to the closely related areas of writing rules and regulations, discussed in the next chapter.

In this area, your most important axiom is:

Axiom Four: Show the reader!

Try to anticipate all problems, and make sure you deal with each one—simply, logically, and *in the right order*. I could give you examples of how not to do it that would (apologies to my old friend and colleague, the late Ralph Gibson) "bring a suspicion of moisture to your steely blue eyes."

Let's look at a typical example. Many years ago, I bought an electronic ignition system for my car. An inscription on the top of the box said the device would be easy to install—"Just follow the simple instructions." Does that sound familiar?

When I opened the box, I was happy to see that the instructions were spelled out step by step—a good sign. That's the best way to write instructions. I immediately began to feel a false sense of security.

I noticed something else. The manufacturers wanted to make sure I wouldn't lose the instructions, so they had glued the instruction sheet on the back of the ignition module. Great!

As I recall, the first step went something like this:

Step 1. Using the ignition module as a template, drill two 3/8-inch holes at a suitable spot on the fire wall of the engine compartment. Using two 3/8-inch sheet metal screws, mount unit firmly to fire wall.

Well, that sounds clear enough, except for the "suitable spot," and I suppose a reasonably bright person could figure that out. So what's the complaint? Surely I don't have to remind you that the instructions were glued on the *back* of the module!

As I say, that sort of mistake is typical. Even though the instructions were well-written in many respects, putting the steps in the wrong order is a most serious offense. As discussed in the previous chapter, you can choose from many methods of development, but in writing instructions, the *sequential* or *chronological* method usually works best. Why? Because instructions usually must be followed in an established sequence. Thus, one of the worst crimes a writer can commit is to present steps out of sequence. Confusion could lead to damaging equipment or to injuring or killing an operator.

Checklist for Writing Instructions

1. **Use short sentences and short paragraphs.** Numbered sequences are usually best.

2. **Arrange in logical order.** (I know you are tired of hearing it, but we *must* get this in the checklist.)
3. **Make your statements specific.** (Once more I'll remind you of the Kipling jingle: Who-What-Where-When-Why-How, not necessarily in that order.)
4. **Use the imperative mood.**
5. **Put the most important item in each sentence at the beginning.**
6. **Say one thing in each sentence.** Don't try to pack in any extra information or thoughts beyond what it takes to do the job. Let's repeat—say one thing *only* in each sentence.
7. **Choose your words carefully. Avoid *jargon* and technical terms if you can**, by using everyday words familiar to the average reader. If you must use technical terms, define them. One good way to do this is to furnish the reader with a glossary of technical terms. See 240 for further discussion.
8. **Give an *example* or an *analogy*,** if you think a statement may puzzle the reader. Using properly captioned diagrams or illustrations is often even better. Remember Axiom Four: Show the reader!
9. **Check your completed draft for logic of presentation.** Make sure you have progressed from (a) the known to the unknown; or (b) from the general to the specific.
10. **Don't omit steps or take shortcuts**, in the belief that something is obvious, and the reader will understand. Murphy's Law promises us that the reader will *misunderstand* if such a thing is at all possible, and probably will even if it's not possible.

How to Describe Simultaneous Operations

Sometimes you may have to describe two or more steps that must be performed at the same time. Here are a couple of suggestions on ways of handling these toughies: (a) Write an introductory paragraph of explanation before you start on the actual step-by-step procedures; (b) include *both* steps in the same numbered item, with a large-print NOTICE that they must be performed together; or (c) use a double-column layout to indicate the simultaneous operations. Take special care not to overload any of the numbered steps with irrelevant detail.

Exercise: How to Write Instructions

You'll find EXERCISE TEN(c) on writing instructions in Part Four, page 282.

13

How to Write Regulations

*Any member introducing a dog into the
Society's premises shall be liable to a fine of
one pound. Any animal leading a blind person
shall be deemed to be a cat.*

—Rule 46, Oxford Union Society, London

*There are two things wrong with almost all
legal writing. One is its style.
The other is its content.*

—Fred Rodell (Retired Yale Law Professor)

Introduction

Writing is far from being an exact science, as we have said. Even
when we try our best to be precise, we fail more often than not.
Readers come up with interpretations totally different from those
we intend to convey.

Law is, if anything, even less exact. After all, laws and regulations are made up of words; they can be no more precise than
their ingredients. No law has ever been written that didn't have an
exception—sometimes many more than one.

It's an age-old problem. How can you write something clearly,
so that it is easy to understand, without oversimplifying? How do
you keep from losing or changing important shades of meaning?
It's hard enough with any kind of writing. But when you deal with
laws and regulations the problems become much more serious.
Laws usually affect lives and pocketbooks, and you can't get much
more serious than that.

But good things have happened during the years since 1977
when I completed the manuscript for the first edition of this book.

In New York State, an assemblyman named Sullivan sponsored a revolutionary "Plain Language" bill that was signed into law (after much hassling and an amendment or two) to take effect in the fall of 1978. It required leases and other consumer documents to be written "in a clear and coherent manner using words with common everyday meanings," and it became a model for other states drafting similar laws. A few years ago these kinds of laws were unheard of. Now they're growing fast. *Progress, it's wonderful.*

In the mid 1970s, the state of Pennsylvania put into effect a regulation requiring auto insurance policies to rate at least 40 on the Flesch Readability scale. (See **readability** entry in the handbook section.)

Time magazine reported (circa 1978) that several other states had legislated plain language requirements for health and accident policies. About the same time, Congress enacted the Federal Pension Reform Act, requiring that company booklets be written "in a manner calculated to be understood by the average participant." And, said *Time,* the new Federal Warranty Law stated that product warranties had to be "simple and readily understood."

But most written legal documents and government regulations continue to be written in difficult, obscure, and ambiguous language. *We've come a long way, baby, but we still have a long way to go.*

Check with the Legal Staff

Unless you are trained in the law, take this advice: check out every word of every regulation you write with the organization's legal staff. This can be good or bad—it's up to you. I know many writers who hate every minute of it. They bypass getting legal coordination every time they can. Frankly, that isn't very bright. More than once a lawyer has saved me from a severe *attack of the stupids.*

Be glad you have a lawyer to check everything out. You need not have an adversary relationship. After all, you are both on the same side, and if you're not, you should be. You can argue over words, phrases, meanings, and intents all day—and still be friends.

Mutual respect is the key. Your relationship is—or should be—symbiotic. Each of you has special knowledge to contribute to the accuracy of the end product, and working together will increase that accuracy. Both of you should have the courage of your convictions, but should be willing to bend a little to achieve the desired goal.

Don't permit yourself to be *snowed* by legal erudition. Some lawyers know the law inside out, but still write the most convoluted prose imaginable. Maybe they know *too* much. Balance things out by injecting a smidgen of common sense. Admit your own ignorance, and point out that if the lawyer can explain things to you, you can in turn explain them to the public.

Much bad legal and regulatory writing stems simply from custom and habit. The old story—you're as tired of hearing it as I am of telling it: "We've always done it this way."

But that isn't the whole problem. Much legal writing is as miserable as it is simply because the writers don't know how to do any better.

Some Steps in the Right Direction

Jim Miner was chairman of the American Bar Association's Committee on Legal Drafting in the 1970s. Miner explained that the main reason regulations are almost always written in gobbledygook can be traced to one thing: only the worst sections of any regulation are handed down and used over and over again in later versions. These obscurely written passages are preserved, he explained, because only the most incomprehensible sections of any regulation or law are litigated in court. "The language has been tested," said Miner, "because it is so bad that no one could understand it."

He pointed out that arguments can be long and bloody, but once a decision has been reached, the words "blessed" by the judge's decision go into the form books for other regulation writers to use.

I particularly enjoy the following paragraph, which Miner distributed to all his classes as a typical example of what's wrong with most legal writing:

> *We respectfully petition, request and entreat, that due and adequate provision be made, this day and the date hereinafter subscribed, for the satisfying of this petitioner's nutritional requirements and for the organizing of such methods as may be deemed necessary and proper to assure the reception by and for said petitioner of such quantities of baked cereal products as shall, in the judgment of the aforementioned petitioners constitute a sufficient supply thereof.*

In case you don't recognize this legalistic version of an extremely familiar passage, it translates to "Give us this day our daily bread."

Cutting Out the Legalistic Jargon

One step to improve legal writing is a simple one: substitute everyday words for "legalisms." Obviously, we can't list them all, but here's a sampling of some of the worst offenders with suggestions for replacing them. Here goes:

abeyance. Try *wait*, or *postpone action*.
accompanied by. Most of the time you can substitute *with*.
affix your signature. Just say *sign the paper*.
afford an opportunity. How about *allow?* Or *permit?*
as of this day. That's saying *today* the hard way.
at an early date. Try substituting *soon*.
at your earliest convenience. What if your reader doesn't find it convenient at all? For best results, be as specific as you can.
claim. Try *say*, *charge*, *contend*, or (rarely) *allege*. (Watch your tone. *Allege* can be dynamite.)
cognizance. Mona Sheppard says: "Avoid this big word both in its legal meaning of jurisdiction and in its common

meaning of heed or notice. Instead of saying "under the cognizance of this office," be specific, as "this office does not audit travel vouchers."

earliest practicable date. Say *as soon as possible*.

e.g. This abbreviation stands for the Latin **exempli gratia**, which means *for example.* Many readers don't know what it means. Avoid confusion. Simply write *for example*.

endeavor to ascertain. That's the long-winded way of saying *try to find out*.

eschew. This means *give up*. Most of the time that's what you should write. But you need not always eschew **eschew.** Sometimes it's useful. It was good enough for Mark Twain, and that's pretty good. Also, Richard Wincor, a lawyer who writes wisely, wittily, and well, defends the word. He goes on to say that ". . . rare words should be used only once in a long while. Whoever uses them sparingly appears reliable, but with hidden depths."

finalize. This miserable abomination of a word is on the forbidden list of most careful writers, but it continues to crop up anyway. Why not substitute *end, conclude, finish*, or *complete?*

fullest possible extent. Try substituting something like *as much as you (or somebody) can*, or—better—leave it out entirely. Mona Sheppard calls it meaningless padding.

hereby. Some lawyers appear to love this word almost more than life itself. Too bad, because it is a real confuser. Sometimes it means *by means of this*, but you can't tell what the *this* is referring to. It could be an entire document, or a part of it, or at a particular moment, but perhaps a little later. You see, it has no definite or fixed position in space or in time. Forget it. Unless you just want to sound fancy and legal, you'd better **eschew** it.

herein/herewith. It won't do much good to define these words, because the meanings are not difficult. Unfortunately, they can often lead to unsuspected ambiguity.

Most of the time you'll make your writing clearer by leaving them out.

hereinafter. This little word, unlike the others, probably deserves a medal. It is a time and space saver, particularly useful for setting up abbreviated names to be used throughout the remainder of a legal document.

i.e. This is an abbreviation for the Latin **id est**. As with **e.g.**, (with which it is sometimes confused) many readers simply don't know what it means. Say *that is*, and avoid misunderstanding.

implement. What would the government do without this word? I don't know, but it would be interesting to find out. The word simply means *carry out* or *put into effect*. Unfortunately, saying it that way simply doesn't sound nearly impressive enough to suit many writers.

in compliance with your request. Say *as requested*.

interpose no objection. How about *I do not object*, or *I approve*.

objective. Try *aim* or *goal*.

obligate. Frankly, I know that the budget and fiscal people won't give up on this one without a struggle, but sometimes *bind* will work. Not always.

obligation can be *debt*.

over the signature of. Why not just say *signed by*?

preclude. You could substitute *shut out* or *prevent*. But I don't always preclude **preclude**, so I shouldn't expect you to.

promulgate. Some people would rather promulgate than eat. We are going to have a rough time stamping this one out, but we can try. A good substitute is *issue*. Sometimes *publish* will work.

pursuant. Old-line members of the military services would probably go up in smoke if they couldn't say "Pursuant to the authority contained in" whatever it is. Just for kicks, I wish they would at least occasionally replace it with *under*.

secure. This is another word that has built-in ambiguity. The military services use **secure** in a specialized way; they are not about to change, and I don't suppose they should. But the rest of us should bypass secure by saying *get*, *take*, or *obtain*.

since. This word is often misused and I must admit with shame that I'm frequently among the guilty. **Since**, in its primary meaning, should carry the idea of *from then until now*, or *from some particular time in the past and on up to the present*. But many writers use it regularly as a substitute for *because*, with resulting confusion to the reader.

subsequent to means *after*.

telephonically. This is a real monstrosity. I am horrified to learn that there are agencies that won't permit their employees to write or say *by telephone*. They must think they are impressing somebody, but all I know is that they are *de*pressing me.

terminated. Let's terminate **terminated**. Say *ended*—it's just as final and much neater.

utilize. *Writers often utilize* **utilize** *when they should use use*. (A tip of the hat to Bill Gilbert, Public Affairs Officer of the D.C. Council of Governments, from whom I "borrowed" this definition.)

verification. Sometimes you can at least unsmother the verb and say *verify* or *verified*. Other times you can simply say *proof*.

whereas. This is a real troublemaker of a word. It doesn't really mean much of anything. Still, some lawyers love to fling it around—I suppose they think it adds a legalistic overtone to an otherwise mundane and unexceptional document. Sometimes they use it to mean *since*, or *considering that*. Other times it means *while on the contrary*. Most of the time it's window dressing. Still, I don't suppose a **Presidential** Proclamation would be considered authentic without a nice **whereas** at the beginning of each paragraph.

One last offense has been saved for special mention: **and/or**. This inseparable pair is greatly disliked by many writers, including the impeccable E. B. White. But Richard Wincor, writing from the viewpoint of the law, calls **and/or** "an essential barbarism." His implication is that the expression has its uses. I agree. At least once or twice in this book you can catch me using it. Nevertheless, I would suggest that there are *usually* ways of writing around it; by avoiding the expression whenever you can, you will certainly improve the accuracy of your prose.

Exercise: Rewriting a Legal Document

Here is the actual language of the old personal-loan note of the First National City Bank. Rewrite it as simply and clearly as you can, but be careful not to change any legal meanings. This is a difficult assignment, but just consider it a challenge! When you have finished, you'll have a chance to compare your version with the actual version now in use. Segal and Gale, a firm that specializes in writing legal documents in plain English, accepted the challenge and managed to do a marvelously clear rewrite. You'll find it below.

In the event of default in the payment of this or any other Obligation or the performance or observance of any term or other contract of agreement evidencing or relating to any Obligation or any Collateral on the Borrower's part to be performed or observed; or the undersigned Borrower shall die; or any of the undersigned become insolvent or make an assignment for the benefit of creditors; or a petition shall be filed by or against any of the undersigned under any provision of the Bankruptcy Act; or any money, securities or property of the undersigned now or hereafter on deposit with or in the possession of or under the control of the Bank shall be attached or become subject to distraint proceedings or any order of process of any court . . .

Suggested Rewrite of Exercise: Rewriting a Legal Document

NOTE: I truly didn't expect you to perform any miracles on this, because you have had to work on the basis of limited information, and probably, little or no experience in legal writing. So, if you came up with something even remotely like the following, you did well. This is the way Segal and Gale did it:

I'll be in default:
1. If I don't pay an installment on time; or
2. If any other creditor tries by legal process to take any money of mine in your possession.

The Rules for *Shall* and *Will*

Thirty-odd years ago, traditional grammarians were still quite concerned about the differences between *shall* and *will.* In those days, the formal rule was that, to express simple futurity, you would use *shall* in the first person, and *will* in the second and third persons. That is, *I shall, you will, he/she/it will,* and so on.

To express determination, promise, or intention, it was the other way around: *will* for first person; *shall* for second and third persons.

Most of these distinctions have just about disappeared in recent years. *Will* is generally considered acceptable in informal usages for all purposes, and few persons hearing it used that way would even raise an eyebrow.

When it comes to the language of regulations and contracts, however, the old rules still apply. In such cases, of course, your primary concern will be the usages for second and third person, not first. For example, if you write "The contractor will furnish . . ." you are implying simple futurity only, and there is no binding force. But "The contractor shall furnish" means that the contractor is under firm direction to perform.

The Rules for *Must* and *Should*

In the language of regulations, the word *must* is used as an imperative to indicate a necessity, a binding force. The word *should* carries the idea of obligation, but not of necessity. It is, accordingly, a weaker word.

Checklist for Writing Regulations

1. State the purpose of the regulation as simply, briefly, and clearly as you possibly can.
2. Tell who will be governed by the regulation. Be specific.
3. Use short sentences and plain words. Define your terms.
4. Prefer the *present tense* whenever possible.
5. Use the *imperative mood.*
6. Put the most important things first. Start with the known and move to the unknown. Start with the general and move to the specific—logically.
7. Say one thing, and only one thing, in each sentence.
8. If there is an exception, put it in the very next sentence.
9. Check your completed draft for possible ambiguity. If necessary—rewrite, rewrite, rewrite.
10. Don't omit any steps or take any shortcuts. Spell everything out, all the way.

NOTE: The legal department of your organization will probably give you a hard time on items 7 and 8. You may lose. But don't give up without a struggle. These two items are highly important. It is a mistaken notion to think that all qualifications, all exceptions, and the like must be packaged within a single set of periods. You will often be told that you must do it this way—to keep people from taking information out of context and twisting it. Don't believe it. A number of excellent lawyers have assured me that this simply is not so. In fact, they say that overpacked sentences can well lead to problems and litigation. Trying to fit too many ideas into one long, complicated sentence will often result in total incomprehensibility—not just to the lay reader, but often to the lawyers as well.

Exception Disclosures

Because courts have ruled that regulations have the same force and effect as law, it is well to include in most regulations an "exception disclosure," such as "Exceptions to the provisions of this regulation may be made only by [fill in organization title]. Send requests for exceptions to [organization title].

Consistency

Let me bring this chapter on writing regulations to an end by reminding you once more to be consistent. Do *not* use different words to denote the same thing. Do *not* use the same word to denote different things. Set a style, choose a vocabulary, and stick with it. In other types of writing, you can commit these "sins" and perhaps even get away with some of them. When you are writing regulations, you cannot. Engrave this next axiom on the tablets of your memory:

Axiom Five: Be consistent.

14

How to Write Reports

I never understand anything
until I have written about it.

—E.M. Forster (1879–1969)

What's the Problem?

After nearly 50 years in the business, one thing I've found is that most of us can tackle a one-page project and finish it. (Okay, so maybe it won't be a masterpiece.) But confront us with a longer project—for example, a 50-page report or a 250-page manual—and watch instant panic set in.

After discussing this almost universal problem with thousands of writing students, I believe I've uncovered the root of the matter: Invariably, inexperienced writers (and some experienced ones who ought to know better) think of the task as one thick, solid, indigestible mass. Quite literally, they get the overwhelming feeling that they're biting off more than they can chew.[1] So, quite naturally, they choke.

No longer am I shocked, or even surprised, by this apparently universal malady. As the radio comedians of my youth would have said, the *guilty finger* is pointing straight at our English teachers, who paralyzed our childish minds by giving us a lot of bad advice.

---

[1]Idiomatic expression meaning "to take on a commitment one is unable to fulfill."

Probably the worst offense was to instill in us the ironclad rule that we must always make an outline before we begin to write. (Let me say here that I'm not really against outlines; they can be valuable tools. It's just that our teachers didn't teach us the right way to go about outlining. I'll show you "the easy way to outline" in the next chapter.)

In this chapter, I'll explain how to overcome the fearsome problem of getting started. If you're perceptive, you'll see that in doing this, I'm simply putting into practice my own advice: break your task up into "bite-size" pieces, and then chew them up one at a time.

What follows is a simple, step-by-step system that will get you started as painlessly as possible.

Getting Started

Identify Your Subject

The first step in writing a report (or anything else) is to identify your subject clearly and sharply. As Norman Vincent Peale brilliantly put it, "Write yourself a telegram." That is to say, jot down, in as few words as possible, exactly what you want your report to accomplish. In considering this, focus your approach on the basic truth that most reports are concerned, one way or another, with stating a problem and offering a possible solution or solutions.

Get the Facts

Far too often, reports are written without full knowledge of the facts. Indeed, many of them should never see the light of day. My first advice to anyone assigned the project of turning out a report is "Get out of it if possible!" That comment is not entirely facetious. It's just that over the years I've seen the wheel re-invented entirely too many times. What I mean is that you should start by doing some basic research—find out what is already in print, and what information on the subject is readily available.

Let me illustrate with a story I heard at NASA many years ago when I was writing speeches for the agency. Old-timers told me that, back in the days of Project Mercury, a large aerospace company spent almost two million dollars and a year of research on a project. When at last the report was published, only then did somebody discover that a competing organization[2] had performed almost identical research, come up with substantially the same results, and published a report, available commercially, that could have been purchased for $14.95! This story sounds too true to be apocryphal.

So, before you begin to think about writing *anything* try one of the following options: (a) go to the library, enlist the aid of a technical librarian, and find out who has written what; OR (b) if (as I now do) you write on a computer/word processor equipped with a modem, check the available "on line" databases and get a full readout of everything published on a given subject, without ever leaving your desk.

Even if this kind of research doesn't save you from having to write your own new report, knowing what is already in print will enable you to do your job a whole lot better.

Start with the "Givens"

Many scientific and technical reports are virtually straitjacketed as to format. To the extent that your report must conform to the established formal pattern, you have, in a manner of speaking, a canned "outline." Beyond that, your organization may even have a traditional format you must follow in developing ideas and presenting factual material.

Recognize these "givens" and learn to live with them, but don't feel hemmed in. They're not all bad. In truth, they give you an easy and virtually automatic way to break the indigestible mass of

---

[2]In earlier editions, I wrote "*competitor* organization." A sharp-eyed editor suggested that I had made a poor word choice, and recommended substituting *competing*. However much I hate to admit a mistake, I couldn't deny that he was right. As the corny old story goes, "I once made a mistake back in 1948. I thought I had written something wrong, but I was mistaken!"

your project into easy bite-sizes. And creativity need not surrender abjectly to form. What you do with your own material within the "givens" is what we are discussing here.

Taking Notes: It's in the Cards!

This book—like all my others—was organized and outlined using a card system. Indeed, most of the professional writers I know use cards as their basic tool in putting their manuscripts together. During long ago days in English Comp I, one of the first things I learned was that index cards are the recommended tool for taking library notes and making bibliography cards.

But that was only the beginning. In another class, an inspiring professor named H. O. Grauel made his students write a daily composition within the space of the two sides of a four by six card. That discipline taught me a valuable lesson and a new trick.

Ever since, I've observed with interest the myriad ways that seasoned writers use the power of index cards. Recently, I heard someone call them his "portable memory bank." In these days of computers, I find the term apt, maybe even endearing!

So, this may be one of the most important bits of advice that I can give you, now or ever:

Carry index cards with you everywhere you go. Get in the habit of making notes all the time. The more I watch—and ask—the more I find how many successful people in all walks of life—not just writers—use three by fives, although their methods may vary all over the landscape. And, of course, a growing number are now taking advantage of new technology: they make their notes on a laptop computer or a dictation machine. I do a lot of that now myself. But surprise! Where do those notes finally land? That's right, printed out on three by fives. More about these methods later.

In case you've grown rusty on note-taking techniques, here are a few reminders:

Bibliography Cards

- Use standard three by five cards. Make a separate card for each reference you check. Put on each card, in the order indicated, the items listed below:
- **Author's name**, last name first. If the book has more than one author, list the rest of the names, first names first, in the order that they appear on the title page of the book.
- **Title of publication**, underscored. (If you're listing an article from a magazine or periodical, put the title of the article itself in quotation marks. Then give the name of the publication and underscore it.)
- **The edition** (1st, 2nd, etc.).
- **Place of publication.**
- **Name of publisher.**
- **Date of publication** (if no date is given, write *n.d.*).
- In the lower left corner of the card, place the library call number or file number. That way, you'll have it handy and won't have to look it up again if you need to track down the reference later.
- In the upper right corner of the card, write your own identifying number, starting with "1" on the first card and continuing with consecutive numbers on succeeding cards. You will refer to these numbers to identify the source of your *note cards*. You don't need to be concerned about alphabetizing at this point. You'll do that later, when you prepare the actual bibliography or list of references for your report or paper.

Note Cards

After you survey a reference work and decide it will be useful, take careful notes in a way that permits you to identify what idea came from what source. Many experts recommend three by five cards for this. For a long time I preferred five by eights because they hold so much more. A few years ago I changed back to three by fives, using computer cards, attached in perforated flat packs. That gives me the best of both worlds; they fit neatly in my inside jacket pocket and can be torn apart into one, two, or three cards, according to how much information goes together.

You might want to use different colors for the various types of material—for example, yellow for bibliography cards, blue for the related notes cards, and white for your own original material.

Most standard references on report writing suggest that you write notes in your own words, rather than quoting the author exactly. When you do quote a writer's own words, enclose them in quotation marks. Quotations must be exact, even to vagaries in grammar, spelling, or punctuation. Use the expression *sic* (Lating for *thus*) to indicate mistakes or special uses for which the original writer is responsible.

In quoted material, indicate omitted words by ellipses (. . .).

If you find it necessary to add any of your own words in a quoted passage, enclose them in brackets [ ].

There are certain cases when direct quotations are necessary and helpful. For example, when—

- The point is important.
- The statement is to be refuted.
- The author's statement is ambiguous.
- The citation may be questioned.
- The point is stated so well that the style will strengthen your own report or paper.

Often you will make a number of note cards from the same reference. Make sure to cross-index each note card with the appropriate bibliography card, using a number system that corresponds with that of the bibliography cards.

Take down more notes and quotations than you expect to use. Err on the side of too much rather than too little. (Using a dictation machine makes this easier; it's a lot easier to talk your notes than it is to write them down[3]—especially if you have someone to tran-

---

[3]An editor suggested I eliminate the word "down." After due deliberation, I decided it would be better to leave it in. There is a difference between "writing something" and "writing something down."

scribe them onto the cards for you later.) This practice will save you time and trouble when you actually[4] get down to writing.

The Creative Organizer

I don't know if my hero, Mark Twain, used a card system, but he did have some wise observations about organizing. In his diary he once observed: "Have a place for everything and keep the thing somewhere else. This is not advice, it is merely custom." Taking an inward look at my own problems, I'm led to suspect that old Mark may not always have been able to find precisely what he was looking for.

As you can imagine, at one time I had thousands of index cards filled with notes, filed away in assorted little tin boxes, file drawers, bundles wrapped in rubber bands, or inserted in portfolio pockets—or just plain lost. What a mess.

For many years, I searched—without success—for a master plan to organize all those cards. Finally, in the summer of 1984, I found my answer: the "perfect" organizer that does everything I had ever hoped for, and a lot more that hadn't occurred to me. It's called *Scan/Plan, The Creative Organizer*™. I've been using the system ever since, and the more I use it, the better I like it. (No, I don't own stock in the company, but I do sincerely hope that it achieves the success it deserves.)

I use the system every day, everywhere. I carry a *Minipak*, a handy pocker-size wallet that holds 20 cards. In my office, I augment this with other sizes, shapes, and configurations—all interchangeable; I'll describe them in the next chapter.

Visualizing the Total Report

Once you have assembled all the facts, the quickest way to get some bite-size pieces is to fit them into the standard format your

---

[4]The same editor wanted me to leave out "actually." Again, I chose to leave it in. Omitting it changes the shade of meaning that I was striving for. I freely break any and all of my own "rules" or principles if the breaking thereof makes my intended meaning more understandable. I think that is the case here.

organization uses. A good way to start is to study a *good* existing report. (For heaven's sake, don't choose a poor example as your standard.)

Make a simple "dummy" of the project,[5] and your task will be much easier. The usual report is divided into three major sections, the *Introduction,* the *Body* (or *Discussion*), and the *Conclusion.* In addition, there will be "front matter" consisting usually of a letter of transmittal, a summary or abstract, table of contents, and sometimes a list of figures and tables, or a glossary of technical terms. If you have extremely complex or technical material that might slow your pace in the body of the report, consider putting it separately, in an appendix. Many readers will ignore such material, but specialists will dote on it.

Here is another way to cut a big job down to size. I'll tell you what I do;[6] then you may want to try your own variations. The objective, whatever device you use, is to break that overwhelming multi-page report into segments you can deal with comfortably. The difference this makes in psychological attitude is astounding; small pieces, no matter how many, seem far easier to deal with.

I use file folders with internal pockets—one on each side—that hold standard sheets of paper. I label one folder for each section of the job and put my notecards into scan pages, using the left-hand pockets. As the report grows, the sheets of typed material go into the right-hand pockets.

When the first draft is completely typed, I check against the cards to make sure I haven't missed anything; then I remove them from my folders and file them in notebooks or hanging files. The first typed version now moves to the left; the new revised draft will

---

[5]I deliberately inserted a comma here, at a spot where most careful writers I know would probably leave it out. Why? Because I didn't want to lump the words "project" and "your task." Adding the comma keeps them clearly separated, and hence helps make sure that readers do not stumble over my intended meaning.

[6]Several editors have suggested that I don't need to say "I'll tell you what I do . . ." but instead should write "You may want to try your own variations . . ." I tried their variation and didn't like it, so I put mine back. Again, brevity is on their side, and you may choose to join them.

go to the right. Watching the folders fill is encouraging, helping you to maintain a full head of steam.

Using Footnotes, Credits, and References

Footnotes can help both writer and reader. Today's technology makes footnotes much easier than in the past, and you can use them fearlessly. The reports *you* turn out will probably be done with a word-processing program. *Word for Windows*, which I am currently using, makes them a snap,[7] as do many other popular programs. One good thing about footnotes is that you can keep your narrative going full tilt without slowing the pace with meticulous details. The footnotes have the extra information there for those who want it, but can easily be skipped by those who don't.

Your "everyday" readers are interested primarily in the narrative; they can read straight through and 'skip the footnotes. If you have specialist readers concerned with minute details, the situation remains well under control. Writer and readers share the best of all possible worlds.[8]

But footnotes should be used properly[9] and *located* properly. My pet peeve is the chintzy (as in cheap) method—used by many publishers—of putting all footnotes (okay, you purists—I know that technically they're called **endnotes**, but a rose by any other name![10]) bunched together, at the end of a chapter or clear[11] at the back of the book. This leaves the reader with several choices, all miserable. One choice involves reading through the chapter and

[7]This word has literally dozens of different meanings, but the one intended here is "easy or uncomplicated."

[8]A quotation from Voltaire's *Candide*. Did you recognize it?

[9]Half a dozen editors have said I should eliminate the word "properly" here, and make the second one serve for both. I say again, the change would soften my emphasis and alter my intended meaning. The first "properly" stays!

[10]This famous Shakespearean reference should need no explanation, but in recent years I've encountered many readers who don't recognize it. The full quotation goes: "What's in a name? That which we call a rose by any other name would smell as sweet." It comes from *Romeo and Juliet*, II,ii, 43.

[11]Do I need "clear" here? Possibly not, but I think putting it in adds a bit of emphasis.

then going back and reading the footnotes. This is frustrating because the reader forgets what the footnotes are referring to. The alternative is just as bad—flip-flopping back and forth between the text and the footnotes—an extremely time-consuming and frustrating operation.

I've been talking here about *explanatory* footnotes. Documentation is different. It's okay to list authors, references, and the like, at the end if this method makes life easier for the production staff.

For more guidance on footnotes and scholarly citations, you shouldn't have any trouble finding a suitable stylebook—quite likely your organization has one, or more. If not, a good (and inexpensive) choice is Kate L. Turabian's *A Manual for Writers of Term Papers, Theses and Dissertations* (Chicago: University of Chicago Press, 1987).

Finally, when the report has been put together, alphabetize your bibliography cards and use them as the basis of your *Bibliography* or *List of References* section. This is where you list all your sources, whether you have actually quoted directly from them or not. However, one word of warning: don't frustrate readers by listing "classified" (top secret, secret, confidential, etc.) sources or other items difficult or impossible for most readers to obtain. If you must mention such documents, make sure to indicate their status, so as not to send anyone on a goose chase.[12]

Using Copyrighted Material

Incidentally, if you publish a report containing quotations from copyrighted sources, give credit where credit is due. Clearly identify all such material and attribute it properly. If you plan to quote more than a few words of copyrighted material from any one source, obtain formal permission from the copyright owner to use it. Read about *copyright* in the handbook section of this book; for more detailed information, a good source is *Law and the Writer*, edited by Kirk Polking and Leonard S. Meranus. (Cincinnati, Ohio: Writer's Digest Books, 1978)

---

[12]Short for "wild goose chase."

Summing up

I realize we've covered considerable territory in this chapter, but I urge you to master it. Follow the instructions faithfully, and you'll turn out reports better and faster than ever before.

A final reminder: for maximum efficiency, always separate the *writing* and *editing* aspects of your work. This is important even for short pieces; it is imperative for long ones. Don't try to edit as you write—get those words down on paper as fast as you can, and edit them later. For more suggestions on increasing your efficiency, see Chapter 16.

15

The Easy Way to Outline

Good order is the foundation of all good things.
—Edmund Burke (1729–1797)

Why the Old-fashioned
Outline Often Doesn't Work

We've all been brainwashed. Back in high school, our English teachers said, "Always make an outline before writing." And we believe them still. Why, then, do most writers hate outlines so?

Mostly, because we know in our hearts that the way we were taught to outline often doesn't work.

Why not?

Let's compare our experience—mine is probably similar to yours; when my teacher assigned an outline to be turned in, corrected, and then followed by a composition, I always wrote the composition first. Then I worked backwards and made the outline. I was close-mouthed and cagey about my method; indeed, I believed I was the only one who used it. Years later, in graduate school, I confessed my "crime" to some fellow English majors; their sheepish admissions of the same deed gave me the first inkling that hosts of others secretly defy the sacrosanct[1] outline system.

---

[1]Adjective meaning "most sacred, most inviolable."

Chances are, our teachers did too. All evidence points in that direction. I know now that most working writers make only the sketchiest of outlines before beginning a short assignment, and not much more before a long one—totally unlike the picayunishly specific blueprints English teachers require of their students.

Writers with practical experience learn the hard way that one idea grows out of another, one sentence out of another, one paragraph out of another. Almost always, a formal outline constructed in massive detail at the beginning will bear only faint resemblance to the ultimate product.

But, as I said earlier, we've been brainwashed—told we must always prepare a full outline according to the timeworn tradition; first, a Roman numeral, then a capital letter, than an Arabic numeral, a lower-case letter, and so on. Unfortunately, the whole routine is usually an exercise in futility. How can anyone realistically outline in advance every detail of a projected piece of writing? During the actual creative process, writing the very first paragraph may alter the writer's entire outlook—and outline.

My longtime colleague Chuck Waterman, who loved to play the devil's advocate[2], once reminded me that—since my system involves keeping all options as open as possible—I should *entirely rule out* making a formal outline. This forced me to admit that, quite truthfully, I don't. All I want to do is teach you an easy way to make an outline that really works. That's what the rest of this chapter is about. In all fairness, I must add here some of Chuck's cogent thoughts about a few cases that may not lend themselves to my approach. Said Chuck:

> Some kinds of creative writing are indeed organized carefully before the author begins the actual writing task. Among these are mystery and detective stories, where the writer conceives the solution and works backward toward the problem. A good example of this is almost any Perry Mason mystery;

[2]Idiomatic expression meaning "a person who tests a position by arguing against it."

Erle Stanley Gardner, a lawyer before he became a writer, loved to build an entire plot around a key point of law.

The outline we are speaking of here is more of a thread of the story that will have to be pursued if all the plot lines are to meet in the big surprise finale.

Even here, of course, the writer probably does not use a Roman numeral, cap A, etc. In this format, the writer may draw something that looks more like a computer diagram or a calendar, or a map, or a spider web, than it does like an outline.

I'm putting some of the key ideas that follow in boldface, to emphasize how important this material is. What you are about to read is the most practical system for making an outline that really works that I have gleaned during a lifetime of writing. Here is the system, which emphasizes my profound belief: *keep all your options open as long as possible.*

Checklist: The Easy Way to Outline

- Get a batch of notecards, **(Preferably five by eight, or three by fives in continuous format.)**
- **Brainstorm. Throw your imagination into high gear, and start putting down ideas about your project. If you can persuade fellow workers or colleagues who are familiar with your project to help you—and this is what the term "brainstorming" really means, the way it is done in advertising agencies—by all means do so. Creativity is compounded; one idea sparks another. (Remember, no one is allowed to criticize anyone else's idea, no matter how far out it may seem at the time.)**

If you end up like the little red hen, with no help, apply the brainstorming process on yourself. Turn your subconscious mind loose. You don't have to know or care where a particular idea is going to fit. All you need do is write it down. Maybe it will eventually land in the first section, or the middle, or the last. You couldn't (or needn't) care less at this point. (**NOTE:** Apply the process at your most creative time of day—for most of us that would be fairly early in the morning, but not if you are a night person.)

- **Put each idea down on a separate card. (Just a few words will be sufficient—write only enough to remind you of the idea later.)**
- Use a fresh card for the next idea. **As soon as you complete a card, put it aside. The beauty of this approach is that it frees you from the whole routine of having to figure out in advance what is important. You aren't concerned with what is going to be subordinated to what. It is really a joyful experience to be so free and easy, and to know that you are not locking yourself in.**
- Work on a different project for the rest of the day. **This is important—it relaxes your mind so that when you tackle the job again, you'll be fresh and ready for it.**

Take the cards home with you; **read through them just before you go to sleep.** That way, your subconscious mind will do much of the hard work for you. Try it. It works.

- **Next morning,** spread out the cards where you can see them. **As you try arranging the cards in various sequences, you can begin shaping them up into an increasingly logical order. As you proceed, you may move cards forward or back in the sequence as ideas begin to gel. Put closely related cards in the same row or stack.**

When you finally get the cards into an order you like, use them to make a formal outline. You're safe in doing this, because your options are still open. The outline isn't engraved on stone, so if things don't work out quite right, you can always shuffle the deck and try again. (Incidentally, when I was writing speeches at

NASA, I never threw any of those cards away. Sometimes by a bit of thoughtful shuffling, I could come up with several different speeches from the same set of cards!)

Since 1984, when I discovered **The Creative Organizer**[3] I've been putting my organized cards into the system's versatile *Scan Pages*. This permits great flexibility in filing—in notebooks, file cabinets, folders, or what have you. The overlapping arrangement of the plastic pockets makes it easy to see all the cards' titles at once, and to refer to any card instantly, front or back. The system offers a beautifully simple way for a naturally disorganized person like me to keep my notes in perfect order. It's hard to believe, but now I know exactly where they are.

At this point, use the cards as building blocks. Build on each card by expanding an idea into a sentence, a sentence into a paragraph. The stronger and more complete you can make each card, the easier your actual writing will be when the time comes. My experience has been that sometimes the report gets more than half finished while it's still on cards. Can't beat that.

As you study the cards, sometimes a phrase, a sentence, or even a whole paragraph may come to mind on how to develop a particular point. Stop and write the thought down directly on the card before those inspired words escape forever. That's why you might want to try using five by eight cards, which offer much more space to write down your sudden thoughts. (The *Creative Organizer* added five by eight *Scan Pages* to their system several years ago, partly at my insistence.)

Often by the time you make these quick additions while arranging the cards in sequence, you'll have a big head start on the report.

That's it—the whole secret. It works so well it's almost scary. By comparison, if you had used a conventional approach, as soon as you had set down your ideas in even the most random of orders on a single sheet of paper, they would have begun to set harder

---

[3]To get information on this beatifully simple system, write **Scan/Plan, The Creative Organizer**, Post Office Box 1662, Santa Monica, CA—or call 1-800-SCAN-PLA(N).

than concrete and a whole lot faster. That seems to be the way human thought processes work: put something down on a page, and even though the order turns out (as random orders usually do) to be illogical or unworkable, your mind (subconscious?) works to justify (rationalize) its illogic. You often find the jumble impossible to change. You'll hate the helpless feeling of being stuck with an arrangement you know in your heart is wrong. Sad, but oh so true.

So, one more time: *Use the card system. Keep all your options open as long as you possibly can.*

16

How to Write Like a Pro

Writing is like walking blindfold: instinct will carry you far, but not always where you want to go. Before long, the instinct-guided writer, like the blinded walker, bumps into things. Like the hard question of when to write. Everyone knows that Hemingway liked to write in the morning, Mark Twain when he was lying down, H. L. Mencken when he sniffed a deadline, and Norman Mailer whenever he gets punched in the mouth. . . .

—Colman McCarthy, *Inner Companions*

Establishing Good Writing Habits

One of the most well-organized and self-disciplined writers I've ever known is Virgil Carrington "Pat" Jones. I hope you've had the pleasure of reading some of his work. He's a recognized authority on everything from the War Between the States to the real story of the Hatfields and the McCoys. His *Gray Ghosts and Rebel Raiders* and *Ranger Mosby* served as the inspiration for the popular Gray Ghost television series of a few years back.

It was my privilege to share an office at NASA Headquarters with Pat Jones for several years. He was one of several extremely talented writers who worked in my shop. (I sometimes wondered why it wasn't the other way around.)

Anyway, when I first met Pat, he was working on a book, even though he was also employed full-time as a NASA ghostwriter. For Pat, that was par for the course.

How did he do it? By getting out of bed at 2:30 every morning and working straight through until breakfast. Pat followed this demanding routine every morning, seven days a week, for many, many years. (He finally retired a few years ago, but he still gets up and writes for a couple of hours early every morning.) And that was only the beginning. After putting in three or four hours of writing and research, Pat would eat breakfast, drive about 40 miles into Washington through the rush hour traffic, and be at his desk next to mine promptly at 8:15—or usually earlier. There he would sit, straight as a ramrod, all day long, turning out more and better copy than many other writers half his age. That is real self-discipline!

Pat Jones's Advice

Twenty years ago, when I was still an aspiring middle-aged writer, I often asked Pat for advice. He gave it kindly and freely. I didn't always have the gumption to take it, but it's a pleasure to pass some of his wisdom on to you. Here are some of the important things he told me:

Try to write at the same time every day. Set up a regular routine and stick to it. Make it a habit. You have to learn what time of day is best for you—Pat is a morning person; other writers I know don't begin to function until the sun goes down—then work at your writing at that time, systematically, every day.

Don't stop—or even slow down—once you get up to speed. Work at least three or four hours, until you feel yourself growing genuinely tired. Pat says it's okay to take a few minutes for a break every hour or so, allowing that the best of us may need to go to the bathroom once in a while. Also, he says, walking around and taking a few deep breaths will help relax those muscles at the back of the neck. They seem to get even more tired than your posterior does when you've been sitting in front of your typewriter or word processor for a long spell.

Don't let anything interrupt you. This is one of several reasons Pat likes those early morning hours—no telephone calls or other annoying intrusions on concentration.

Make your surroundings conducive to good work. After I moved to Fairfax, Virginia, I seized the opportunity to visit Pat in his home, which was situated in a beautiful wooded area. His land was once a battlefield; it even had a historical marker at one corner of his front yard. Pat, as handy with tools as he is with a typewriter, had built his own office. It covered most of the top floor of his house. Bookshelves lined every wall; every book was catalogued. (Pat could—and still can—even tell you the date he finished reading each book.) His many file cabinets were all clearly labeled. Within arm's reach of his desk was an ingenious four-sided revolving bookshelf that held all the references he had to check most frequently during a particular project.

At each end of his office were huge windows. Just outside was a balcony where he sometimes set up his typewriter when the weather was right. From his desk he could see woods and what we Virginians call a run.

I envy all Pat's arrangements except the view. For someone with my lack of self-discipline, it would be murder. I have long since discovered that I would rather admire scenery than sit at my word processor and tackle a difficult writing task. My self-discipline improves only when I face austere surroundings and an inescapable deadline.

Don't try to write when you are starving to death, are having a nicotine fit, or are worn-out and exhausted. It's hard enough to work when you're fresh and have everything going for you. Don't make things any harder for yourself than you have to. If you aren't careful, you could actually build a conditioned reflex against writing. (I don't smoke, so I don't have that problem.) One of my fellow ghosts at NASA was constantly trying to give up smoking. Like Mark Twain, he had done it a thousand times. When he didn't have any writing pressures on him, he could hold out bravely. He would go on for hours or days without a single drag from the noxious weed.

But let a deadline assignment come up, and he couldn't cajole a word out of his typewriter unless he had a cigarette dangling from his lips. Smoking was, to him, such an ingrained habit that it had become a conditioned response. It was an inescapable part of his whole creative process.

Production Rates for Writers

How many pages of manuscript should a disciplined writer be able to turn out in a day's work?

There aren't any standard answers. Writing speeds, even among professional writers, seem to vary all over the lot. Still, after observing dozens of writers (some of them professionals and a helluva lot more who were not), I'll stick my neck out. In my opinion, a good average would probably be about five to ten double-spaced, typewritten pages a day.

If you manage that kind of production, you can be confident that the boss has no right to complain. But let's elaborate on this subject a bit. Bear in mind that, even with *professional writers, production rates can and do vary considerably from day to day. What is more important to a disciplined pro is that those five or ten pages represent his or her best efforts.*

Let me tell you about another of the really fine professional writers I have known—my former boss and longtime mentor, James R. Aswell. I worked with Jim for almost a decade, and never ceased to marvel at his dedication to excellence. Many times I watched him put his daily five or ten pages of copy through the equivalent of four—or even five—separate and complete drafts. Each would be slightly different from, and undeniably better than, the one that went before. Katie Egland, the patient and long-suffering secretary who typed our manuscripts, would put on her most resigned look. Then she'd bravely type another draft from Jim's henscratch revisions. She knew, and we all knew, full well that she would be typing at least three or four more versions before the day was out.

I once overheard Jim's boss say, "That damned Aswell—everything he writes is for the Pulitzer Prize." Well, the boss may have thought he was putting Jim down with that remark. The scorn for Jim's dogged and continuing search for writing perfection was not the least bit subtle. But to me—and I feel quite sure, to Jim himself, if he had known about it—the remark wasn't a putdown at all. It was the highest possible compliment. For, in all the years I knew him, and that was more than a quarter of a century, one fact stands out.

James R. Aswell was constitutionally incapable of writing anything without giving it his best shot.

Another of my ghostwriting colleagues at NASA was Jack Doherty, a former newspaperman who had covered the White House beat for the *New York Daily News*. Like many other ex-newspapermen, Jack found it difficult to get up a head of steam until a deadline had him cornered. Once in that position, with no possible escape, Jack would write like an angel. He could turn out four or five double-spaced pages of really singing copy in less than an hour. I suspect that not too many writers in this world can manage that much production. An average of about two pages an hour, or roughly 500 words, probably is closer to the norm.

All I can say is, don't let any of this scare you. You—my readers—are almost undoubtedly not professional writers. Granted. Still, you are writing on a subject you know about—you're the expert. Use the tricks I've shown you, and you can produce as much as a pro, day in and day out. Realistically, neither you nor I will expect you to turn out prizewinning prose. But *I do expect, and I hope you'll agree, that you'll produce five to ten pages of clear, useful writing every day that your job requires it. You can do it—and I hope you will.*

Axiom Six: Rewrite—rewrite—rewrite!

The Mechanics of Writing Production

Most writers who do not type their own manuscripts have no idea of how long it takes simply to perform the *mechanical details* of getting a manuscript out: typing, collating, stapling, distributing, printing out, and so on. Even the most experienced executives are likely to have a vague notion that a person who holds a typing job in a business office or a government agency should be able to type at least 40 to 50 words a minute—minimum. Furthermore, they have probably read somewhere that really proficient typists can go much faster than that—60, 70, perhaps even 80 words a minute.

Well, they're right in theory, but wrong in practice. What they don't know is that nothing in this world is ever that simple. You can't just count the total number of words in a manuscript, divide by 80 words a minute (or 70, or 60, or whatever), and come up with a time estimate.

For one thing, this simplistic approach doesn't begin to allow for all the other necessary but time-consuming details that executives are not accustomed to thinking about. Of course, with modern word processing equipment, things are easier than they used to be. Old-timers like me can remember when the typist had to line up an original (bond paper) copy with about umpteen different colored carbon copies. At the Pentagon, this was known as the rainbow. Each colored sheet went to a different office or a different file.

Typing in those days on a regular office typewriter, the typist encountered problems that would curdle the blood. Every single time one wrong character was struck, the procedure was to insert a shield behind the carbons, one at a time, and erase each sheet separately. The top sheet had to be erased with all the care of a brain surgeon. Bosses had a mean habit of holding the paper up to the light, and if they could detect a single erasure, they'd demand a retyping of the entire mess. Murder!

Today, with word processors, the correcting process is relatively hassle-free. The operator can correct mistakes simply by backspacing and striking the key for the correct character. This saves much time—but not so much as you might think. What you may not have realized is that the finished rough draft, even though it has been corrected, is usually not the final product. Each page must be processed and printed out again. Even at 175 words (or even 400 or 500 words) a minute, which many of the late model machines can easily do, these operations often take an extra couple of minutes for each page. (My pride and joy, an HPIII laserjet printer (a year old and already obsolescent!), **turns out eight pages a**

minute. Does this speed up my production? I doubt it. (What it does is to increase the amount of wastepaper I must recycle or otherwise dispose of!)

Also, we still have not allowed for the inevitable interruptions that most typists face constantly—answering the telephone; hunting things up in the files; and performing all the other necessary tasks of keeping the office going.

Ask the most competent typist you know how many words a day are turned out, in finished form, on an average day, and the answer will probably surprise you.

When I wrote the original version of this book in 1977–1978, the year-round average of production in American offices was about *three lines of typing per minute*. I didn't make this figure up. It came straight from a formal study conducted a year or so earlier by a magazine called *The Secretary*. The study concluded that the average letter or report was being typed at a rate of approximately five pages an hour—certainly no faster.

I'm not aware of any current studies, but I suspect the rate may now be a little higher, but probably not more than six pages an hour.

One thing you need to know—and you probably don't—is how many words you usually get on a typewritten page. I suggest you try a few experiments. Figure out how many words per page, on the average, you put in your own writing. It's an awfully handy figure to know.

I keyboard my own final drafts. You may not, although many more people are doing it nowadays than there were in the 1970s. When I finish typing, the work is ready to go. But if you are going to be turning your copy over to a secretary or a word processing center, you must allow for a built-in time lag of between two and three hours before your product can go out. You cannot relax and assume you've met your deadline when you have given your draft to the typist. Remember: allow time for all the required mechanical steps—these may include not only the typing, but perhaps also such other time-consuming processes as duplicating, sorting, collating, stapling, and distributing. I wish I had a dollar (or a nickel, for that matter) for every time that a writer has completed the job itself on time, but has missed a deadline because of not having allowed for the built-in delay factors.

If you're wise, you'll put a fudge factor in your planning.

> **Axiom Seven:** Allow in your planning for production delays.

Deadlines and Supervisors

Many so-called management experts—who, as a concomitant fringe benefit of their position can set deadlines for working writers—do not have the faintest idea how long a writing job should take. Unfortunately, it is very difficult to explain to them the facts of life. They often have the obtuse mentality that is inevitably prevalent among those who can draw their pay without having to write themselves. (If you detect a note of bitterness, you're right!) Nothing can be so exasperating as having to explain, with great care, what some of the problems are, only to hear the response. That's all very well, but have the manuscript on my desk by close of business today. Those rotten (expletives deleted) obviously do not hear a word of what you say.

Chances are, you'll run into another problem—not quite so bad, but still plenty bad enough. Your supervisor will come charging in and say, I want you to do a report on (fill in an appropriate subject). How long is it going to take?

How does anyone answer a question like that? I've never found out. Until you've done some research, you can't possibly have any idea what the job requires. You won't know whether you'll have to look up all sorts of obscure data. You also won't know whether you will be lucky enough to find some quick resources, so that difficult questions are already sorted out in advance.

It's a good bet that you will have to send out of town for certain items. There are always imponderables—problems that cannot possibly be predicted.

Well, one thing you can do with these obtuse characters is to quote an authority. Here's one that might carry a certain amount of weight: *Writing Guide for Naval Officers*, published by the U.S. Government Printing Office. Because the book has been out of print for some years, I'll do you a favor and quote some of the appropriate passages here:

> Estimating writing time is a difficult process. Some reporters and fiction writers can turn out a million words a year, the equivalent of a 20-page report every day. But the author of one hundred western stories a year will find his production slowed down if he undertakes a new form of writing. He'll have to do research. He'll have to think out new lines of action, characters, and dialogue. Similarly, a newspaper reporter can write rapidly about what he observes; he can report on what people say and do. But assign him the task of reporting in depth or analyzing the reasons and the trends behind events and he too will sweat over his words.

Let me pause for an aside here, before continuing the quotation. In the late 1950s, Jim Aswell and I worked for a couple of years with a gifted writer named Norvell Page. (Norvell was an exwriter of pulp-paper thrillers. For those of you too young to remember, pulp-paper magazines were what old galoots like me used to read before World War II—the predecessors of today's comic books.)

For most of a decade, Norvell Page had turned out, singlehanded, an entire magazine called *The Spider*. (Don't confuse this with today's comic book *Spiderman*.) Each month, Norvell would have to write a lead novelette of at least 80 printed pages. Then he would write a half dozen or so short stories, not connected with his main novelette in any way. *The Spider* magazine would be roughly 200 printed pages per month, all written by one man, month after month, year after year.

That's an incredible performance. It would give the willies to most of the professional writers I know. That kind of pressure might be okay once in a while, but not when sustained over months and years.

Just for comparison, and this is a comparison to, not a comparison with: the complete works of Shakespeare total slightly more than one million words. The complete King James translation of the Holy Bible also adds up to something more than one million words. Norvell Page annually turned out more than a half-million words of not-quite-so-deathless prose for many, many years.

In all the history of writing, only a handful of writers have done that. In modern times, the late Dr. Isaac Asimov probably takes the cake. It's futile to say specifically how many books he wrote, because posthumous publications keep appearing. At last count I believe his total had reached almost 500 books.

Many of the other writers whose production feats I admired in my younger days are now long gone. They include Erle Stanley Gardner, of *Perry Mason* fame, who broke quite a few records; in his later years he dictated to several secretaries, working in shifts, since a single one couldn't keep up with him. (Dr. Asimov always typed his own manuscripts, converting to word processing relatively late in his career.)

The late Georges Simenon, French writer of detective stories, was noted for prodigious speed, and is reported to have completed many of his hundreds of books in a matter of two or three days of almost uninterrupted production. Add to the list Zane Grey, Edgar Rice Burroughs, Kenneth Robeson (creator of *Doc Savage;* Robeson's real name was Lester Dent). Add Max Brand, whose real name I can't remember, and a few others, and that just about does it. In earlier times, add Charles Dickens (who was accused by his contemporaries of writing pot-boilers), Victor Hugo, Alexandre Dumas (who was accused of running a fiction factory), and a few more.

Yes, Norvell Page was one of a rather select group when it comes to production. He had things down to a formula—a formula that worked great for grinding out pulp-paper detective stories and science fiction.

But now the scene changes. When Jim and I worked for Norvell Page, he was in charge of producing the Atomic Energy Commission's Semiannual Report to Congress. And believe me, Norvell didn't crank out that complicated opus in a couple of weeks. The task took months of effort on his part, and he had the incredible talents of Jim Aswell and me to back him up.

The moral of this true-life fable is that you may hear wondrous recitals about the enormous productivity and speed of a given writer in a given situation. Those stories may well be true. But keep in mind the chastening truth that the dazzling speed will inevitably slow to a crawl any time the writer is forced to tackle assignments that fall outside the familiar territory.

Okay, it's time to return to the Navy treatise. Again I quote:

A captain with considerable experience advised students at the Naval War College concerning their term papers. He recommended that they allocate at least two hours a day over a two-month period to prepare papers running from 8,000 to 12,000 words. [He was, of course, addressing students, not professional writers.] The famous novelist and short-story writer, W. Somerset Maugham, once remarked that in his experience a professional writer can write at most about three hours a day. He knew of some authors that wrote only one hour a day, and he admitted that others might sometimes go on for ten, twelve, and even sixteen hours at a stretch. But, he added, such authors usually balanced out productive periods with weeks in which they wrote little or nothing. The average administrator cannot expect to concentrate on a writing task for more than three hours a day, and often these hours must be spread out because of the other demands of the job. For most administrators whose writing is assigned as a secondary task, you may well be spending about one-third of your time in actual writing.

17

Retaining and Using Your New Knowledge

I've forgotten more about this than
you'll ever know. The only trouble is,
I've forgotten more about it than
I'll ever know, and I can't even remember
what it was.

—Famous saying by *Groucho Marx*,[1]
or maybe somebody else whose
name I can't remember.

Training Is Big Business

The powerful principles you've learned from this book can improve all the writing you do, of any kind, for the rest of your life. Notice, however, that I say can, not will. It's up to you. The old saying, "Use it or lose it" applies. Use your new knowledge right away, every day, and you'll have it always. Fail to use it, and within six weeks you'll have forgotten all but five percent of what you've learned.

Training represents one of our country's strongest weapons for keeping our citizens out of the unemployment offices—if it's used for optimum benefit. Training in the U.S. is a $200-billion-a-year business. This figure does not include the traditional formal schooling presented in public and private elementary schools, high schools, prep schools, colleges, vocational schools, and the like.

It does include: (a) all training seminars of the types marketed

---

[1] I used to think that everybody knew who Groucho Marx was, but younger readers may not. He was the leading member of a vaudeville and movie team known as "the Four Marx Brothers." In later life he became the quiz master of a television show and renewed his fame as a raconteur and wit.

by producers such as Career Track Seminars, Tony Robbins, Brian Tracy, and Zig Ziglar; (b) self-teaching courses available on video and audiotapes; and (c) the less visible but very large segment of "in-house" corporation programs—both to train new employees and to enhance skills of older employees. Corporations and many smaller businesses have full-time trainers and training facilities with constant programs. Is training of this kind useful and valuable? You bet it is. But do the students or employers who pay for these courses receive full value?

Here are some depressing facts:

Typical trainees forget 40 percent of what they have heard within 30 minutes. By the end of the day, that figure jumps to 60 percent. And within a week it has skyrocketed to 90 percent. Not much of a return on that original $200-billion-a-year investment. Can we afford that kind of waste in time, effort, and dollars?

What about the minimal amount of learning that remains? Do the trainees actually *use* any of this valuable new knowledge that they (or their employers) have paid all that good money for?

Within four to six weeks, only five percent of the people who gain information in this manner are actually *using it. And that five percent drops to less than one percent within six months*.

What can we do about it? Sounds pretty hopeless. Why do we keep on having training courses at all?

Some Ways to Help You Remember—and Use—Your New Knowledge and Skills

Fortunately, I can tell you some proven methods that you can employ to remember far more of what you have learned, and how you can put every bit of it to use. Get ready for a miracle.

Let me take you back more than 50 years, to the time I enrolled in my first undergraduate course in Educational Psychology.

You have undoubtedly noticed that bashing "education courses" is one of today's favorite sports, Too bad. I'm still delighted that I majored in that subject as well as in English. I did gain some knowledge that's served me well ever since.

Truth to tell, though, I learned at least as much about practical ways of improving short- and long-term memory and fact retention from a fellow student than I did from my professor.

Our professor inspired terror in us students because of his nasty habit of giving "pop quizzes" nearly every day. I soon grew frantic. Although I'd always been a good student, my test grades in his class were miserable. I didn't know how to cope with such low scores.

No matter how hard I studied, my grades didn't get any better. I envied a good friend of mine named George Lowe who kept on "acing"[2] every quiz with seeming ease.

I didn't think George was any smarter than I was (I was wrong about that too!), so I swallowed my pride and asked him if he'd be willing to share his secret. The tips he gave me so long ago have revolutionized my working methods ever since. (If some of this seems reminiscent of earlier chapters, bear with me a moment longer.)

"Have you paid any real attention to what Prof has been telling us in all these dull Education lectures?" he asked me. "You know he makes the point that just *listening to lectures won't cut it*. He says *students have to get actively involved; take notes, and take them selectively. Writing things down means you'll remember a lot more. The act of thinking and deciding about what is important enough to remember, and then the physical act of writing it down helps students remember more than twice as much as they would from simple, passive listening*."

"Heck, George, I already do that," I said. "So why is it you can ace all those quizzes while I'm practically flunking?"

The Big Secret of Learning and Remembering Information

"What's the other big point Prof keeps harping on? *Distributed study is best*. That's not just education theory. Jeff, you know—

---

[2] "Acing" is a slang term, probably carried over from popular sports such as tennis or handball; an "ace" is a point that is won with a single stroke. By extension, American students (and perhaps others) have grown to use the term to mean something like "making a perfect score."

every college student knows—that most of us put things off and then cram for exams at the last minute. Learn things one day, forget them the next. Doc's theories make sense. I review my lecture notes every day. Look, here's my system."

George pulled a bundle of three by five cards from his inside coat pocket. "Remember the flash cards your teachers used to help you memorize things when you were in first grade?" he said. "Look at these." He handed me the top card. On it he'd written a short question. "Flip it over," he said. On the other side, in succinct language, he'd written the answer. While I was looking, he kept on talking.

"I review my lecture notes every day. Then I get out a stack of these three by five index cards and go through my notes again. I spend a few minutes making up the best questions I can to cover each important point in the notes. I write each question down on a separate card. Any time I get a spare moment, I whip out the cards and run through the questions until I no longer need to turn the cards over and check the answers. As you seem to have noticed, it really works."

It all sounded much too simple, but I tried his system and sure enough, it worked. The result: soon thereafter, my name appeared on the Dean's List ahead of George's. (All right, so my name starts with a "B.")

On to the Millennium

Let me remind you once more—most people quickly forget much of the valuable information they have gained (at considerable expense) in courses. What's even worse is that only the smallest percentage of them actually *use even a small portion of that expensive knowledge.*

Using cards in the way I've described works great for reviewing information learned from books or in training programs. I've already explained to you how I write down facts and figures I need to remember on three by five cards and keep them in *Scan/Plan Minipaks*. That seems to be the only way I can still manage to have a steel-trap memory.

Rhoda and Hal Neiman, developers of *Scan/Plan,* have been researching ways to help people develop habit patterns that will enable them to make real changes in their lives. Their limited studies indicate that the *Scan/Plan* system of organizing information on three by five cards offers great potential. Trainees using the system have substantially increased the extent to which they actually utilize their new knowledge or skills.

Those gains multiply exponentially. First of all, trainees who review their work with *Scan/Plan* remember a much higher proportion of what they have learned. And second, in comparison with trainees not using the system, they double or triple the amount of information they actually put to practical use.

That's worth thinking about. When you consider that training is a $200 billion business, an increase of even 10 percent or more likely 20 percent or better, would offer a substantial return on America's investment in training programs.

Books on Cards

In a related project, *Scan/Plan* has developed a program called *Books on Cards*™—a system of presenting important ideas from books on three by five cards. They are available either in the pocket-sized *Minipak* or the notebook-page size *QuickScan Learning Page*™. They offer a quick, highly efficient way of either studying or reviewing concepts and information, learned from books or in training programs.

Rhoda Neiman, *Scan/Plan*'s inventor, recently sent me a sample *Book on Cards* called *Creating: Become the Creative Force in Your Own Life,* excerpted from the popular books *The Path of Least Resistance,* and *Creating,* both written by Robert Fritz. I found it presented Fritz's innovative ideas and methods in an amazingly quick, easy-to-learn way. I think all writers could profit from using it.

Forgive me for putting in a plug here, but as my dear grandmother used to say, "It's for your own good." I hereby (notice how much more official this legalistic term makes it sound!) immodestly announce that *Scan/Plan* has published a *Book on Cards* version of *Writing with Precision.*

After looking over the "Beta test" version, I found that it exceeded my fondest expectations. It should be a valuable study tool and memory aid to remind users of the ten principles and seven axioms.

Books on Tape

Audiocassettes

Before I close, I must mention another simple but valuable tool made available by modern technology: books on tape. I have learned, primarily at the national conventions of the National Speakers Association, that the most highly motivated and truly successful people spend a good percentage of their time listening to audiocassette tapes as a learning device. Repeated listenings to such tapes offer an efficient way of remembering newly learned information. The method can also be fun. It comes as close as anything I know to being a painless way to bone up on the latest techniques in fields ranging from time management to sales to foreign languages.

Many professional trainers and seminar leaders have discovered the value of offering their students audiocassette versions of their courses.

The last time I counted, more than a hundred companies were producing audiocassette learning materials. *Career Track Seminars,* a national seminar company that occasionally offers seminars based on *WWP,* produced a multi-cassette album narration of *Writing with Precision,* complete with exercises, several years ago.[3] The reading was done by an old pro with a good sense of humor and an excellent voice, so listeners didn't have to put up with the cornpone[4] accent I've never managed to lose.

---

[3] For information, write Career Track Seminars, 3085 Center Green Drive, Boulder, CO 80301-5408. Telephone: (303) 447-2323.

[4] Cornpone is a low-cost food, consumed mainly by poor families in the south. It is a king of corn bread made with water, and without eggs or milk. By extension, a "cornpone accent" is a rather derogatory way of referring to the regional characteristics of southern folk.

Videotapes

Videocassette tapes are now also gaining in popularity. You might want to consider trying some of them, particularly for learning how to use new computer software. They do have one drawback, and it's a big one. They lack the flexibility of audiotapes, which permit listeners to use them in their cars or other unlikely places.

Department of Anticlimax

For 17 chapters I've regaled you with the best advice on useful writing that I know how to give. Of the wondrous things I've told you, what's good is probably not original, and what's original may or may not be good. (Don't be taken in by my false modesty. That statement itself is a mild paraphrase of a famous putdown directed to a would-be author. The great lexicographer Samuel Johnson, one of the top putdown artists of all time, is the source of this particular "borrowing.")

Very little that is new has been written on the subject of writing—any kind of writing—since the time of Aristotle. But I do hope I've hung a few new ornaments on the ancient Christmas tree. I sincerely hope, also, that you have at least been reminded of some important things you may once have known but have probably forgotten. And I hope even more that you may have gained a new perspective—a way of looking at things so that you will be motivated. Get that missionary spirit. Strive to improve all the copy you must write or edit.

Go forth and preach the gospel. Whatever you can do will be a help to your customers or clients or the taxpayers, as the case may be—and that's you and me. In your spare time, please browse through the handbook section that follows.

As a writer, I'm aware that I've made heavy demands on your time and trouble. If you've stuck with me this far, thanks for your courage.

And now, I pray you, keep the faith.

Epitaph

You may recall that I suggested in Chapter One that writing your own obituary might be an interesting exercise. I haven't written my own yet, but I have done my **epitaph.** *I'd hate for it to go to waste, so here it is.*

> *His vice was verse,*
> *Please don't ask twice.*
> *His verse was worse*
> *Than his advice.*
>
> *And on this stone,*
> *His verse is terse,*
> *With no encores,*
> *He won't re-hearse.*

—Poems for Old Geezers and Young Whippersnappers

Part 2

Editing (and Self-Editing)
with Precision

18

An Editor's Credo

Make any changes you want. I have no pride of authorship.
—Biggest lie ever told

What Is an Editor's Job?

I've been thinking about that subject for a long time. In the '80s, I wrote a series of articles for *The Editorial Eye,* (a newsletter for professional writers and editors) which I have now consolidated into this new section called *Editing with Precision.* It contains discussions of thorny subjects that can't always be found in regular reference or style books.

Scribble, scribble, scribble, eh, Mr. Bates? Aren't there already plenty of books on editing available?

The answer, of course, is yes, and some of them are very good indeed. (On the other hand, a surprising number are remarkably bad.) I suspect that most professional editors already know which ones are which, and what's in them. I, like you, have done my homework. For many years I've been reading everything on the subject that I can find. To date I haven't found a single book that is as good as it ought to be, in terms of teaching editing skills rather than simply setting forth rules in take-it-or-leave-it fashion. Furthermore, many so-called style manuals are atrociously written.

If I had good sense, I wouldn't rush in where better editors than

I may fear to tread. But "somebody's got to do it." My aim is to craft a practical handbook (based on sound teaching methods) that systematically explains (and illustrates with real-world exercises) some easy-to-learn, common-sense principles. Many of the exercises will not readily respond to arbitrary, inflexible stylebook rules.

I anticipate that my readers may sometimes find solutions superior to my own less-than-perfect wrestling with thorny, confusing problems that traditional style manuals ignore. Let's hear from you—my email address is jefbates@erols.com. I'll credit all suggestions that I use in subsequent editions of this book.

After half a century in the business, I'm still amazed at how much others continue to teach me. I sincerely hope that any experts among my readers will straighten me out if I get off the track. All I ask is that you please be gentle.

I'm not a professional editor—I'm a professional writer who has long believed that editing one's own copy is the best way to ensure that it meets one's own standards of what good writing is. And I know, further, that self-editing alone is not enough; no conscientious writer can safely forgo the insurance of an equally conscientious editor.

During my 50-odd years on the job, I've learned by osmosis from some superb professionals—those painstaking, nit-picking, frustrating, know-it-all practitioners who spot mistakes and infelicities that somehow elude the most careful self-editing. Here are some of the lessons I've learned—what I've come to call "an editor's credo," and which have made me a better writer and editor.

I believe the editor's (or self-editor's) job is to improve the clarity, accuracy, and effectiveness—the *precision,* if you will—of any manuscript lacking in these qualities. It is emphatically not the editor's responsibility to make changes for the sake of changes, or because of personal preferences (or prejudices). I believe that the editor has a responsibility to point out errors tactfully. (A good editor must be good at human relations, not just grammar and syntax.)

I believe that TEAMWORK is the key to a good relationship between writer and editor. (Avoid the adversary attitude.)

I believe that if writer and editor hold seriously conflicting opinions, both parties should strive for an acceptable compromise. (If no compromise is possible, the writer should win.)

I believe that a good editor must read widely and voraciously, with a mind open to new ideas and new (and old) knowledge.

I believe that a good editor must know the rules contained in such editorial bibles as the *Chicago Manual of Style* and the *GPO Manual,* but need not follow them slavishly if bending the rules (judiciously) will increase clarity and help the reader.

Undoubtedly, I look at the editor's task with eyes that are both myopic and jaundiced. But I count myself fortunate in having learned my crotchets from two inspiring mentors: a salty, erudite technical editor—the late Mazie Worcester, who was my supervisor early in my career, at the Harry Diamond Labs; and an intense blue-flame of a man—the best writer and editor I've ever known— the late James R. Aswell. It was my privilege to work under Jim's fiercely blazing editorial eye for almost a decade. I owe some of my formal training to other teachers that I loved and admired, but these two administered my baptism of fire.

The editorial gospel according to Mazie was, "Don't believe anything until you've checked it out." (We'll be talking about this and some of her other precepts in later chapters.)

Jim Aswell said that the first task of an editor is to make things easier for the reader. (In the same breath he'd tell me that William Faulkner was the best writer of our century. Fiction writers and poets, Jim patiently explained, can make an art form of obscurity. Nonfiction writers cannot be allowed that prerogative.)

From Jim I learned more about the practical approach to editing I've already outlined in the credo: don't make changes for the sake of changes; don't be afraid to bend the rules to increase clarity (but know the rules first); and always remember there are exceptions to everything.

Most professional editors I know have crotchets; that's fine with me—nobody has a better right. They practice a profession that is much abused and, I believe, misunderstood.

I can sympathize with all the writers who have waxed wroth with their editors. (Sorry, Groucho!) I happen to be one of them, particularly after some whippersnapper editor has dared tamper with my inimitable prose.

Even so, I take a crude and wicked delight in catching my fellow writers in boo-boos. (Maybe that's the editor in me.) I fear that all of us must have an overdeveloped mean streak. But we must strive not to be intemperate and ill-natured in the way we express our displeasure. Editors are people too.

If you've been editing—or edited—for very long, you undoubtedly have crotchets of your own. Fine. You wouldn't be much good at your job if you didn't. In the chapters that follow, I hope to reinforce your "good" ones, and make you at least take a fresh look at what I conceive to be your "bad" ones.

19

Hyphenation and Word Compounding

*The Art of Hyphenation
can be twice as mysterious
as a Hitchcock thriller.*
—Jeff (No relation to Norman) Bates

Doormats, Floormats, and Fruitflies

What should an editor do when the style books don't agree?

Or should it be stylebooks?

I don't know about you, but some of the thorniest problems I face every time I edit copy is whether two closely related words should go together, or be hyphenated, or simply be allowed to remain as two separate words.

Would you prefer *door mat?* Or would you choose *doormat?*

I think the two words are so closely related they should go together—*doormat.* The same goes for *stylebook.*

My beloved old second edition of the *Merriam-Webster International* (1954) accepts *stylebook.* Strangely, it has no definition of *door mat,* whether one word or two.

I'm happy to report that *Webster's New World Dictionary* agrees with me on both choices. With dozens of dictionaries and dozens more stylebooks in my reference library, I can almost always find at least one that is right!

So What's the Problem?

Well, if it's *doormat,* how about *floormat?* Seems logical, but most dictionaries don't recognize *floormat* as a word. Neither does the spelling checker on *WordPerfect.* As a matter of fact, it was that marvelous technological achievement that brought the word compounding (word-compounding?) problem to a head for me. In a book I was working on, I'd written *fruitfly,* and the spelling checker refused to recognize the word. I looked it up in at least half a dozen dictionaries, and unhappily discovered that every one of them said *fruit fly.* I was appalled that not a single one of them was right!

This situation gave me pause. Reluctantly, I caved in and used the two-word (two word?) version. The spelling checker seemed happy with the solution, but I can't say that I was. After all, dictionaries do recognize *housefly* and *horsefly.* (So does the spelling checker.)

In the next chapter, I talked about how my late father always carried a *flyrod* and *tacklebox* in his car. The spelling checker blew the whistle on both combinations. I was, to put it mildly, annoyed—especially when none of my dictionaries came to the rescue.

Research

That's when my research started. Here's what I found:

The *GPO Style Manual* has two chapters—[*6. Compound Words,* and *7. Guide to Compounding*]—with 58 pages of very elaborate lists. Helpful, but *GPO* still chickens out on the tricky ones. [6.3] "The rules as laid down cannot be applied inflexibly. Exceptions must necessarily be allowed, so that general good form will not be offended."

The *Chicago Manual*'s Table 6.1 gives a helpful "Spelling Guide for Compound Words." But like the *GPO Manual,* the *Chicago Manual* resorts to an escape hatch [6.24], admitting that "there will yet be some noun forms and a great many adjective forms for which no 'authoritative' spelling can be found." The approach in

The Elements of Style is more to my liking—a down-to-earth discussion of basic principles:

> Do not use a hyphen between words that can better be written as one word: *water-fowl, waterfowl.* Your common sense will aid you in the decision, but a dictionary is more reliable. The steady evolution of the language seems to favor union: two words eventually become one, usually after a period of hyphenation.

Strunk and White give several illustrations of such words, showing the evolution of bed chamber through bed-chamber to bed-chamber; wild life, wild-life, and wildlife; bell boy, bell-boy, and bellboy. (Interestingly, the *WordPerfect* spelling checker doesn't approve of bedchamber, but most dictionaries do.)

I remember reading somewhere that baseball started out as base ball. (I suppose Abner Doubleday introduced the words as well as the game.) The same evolutionary process goes for basketball, also originally two words. Those now happily married pairs have followed the same pattern as the examples cited by Strunk and White. The same pattern has led to many other unions accepted today without a quibble.

Most dictionaries recognize data base, but not database. Look in computer magazines and books, however, and you'll find that the union has been consummated. The same goes for lap top computer. Maybe in this age of POSSLQ's ("Persons of Opposite Sex Sharing Living Quarters"), words can live together without formalities more quickly and easily than they used to in my day. (I was born too soon.) The cold and water in, for example, "coldwater detergent," now have the comfortable appearance of an old married couple. The *Merriam-Webster Second* separated them with a hyphen. All of these developments would seem to me to reinforce the pronouncements of *The Elements of Style.* As Strunk and White put it:

> The hyphen can play tricks on the unwary, as it did in Chattanooga when two newspapers merged—the *News* and the

Free Press. Someone introduced a hyphen into the merger, and the paper became *The Chattanooga News-Free Press,* which sounds as though the paper were news-free, or devoid of news. Obviously, we ask too much of a hyphen when we ask it to cast its spell over words it does not adjoin.

Getting Down to Common-Sense Principles

Observations are one thing but principles are more helpful. In Part Three (236), I state that:

> . . . My first rule is that two-word (or sometimes three-word or four-word) modifiers that express a single thought should be hyphenated when they precede a noun. For example, an *out-of-order* machine, or a *state-of-the-art* component. The trick is to see whether the individual words can be used to modify the noun, or whether they must be used all together, as an entity. Thus, it wouldn't be an *out* or an *of* or an *order* machine—it has to be all three locked together. If each of the words could modify the noun without the aid of the other modifying word or words, you should *not* use a hyphen. Also, if the first word of the group is an adverb ending in *-ly,* do not use a hyphen. If you are in doubt, look it up.)
>
> . . . The next rule is this: when the modifying words follow the noun, do not hyphenate. For example, "Our writing textbooks are hopelessly out of date. (No hyphens.)

That pretty well takes care of modifiers. Now for some common-sense principles about nouns and noun adjuncts. (Why didn't I write "common sense," or "commonsense"? I hope this section helps you decide.)

Common-Sense Principle Number One:

Decide which version (two words, hyphenated, or one word) will best help the reader understand exactly what you mean to say. Example: In Chapter 18, I wrote about "an intense blue-flame of a man." Why the hyphen? Well, I want my readers to see the words as a single entity, not as an adjective modifying a noun. I deliberated on whether to write "blueflame" as a single word, and decided against it. It just didn't look honest. Virtually every dictionary I know says that the prefix "non" must never (well, hardly ever) be hyphenated. To me, that is nonsense, and I unblushingly break the rule whenever I feel like it—IF breaking it helps the reader.

Example: Take the word "nonnative" as in "nonnative speakers of English." Most readers (including me) have to read the word about three times before its meaning emerges. Now look at the difference when we add a hyphen, thus: "non-native." Readers get the idea instantly. That's why I advise deliberately adding the hyphen to such words, dictionaries and stylebooks to the contrary. Devil take the hindmost.

Common-Sense Principle Number Two:

Take note of the way the words are written by experienced writers who use them frequently, and follow their lead. Examples: database, not data base; laptop computers, not lap top computers.

Common-Sense Principle Number Three:

If words go together so naturally that the readers probably won't even notice, feel free to unite them without benefit of clergy. Examples: *flyrod* and *tacklebox,* not *fly rod* and *tackle box,* even though I cravenly gave in the last time the problem arose. I wouldn't do it again.

Common-Sense Principle Number Four:

If you find yourself using similar pairs, such as *door mat* and *floor mat* in the same paragraph, or even on the same page, be consistent, even if the dictionaries disagree. You'll cause fewer *doubletakes* (*"double takes"?*) from your readers.

20

Avoid "Second Cousin" Words

*A word to the wise
is sufficient, but only
if it's the right word!*

—Old Chinese proverb that I just made up.

Second Cousins and Lightning Bugs

In my youth, when my great ambition was to become an operatic baritone, I met—and envied—a musician who had perfect pitch. Then my new friend and I attended a concert, and I learned that even a God-given gift can be a mixed blessing.

While I listened blissfully, my friend was in torment. Her ears had instantly detected what mine—and presumably, the performer's—could not: the piano was a smidgen flat. I would never have known if Marjorie hadn't told me.

Perfect pitch would be fine if we lived in a perfect world. Since we don't, accurate relative pitch is often more enjoyable, and sometimes more practical.

People can have tin ears for language just as they can for music. Mark Twain made me aware of this when I first read his celebrated essay on the literary offenses of Fenimore Cooper. The great man's observation about using the "right word and not its second cousin" struck my young mind like a lightning bolt. In another essay, Twain wrote, "The difference between the right word and the almost right is really a large matter—'tis the difference between the lightning and the lightning bug."

A common literary sin of many writers—not just the lamented (or more accurately, lamentable) Fenimore Cooper—is what I call the "second cousin syndrome." Many such mistakes can be ascribed to carelessness. That's why writers need editors!

Such mistakes plague even the best of the breed; not only did good old Homer occasionally nod, but so did E. B. White, Winston Churchill, and a host of other eminent writers that I deeply admire.

Only a chosen few are born with a perfect ear for language. In music, the many of us who don't have absolute pitch can accomplish wonders with systematic exercises in ear training. But can we train our ear for language? Do suitable exercises exist? Offhand, I don't know of any.

Some of my favorite authorities on usage—Strunk and White, Fowler, Bergen and Cornelia Evans, among others—address the task only obliquely. Having compiled my own lists of confusing word usages in this book, I've observed that my lists, and theirs, share almost incestuous similarities, focusing on distinctions most writers and editors already recognize.

The time has come to practice some new tunes. That's why I've put together this medley: a collection of words constantly mistreated in books, abused in magazines, and savaged in newspapers. Few of these problem words are mentioned in standard references. (Please tackle the exercise before you look at the suggested answers on the next page. Should your answers disagree with mine, I'd like very much to hear explanations of your choices. Hopefully—oops, we know better than that, don't we?—I'll learn something.)

Exercise

In the following sentences, replace the "second cousin" words with more accurate choices.

NOTE: These sentences are not manufactured. All of them (including some by distinguished writers who undoubtedly know better) have appeared in print.

1. Good organization is the cornerstone of good dictation.
2. The speaker placed her notes on the podium.
3. We should try to hone in on what the real problem is.
4. The hungry beggar scarfed down all the food in sight.
5. The young man dove off the dock.
6. The circus horse harrumphed around the ring.
7. He poured over the dusty manuscript for hours.
8. Bill said, "What are you up to these days?"
9. The Eisenhower Theater seems too small by half to contain the foment of ideas and images [in the Kennedy Center production of *The Count of Monte Cristo*].
10. Beset by grizzly phantoms, they lurch and writhe.
11. From time to time, members of the press are assailed by a curious malady.
12. Mrs. Jones considered it fortuitous that her husband had bought the winning lottery ticket.
13. When the *Esmeralda,* Chile's tall ship, hoves to in Baltimore Harbor this weekend, it will mark the beginning of an eventful week for sailing enthusiasts.
14. The governor was delighted to hear such fulsome praise.
15. Circumstances mitigated against a successful conclusion of the problem.
16. He was the worst knitpicker I ever saw.
17. Jack's action showed blatant disregard for the safety of his friends.
18. More importantly, he said that the whole problem centered around a misunderstanding.
19. The editor carefully amended the text.
20. To prevent the enemy from importing missiles, the President ordered a boycott of the harbor.
21. Joe tried to convince me to buy a 40-volume encyclopedia.
22. The engineer sighted several discreet examples of poor design practice.
23. There seemed to be genuine solicitation in his voice.

You'll find some suggested answers on the next page.

Suggested Answers: Second Cousin Exercise

These suggested answers are provided by the author, along with some explanations. I suggest that you check the shades of meaning in your favorite unabridged dictionary.

1. Good organization is the *wellspring* of good dictation. (Jim Aswell said, "Dictation is a living, moving thing, and a *cornerstone* just sits there. This is something I'd walk the floor with if it were my writing . . . Try for a word that implies creativity." After considerable floorwalking, I came up with *wellspring*. Jim approved.)

2. The speaker placed her notes on the *lectern*. (The term *podium* is frequently misused. Reserve the word for the small platform an orchestral conductor stands on.)

3. We should try to *home in* . . . (I'm amazed at how many good writers make this mistake. *Hone* means to sharpen. *Home in* comes from the early days of aviation, when pilots navigated by tuning their receivers to radio beacons and then *homing in* on them. A change in the pattern of dots and dashes indicated they were off course.)

4. The hungry beggar *scoffed* down . . . (The word *scoff* in this sense is listed in most unabridged dictionaries, although it may be described as slang or dialect. Another accepted spelling is *scorf,* which apparently has been mistaken for *scarf* because they look and sound so much alike. I suppose I'm being pedantic—*scarf* is already firmly entrenched, no matter what I say.)

5. The young man *dived* off the *pier*. (*Dived* is the preferred past tense. When I was young, the definition of a *dock* was "the water adjacent to a pier," and *Writer's Digest* cleverly pointed out that one can dive off a pier into a dock, but it's not a good idea to dive off a dock into a pier. But language and definitions change. A second definition, listed in *American Heritage* third edition, is "pier or wharf." I must acknowledge this, but it still sounds weird to my elderly ears.)

6. The circus horse *galumphed* around the ring. (This example came from the collected essays of E. B. White. Of course he

knew better, but isn't this fun! *Harrumph* means *to clear the throat ostentatiously. Galumph* is a "portmanteau word" coined by Lewis Carroll, probably to convey simultaneously the idea of *gallop* and *triumph*.)

7. He *pored* over . . . (I first ran across *poured* for *pored* in *The Washington Post*'s book section, in a review of a biography of Thornton Wilder. In my mind's eye, old Thornton was pouring molasses on an ancient music manuscript—a stirring picture! I've come across the same confused usage many times since.)

8. Bill *asked,* "What . . ." (This is from a sentence that I wrote in the original draft of *The Portable Office*. My editor pointed out, quite properly, that I use *said* entirely too much, and that *asked* is more appropriate for a question.)

9. . . . to contain the *ferment* of ideas . . . (I found the misuse of *foment* in *The Washington Post*'s review of the Kennedy Center production of *The Count of Monte Cristo*.)

10. Beset by *grisly* phantoms . . . (A *grizzly* is a bear.)

11. From time to time, members of the press are *struck* (or *stricken*—either form is technically correct) by a curious malady. (To *assail* is to attack. Members of the press aren't simply attacked by the curious malady, they fall victim to it. So either *struck,* or *stricken*—both past participles of *strike*—would be a more accurate choice. To my archaic ear, *stricken* sounds better here, even though most dictionaries say to reserve the usage for poetics. If you don't like either word, possibly you might say, ". . . members of the press *succumb to a curious malady.*" Or perhaps easier for today's plethora of semi-literate readers to understand, *fall victim to* might be the selection of choice.

Incidentally, *plethora* is another frequently misused word. It does not imply simply *plenty,* or *ample,* or *enough,* but *more than enough, superabundance,* or *excess*.)

12. . . . considered it *fortunate* . . . (*Fortuitous* means *by chance,* whether the results be good or bad.)

13. . . . *heaves to* . . . (*Hoves* is not a legitimate word, but I saw it in the newspaper article from which this example was taken.)

14. The governor was delighted to hear such *heartfelt, ringing, abundant, copious* [choose any of these, or simply leave out

the adjective entirely] praise. (*Fulsome* has not meant *copious* for a very long time. It means *nauseating,* and other equally unpleasant things.)

15. Circumstances *militated* against a successful solution.

16. He was the worst *nitpicker* I ever saw.

17. . . . showed *flagrant* disregard . . .

18. More *important,* he said that the whole misunderstanding *stemmed from* . . . (One of my pet hates is the use of *importantly* when the writer means *important. Importantly* implies doing something "in an important manner." *Centered around* is probably misused so often that I should give up the battle, but I don't intend to. *Stemmed from* is the preferred choice here.)

19. The editor carefully *emended* the text. (A legislator *amends,* an editor *emends.* Look it up.)

20. . . . the President ordered an *embargo* of the harbor.

21. Joe tried to *persuade* me . . . (The use of *convince* for *persuade* is one of my wife's pet hates. Like me, she is a former English teacher. She points out that *convince* should not be followed by an infinitive, but that more and more writers are making the error. We hope it's not too late to try to stamp it out. We are *convinced* of it. And we hope we can *persuade* you to agree with us!)

22. The engineer *cited* several *discrete* examples . . .

23. There seemed to be genuine *solicitude* in his voice. (I found the misused *solicitation* in *The Brass Go-Between,* by the late Ross Thomas, who wrote some of my favorite thrillers. Mr. Thomas seldom erred; I'm sure he knew better.)

21

Capital Crimes

Capitalize on your own experience
—Motto used at the
National Speakers Association
at the Washington Convention (1986)

To Cap or Not to Cap?

If the rules for capitalization are as simple as they seem on the surface, why do they cause writers and editors so many problems?

Checking the index of *The Chicago Manual of Style*, you'll find at least 72 entries on the subject of capitalization. That's simple? And even after you've studied all the rules (good luck!), you'll encounter many cases that fall through the cracks—especially if you look in some of the many other respected manuals. In recent years, I've grown fond of *Reader's Digest*'s excellent handbook, *Success With Words*—probably because I agree strongly with its philosophy. On the subject of capitalization, it points out that "One authority says *Federal Government,* another says *federal government* or *Federal government.* One approves of the *Mayor of Waukegan,* another endorses the *mayor of Waukegan.* One urges you to write *Board of Directors,* another says the correct form is *board of directors.*"

Using Style Manuals

Your life as a writer and an editor can be simpler, but not necessarily better, if you choose one authoritative style guide and stick to it. Sometimes that guide is chosen for you—for 25 years I had to live by the *Government Printing Office* (GPO) *Style Manual,* but I disagreed with it vehemently in many cases. A decade too late for me, the edition of March 1984 cleaned up the act and eliminated a lot of my pet hates. In light of the preceding paragraph, you might be interested to know that *GPO* says "Federal government"; *Chicago* says [7.53] that federal and government are "not usually capitalized." *Success With Words* shrewdly points out that government insiders are more likely to write Federal Government and Mayor than those outside.

I'm acquainted with professional editors who have memorized all the rules of capitalization set forth in *The Chicago* (or the *GPO*) *Manual.* Frankly, that approach is out of the question for me—my memory isn't what it used to be, and probably never was. Furthermore, even if I could recall everything by chapter and verse, I wouldn't want to. My editorial philosophy is to make clear communication easier for writers, editors, and most of all, readers. And the best way to do that is to use a practical, commonsense approach. If this be heresy, make the most of it!

The best professional editors I know are thoroughly familiar with many manuals. If they run across a thorny problem, they check various pertinent authorities and pick a solution that fits the situation best. I repeat: Using only one manual can make editorial decisions easier and more consistent, but not necessarily better.

Top Editorial Priority: Reader Understanding

If you want to be the best writer and editor you can be, please become familiar with at least three or four of the recognized authorities, and then choose judiciously and practically. Consistency is extremely important, but it isn't everything. Ask yourself, which recommendation makes the meaning clearer to the reader in a given situation? Which is least likely to cause misunderstanding? Which communicates best?

My experience from the writer's side of the table colors my next statement, but I'll say it anyway. When you edit the work of writers whose punctuation and capitalization are logical and consistent, and who clearly know (and care about) what they are doing, don't be procrustean. Even if you consider *The Chicago Manual* to be the authority, be aware that some other respected manuals differ markedly. I implore you to tread softly.

Why Do We Use Caps, Anyway?

Space considerations prevent my setting forth a full-fledged set of "rules" here. A commonsense principle or two must suffice. Let's start by analyzing why writers and editors use capitalization in the first place. I'm sure all the professionals who read *The Editorial Eye* already know these things, but bear with me.

Capital letters add emphasis and importance. Basically, that's why sentences always must begin with a cap, signaling the reader that a new thought or idea is coming up. It's like a road sign.

Sometimes we signify respect or reverence by using capitals. That's why we capitalize the name of the Deity, or the Holy Bible, or the Koran. We also use initial caps for the names of religious or religious denominations or orders.

You're all aware of the concept of proper nouns (and proper adjectives) and common nouns. *Success With Words* says: "The formal or official names of particular persons, places or things—in short, proper nouns—are always capitalized because of the distinction these names deserve . . . "

My point is this: If the caps you add make life easier for the reader, you must be doing something right. And remember there is always room to learn.

Admittedly, I have much to be modest about, so I'd like to close with a learning experience 25 years ago when I struggled with a new problem of capitalization.

A "Sea Story" from Space

I joined the National Aeronautics and Space Administration (NASA) in 1959, when the U.S. space program was just getting off the ground. With the program came a whole new vocabulary, as thousands of new, highly technical words and terms began entering our everyday language. Today many of those words are a part of every schoolchild's vocabulary, but in 1959 only scientists and engineers understood them.

My first major writing assignment at NASA was to put together a glossary of space terms, written in simple language. The task was fun, but difficult. Scientists and engineers did not always agree among themselves on the definitions, and many took umbrage at what they conceived to be my overly simplified versions.

One big problem was what words to capitalize. For example, the words "earth" and "moon" are customarily written in lower case, but the names of planets, such as Mars, Venus, or Jupiter, are accorded upper case. To keep things orderly, when referring to the earth as one of the planets, I felt constrained to capitalize "Earth."

My bible (please note lower case—there's a reason for it) was my beloved Second Edition of *Webster's New International Dictionary*. It said that in planetary contexts, "Earth" (capital E) was okay. For consistency, I decided also to capitalize "Sun" and "Moon." Somewhat arbitrarily, I used upper case for all three heavenly bodies throughout the manuscript, even though some entries, under conventional rules of capitalization, were not in a "planetary" context, and would ordinarily have been lower case. Frequent usage of the convention must have dulled my editorial judgment. By the time I had finished the first draft of the project, Earth, Sun, and Moon looked great to me.

But when the review copies came back with comments, here's one that hit me right between the eyes:

I am Unable to fathom your Rule Of capitalization. If you wish to capitalize Earth and Sun, suggest you drop the "the" in front.

The lighthearted humor took away some of the sting, and the logic of the comment removed a mote from my editorial eye. (Lower case). I trust I won't make that same mistake again. (Of course, I still Have plenty of Room for new Ones.)

22

Vogue Words and Technical Jargon

A flow of words is no proof of wisdom.
—Anonymous

A Definition of Terms

Bergen and Cornelia Evans, in *A Dictionary of Contemporary Usage*, say that "An *argot* is a language, usually esoteric, used by a peculiar group, class, or occupation," and that "*Jargon* means unintelligible writing or talk." They add that "Jargon is a term of contempt and must be used carefully." H. W. Fowler, in *Modern English Usage*, coined the expression "vogue word," saying that such a word or phrase "emerges from obscurity, or even from nothingness . . . into sudden popularity." Fowler felt the popularity of such words was fleeting. He went on to say that "The reason for collecting them under a common heading is that young writers may not even be aware, about some of them, that they are not part of the normal vocabulary, but still repulsive to the old & the well-read . . ."

What should an editor (or a writer, for that matter) do about the use of argot, technical jargon, and "vogue words" in publications addressed to lay readers?

The answer used to be easy, especially for language purists. Virtually every authority (beginning with Fowler and more recently,

Bergen and Cornelia Evans and William and Mary Morris) simply commanded us to get rid of jargon and vogue words, substituting standard English words that everyone knows.

Fifty years ago, as a newly hatched liberal arts graduate, I too was a purist. But after a lifetime of working closely with scientists and engineers who talk that way, I frequently fall by the wayside. Even so, I always strive to be consistent in my inconsistency. I'll describe a few commonsense principles for you at the end of this chapter.

Changing Patterns of Language

Very few questions on English usage are as easy to answer as they used to be. The patterns of language are now changing with incredible and unprecedented speed. So pervasive is the enormous power of the media (the term "media" itself might be considered a vogue word) that the general public is continually barraged with vogue words and technical terms. As a result, many of these words no longer simply disappear the way they used to—instead they become useful components of everyday language.

In 1975, the Morrises considered all these to be vogue words and predicted they would soon go into limbo:

> *input, output, hang-up, freak out, flap, camp, kitsch, watershed, bench mark, overview, empathy, infrastructure, phase (in and out), ongoing, seminal, in depth, feedback, escalate, relevant, generation gap, clout, biodegradable, interface, parameter, in-group, out-group, peer group, synergy, and synergistic.*

If these are truly vogue words, how did they escape the limbo the Morrises predicted?

My answer is that (a) they are useful; and (b) most members of the general public have learned what they mean.

The Two Cultures

The recent deluge of books about "what educated people should know" invites our attention once again to the chasm between the scientific and liberal arts communities. Read William and Mary Morris's mistaken definitions of such neologisms as *kludge* and you'll find that those two dedicated scholars of language lacked comparable scholarship in electronics and computers. In fairness, they were writing more than quarter of a century ago, when the computer revolution had scarcely begun. Schoolchildren today are familiar with words that were known only to specialists in those days.

Are the members on both sides of the "cultural chasm" equally lacking in knowledge about the others' fields? Experience leads me to believe that more scientists and engineers know about, say, the Battle of Hastings or the rhyme scheme of a Petrarchan Sonnet than liberal arts people know about Newton's Second Law or the difference between a *perimeter* and a *parameter*. We face a constant danger that some technical words, quite tractable in the controlled atmosphere of the laboratory, will go wild in the freedom of an ill-informed larger world, and lose the precision that made the terms so valuable.

On the one hand, I sympathize with scientists or engineers who use technical words within the rigorous technical definitions employed by their disciplines. These specialists believe—rightly, I think—that the more sloppily (and mistakenly) lay writers use the jealousy guarded technical terminology, the harder it becomes to speak or write intelligibly within the confines of the discipline. Specialists are not delighted when their precise words become generic, especially when they know all too well that the newly ascribed meanings lose precision through misunderstanding.

On the other hand, I grow impatient with purists who passionately inveigh against certain "new" words just because they've taken a dislike to them. Even more annoying are those erudite souls who demonstrate their moral superiority by trotting out what they deem to be more respectable Middle English or Latin or Greek or French or German words.

I commit this seeming treason in spite of years as a classroom teacher, seeking to impart the joys and beauties of English to sometimes reluctant pupils.

Those who feel that the technical vocabulary is growing too fast, and is somehow illegitimate, are apparently not familiar with the history of the English language—particularly American English.

In light of all these things, here's a summary based on 40 years of pondering. I'll appreciate your feedback (NOT a vogue word).

Common-Sense Principles—
Vogue Words and Technical Terms

1. If a word or expression appears frequently and regularly in current newspapers and magazines for general reading, it probably isn't a vogue word any more, or will stop being one soon. Use it freely.

2. If such a word or expression, or a technical word or phrase (no matter what its origin) helps convey an idea clearly and accurately to lay readers, don't be afraid to use it.

3. If such a word or expression is sloppy or inaccurate, or if it serves only to confuse, forget it. The purpose of language is to communicate, not to obfuscate.

4. If you yourself don't know exactly what a word or expression means, beware of using it! If you feel at all hazy, that in itself is good enough reason to steer clear.

23

Tell Me Not in Mournful Numbers

There's safety in numbers.
—Ancient proverb

Figures? Or Words?

Way back when I was writing speeches for a living, I once hid under my seat when my speaker looked up confidently from his manuscript and told the audience about "World War Eleven." From that day forward I've always written out "World War Two" in speech manuscripts, but boldly write "World War II" in articles and books.

A decade of technical writing and editing supplied the foundation for many opinions about using numbers that I still hold. But the changeover to speech writing during the sixties gave me an entirely new perspective on the way speakers and readers perceive numbers on the printed page. (Incidentally, would you have written sixties as I did, or perhaps with a cap? Or would you have chosen 60s or '60s or 60's? If you check enough style books, you'll find that most of these variations are supported somewhere.)

My prime concern—with writing numbers as with everything else—is clear communication. I must regretfully report that many style manuals, even those most revered, don't give uniformly good advice on when to spell out and when to use arabic numerals. Some, however, are much better than others.

From my strictly practical point of view, the *GPO Style Manual* offers the most practical guidelines on numbers. I recommend that you study it religiously if you haven't already. You'll find other similarly useful guidelines on numbers in *The Washington Post Deskbook on Style*.

Regrettably, *The Chicago Manual* seems more concerned with aesthetics than with ease of understanding. (One principle that I consider supremely important is relegated to a footnote.)

Numbers Speak Louder than Words

The GPO Manual [12.1] sets forth "the general principle that the reader comprehends numerals more readily than numerical word expressions, particularly in technical, scientific, or statistical matter. However, for special reasons numbers are spelled out in indicated instances . . . *The GPO Manual* goes on to say [12.4] "A figure is used for a single number of 10 or more with the exception of the first word of the sentence . . . " and [12.5] "When 2 or more numbers appear in a sentence and 1 of them is 10 or more, figures are used for each number . . . "

The Washington Post Deskbook on Style presents [p. 113] a similar philosophy and approach, and perhaps expresses it a little better: "In general: It is easier to understand numbers expressed in figures than in words. As a rule spell out numbers one through nine in ordinary text. Use figures for higher numbers and for statistical and sequential forms. Arabic numerals are easier to read than roman numerals; use the latter sparingly."

The Deskbook continues [under A. ORDINARY USAGE:] "1. Spell out numbers one through nine and use figures for numbers 10 and higher."

one horse, 10 customers

The Chicago Manual takes a different tack, telling us [8.3] to spell out "whole numbers from one through ninety-nine" and "Any of these followed by *hundred, thousand, million,* etc." A footnote explains that "It should be noted, perhaps, that newspaper style, as well as that of some general publishers and scholarly journals, decrees that only the numbers from one through nine and such multiples as one hundred or nine thousand are to be spelled out."

Numbers and Cases

Now let's get down to cases (or more accurately, numbers). Suppose you're a speaker, glancing down quickly at the manuscript on your lectern. Your speechwriter has furnished you a figure of, say, $10,937,837,444.27, and you must read it to your awestruck audience. (I suggest you fire the miscreant immediately, but for now you're stuck.)

Maybe you'll do fine. I guarantee you that I won't; I have enough problems with 2 + 2. (This, incidentally, would be written as "two plus two" according to the rules set forth in many style books. I hope you'll agree that the 2 + 2 version is easier to comprehend.)

When dealing with relatively small amounts, numerals do have the advantage of quickly sending information from the page to the reader's brain. "$275,000" is easier to comprehend than "two hundred and seventy-five thousand dollars."

Billions and Billions and Billions

But when we start dealing with multimillions and multibillions, and (heaven forbid!) multitrillions, it's a different ball game. Let's consider again the $10,937,837,444.27 example. What's the best way to write such a number? As a speech writer, I would strongly recommend something like "nearly 11 billion dollars." Because few of us comprehend billions all that well, the final eight figures can be safely dropped with no important loss in precision or accuracy.

If I were using the same number in an article, I'd probably write "nearly $11 billion." (But admittedly, I'd be nervous about using the dollar sign approach in a speech.)

All Numbers Great and Small

Let's move to the other end of the scale. How do you think most speakers would read aloud the numeral 6.55%?

From experience, I can tell you confidently that almost all of them would say "six-point-five-five percent." A few would say "six-point-fifty-five percent." Reading it either of those ways does no great harm, but again, the degree of accuracy achieved by the final "five" adds little. And it definitely makes comprehension more difficult for the audience. The difficulty is compounded if the speech contains a multiplicity of facts and figures. I would therefore suggest that writing "six and a half percent," while not supremely accurate, would make the numbers easier for both speaker and audience to comprehend.

I once submitted to a publisher a booklength manuscript that had a great many numbers in it. I meticulously followed GPO/newspaper practice, spelling out one to nine and using arabic numerals the rest of the time.

A zealous line editor changed virtually everything I had written, pockmarking every page with "corrections." This episode raised my blood pressure to about two hundred and twenty systolic over one hundred and twenty diastolic, and gave me a case of the shivering fits. Perhaps that experience helps explain my present firm opinion on the subject of numbers:

Follow the rules of a recognized authority, but choose a sensible authority. And never, never, *never let a foolish consistency stand in the way of clarity and understanding.*

24

The Dangerfield Syndrome

"I can't get no respect."
—Standup comedian
Rodney Dangerfield

Must We Die to Get Respect?

Rodney Dangerfield is no longer alone. In today's society, nobody "can't get no respect" except when his or her obituary is published, and sometimes not even then.

Are honorifics obsolescent? Good manners and good taste extinct? Is "everyday politeness" an oxymoron? Is "common courtesy" uncommon?

Don't put the blame on Mame, folks, put it on influential newspaper style guides, which seem more infectious than AIDS. Now radio and television are succumbing to the blight.

Dictums from a Newspaper Stylebook

Here, in brief, are the culprit rules (under the heading "Courtesy Terms and Professional Titles" from a respected newspaper stylebook.

1. Use *Mr.*, *Mrs.*, and *Miss* only in obituaries, in reference to couples, in direct quotations, and where essential for effect, as in

editorials and critiques. In particularly, do not use the terms with surnames after first reference . . .

.   .   .

3. Use civic, military, and professional titles as infrequently as possible after first reference . . .

.   .   .

5. Use the title *Dr.* for practitioners of the healing arts (including chiropractors and osteopaths) but not for holders of Ph.D.s or honorary degrees.

.   .   .

Manners of Style? Or Style of Manners?

How do these dictums affect writing practices in the real world? And why should writers and editors be concerned? We're not supposed to be the arbiters of good manners—just good style. Perhaps we should leave the problem to Judith Martin, the delightful and witty "Miss Manners" who serves as arbiter of etiquette for *The Washington Post* and its syndicate.

Fortunately, Miss Manners has already sounded the alarm. In a delightful and perceptive column entitled "Mustering Up a Mister" (January 3, 1988), Judith Martin wrote:

Miss Manners is dismayed to find more and more people addressing envelopes with the names totally bald of any titles of courtesy: "Archibald Twimbal." Miss Manners always thinks an exclamation point has been left out, and it was intended as a ringing summons: "Archibald Twimball!"

Under this horrid system, a couple will be "Adelia and Archibald Twimbal," or will include those additions so flattering to ladies, "Archibald Twimbal and Wife" or "and Guest." And that's the formal social style. Should the gentleman or lady be distinguished for heroism or indicted for murder, rather than being so bluntly bidden to attend a wedding, the newspapers would call him or her merely "Twimbal." And if the couple accomplished one of these things together, each would be called "Twimbal" until the poor reader was totally confused.

That last sentence, gentle readers, writers, and editors, pretty well sums up the urgent need for members of our profession to take up the cudgels: bad manners are leading us into faulty communication.

For Example?

Some years back, an article about Mamie Eisenhower in *The Post* referred to her as "Eisenhower" repeatedly. The result? The confusion Miss Manners was talking about.

Do you find yourself constantly forced to re-read news stories in which a number of persons are briefly introduced early on, and then referred to by last name only? Are you often baffled about which of several persons they might be writing about? Do you ask yourself, as I often do, why they can't serve clarity and precision by adding identifying titles or labels when they are needed?

A few years ago a multi-talented young professional woman was attacked, raped, and murdered early one morning while she was out jogging. On the evening TV news, commentators recounted the story time after time in gruesome detail. Every single one of them repeatedly referred to the victim, after an initial reference to "Ann Jones" (not her real name), as "Jones."

The lead sentence of a front page story in *The Washington Post* (5/30/88) informed us that "Ronald Reagan finally got his wish to meet the Soviet people today."

When "Ronald Reagan" was working as a movie actor, he might properly have been called "Ronald Reagan." But, dammit, when *President* Ronald Reagan attended a summit conference in Moscow with Soviet leader Mikhail Gorbachev, let's remember that when the late President Harry S. Truman was in office, he pointed out that the office, regardless of its occupant, deserves respect.

Apropos of Chapter 21 (about the problems of capitalization), the lead sentence of the next paragraph of the same *Post* article refers to "An unscheduled stroll by the president [initial lower case] and First Lady [initial upper case] Nancy Reagan."

As a sidelight, I note that *Time* magazine regularly uses initial caps on the words "President" and "Vice President," while *The Post* capitalizes neither. Is it not helpful to readers to demonstrate a clear-cut and easily discernible difference between the president (initial lower case) of, say, Schlock, Inc., and the President (initial upper case) of the United States?

An adjacent front page story led off with "Pope John Paul II yesterday named as cardinal the Most Rev. James A. Hickey . . . " but in accordance with the *Deskbook*, the Pope is called simply "John Paul" throughout the rest of the story.

Ironically, the editorial page of *The Post*, going strictly by the book, customarily refers to a murderer, or a rapist, or a criminal who has ripped off millions of dollars through insider trading as "Mr." so-and-so. Check this out, in any editorial, any day of the week. You'll find I do not exaggerate.

Granted that newspapers are enormously influential, must the rest of us blindly follow down the primrose path? I'm thankful that at least a few respected newspapers, including *The Wall Street Journal*, *The New York Times*, and the *Washington Times* are still holding the line. If you'd like a quick lesson in what *can* be done, read a story in *The Post* and then read its counterpart in *The Wall Street Journal* or the *Washington Times*. Compare the versions side by side; then decide for yourself which is clearer and easier to read.

Once More Unto the Breach!

Let's continue with Judith Martin's insightful observations on the use of surnames only:

> . . . Miss Manners must put a stop to this; no one is going to address her as "Manners." Her indignation is, however, tinged with sympathy because she understands the cause of the problem. It is a complex cause. Hardly anyone knows

what is correct anymore in the usage of courtesy titles, and hardly anyone knows what a given person's preference is.

Therefore, many figure that leaving off all such designations will eliminate the possibility of offense. Wrong.

Stripping the language of honorifics makes us all sound like children. Surnames-only is a non-gender-specific prep-school custom, as in: "Hey, Twimbal! Can I borrow your notes the week before the exam?"

25

Writers and Editors—Can't We Be Friends?

Do anything you like with this copy—
I have no pride of authorship.

—Second biggest lie ever told

Crotchets, Anyone?

In the preface to *The Portable Office* (Acropolis, 1987) I used the word "overlong" in a sentence, thus: "To keep chapters from being overlong . . ."

A line editor reviewing the manuscript suggested changing the sentence to read "overly long." She was making the suggestion to help, not to hassle. That's what editors are supposed to do. Clearly, the editor felt that her substitution would improve my choice of words. So why did my adrenaline suddenly start to flow? Jack Kilpatrick, whose style I admire, would probably say that my crotchets were showing. (If you haven't read his superb book *The Writer's Art*, you'd better rush out and get it right away.)

Two Words Better Than One?

I respect the editor's opinion; she has saved me from several major embarrassments. So I tried to be analytical: Why would a practicing professional editor think that two words were better than one?

Perhaps my editor did not consider "overlong" a legitimate word. Or maybe she felt that "long," an adjective, must necessarily be modified by an adverb. (And, of course, with "overly long" being considered as two words, that reasoning would be impeccable.)

I mentally tried to put myself in her shoes. A faint suspicion was entering my mind. Could she possibly be right?

I hastily looked up "overlong" in my good old *Merriam-Webster Second* (still my favorite). I found the word listed not once, but three times—as an adjective, an adverb, and a preposition. My judgment was vindicated, at least for the moment.

Blue Pencils and Blue Language

I returned to the blue-penciled manuscript and wrote NO!!! in big letters beside the comment. Feeling better, I resumed reading. On the next page I found a suggestion to change the phrase ". . . you'll stand a good chance of getting prompter and better service" to ". . . getting better and more prompt service."

Again I over-reacted. Once more I pondered why an editor would want to exchange one good word for two. The process would sacrifice the pleasant cadence of a nicely balanced parallel construction for the ragged arrhythmia of a stuffy nonparallel version. Jim Aswell would have said the rewrite had a "hitch in its getalong." This time I wrote NO!!! with underscores.

The crowning blow came when I discovered that Mr. William F. Buckley's foreword to the book had fared little better than my own prose. Mr. Buckley, whose erudition few would question, had written ". . . frit away flight-time on movie watching . . ."

The line editor suggested changing "frit" to "fritter." (Granted, one cannot find "frit" in the dictionary. But if Bill Buckley chose to coin such a word, that was good enough for me. I wasn't just about to change it, and I didn't think the line editor should have done so either. Mr. Buckley needs no lessons in vocabulary or grammar from either of us.)

How Far, O Lord, How Far?

This cumulative experience surfaced a question that has troubled me intermittently for years: Just how far should a conscientious editor go in changing a writer's choice of words, or sentence structure, or even spellings? If the manuscript is illiterate, slipshod, or slovenly (and sad to say, many manuscripts are "all of the above"), that's one thing. But suppose an author (we won't mention any names, of course) has several books in print that relate to usage, and those books have been well received by peers and critics. Isn't that fact admissible as evidence of reasonable proficiency at the writing trade? If there is more than one acceptable way of saying something, or spelling something, shouldn't the editor defer to the author's preference?

But there is another side to the coin. Sometimes an editor stirs my ire, but often that same editor will keep me from making foolish errors that I had overlooked through carelessness (mostly) or ignorance (sometimes). Even when I disagree with the suggestions, they make me take a second look, and that's all to the good. So I must appreciate editorial advice and counsel even when I'm writing NO!!!

Peggy Smith, author of the definitive book on proofreading, and one of the best editors I've ever known, addressed this problem in an article in *The Editorial Eye,* in June 1978 (Issue #8)

Two Schools of Thought

At the time I first read her article, entitled "More on Judgment/Judgement and Related Issues," I had only recently endured the rigors of having *Writing with Precision* copyedited and published. In retrospect, I had an excellent and understanding editor. But what did I know? (A lot, I thought!)

That's doubtless why Peggy's ideas impressed me so deeply. Here, in part, is what she wrote:

Editors seem to belong to one of two schools of thought. When no style is specified, the first, the Mama-Knows-Best school, believes in imposing style on the authors and argues that they do this successfully because few authors know their own preferences.

I belong to the second, the Author-May-Be-Right school. I believe that editors need the ability to make changes that are improvements and the ability to recognize what should be left alone.

To the second school, the number of style manuals that prefer the spelling "judgment" to "judgement" is irrelevant. In this and a thousand other matters, when no style is specified, editors should not follow their personal preferences (nor the style they are used to working in, nor the prejudices instilled by their former teachers). Editors should not be rigid; they should follow the author's preference whenever it is accepted by a standard reference work or whenever common sense dictates.

Honesty compels me to tell you that Peggy softened her position a trifle as the article progressed. Indeed, she went on to say that she "may join the first school any day," explaining that her research had indicated that variant word forms were so numerous that no editor could possibly know all of them.

Well, Peggy Smith is much kinder and nobler (please notice I didn't say "more noble") than I am. My own uncompromising position is that an editor can always take a moment to look up a doubtful word or spelling. As a writer, I always do. (Well, almost always.)

Pride of Authorship

In Part One of this book, I spelled out what I still consider to be the duties and responsibilities of the editor. I also offered the following CAUTION:

Any time you hear someone say "Do anything you like with this copy—I have no pride of authorship," watch out! What the writer is really saying is that there will be a knock-down-and-drag-out fight over every single word you change.

Twenty years later, I'm astonished at how much I knew about pride of authorship when I had published only one book. And the years haven't changed another statement that I made in Part One.

TEAMWORK is the key to a good relationship between writer and editor. Avoid the adversary attitude; even if you use all the tact at your disposal, there still may be times when you find yourself involved in a shouting match. Be aware that you'll win a few and lose a few. The more editing skills you learn, the more battles you'll win.

The writer and editor are on the same team. Their common goal is to produce the best final product possible. Knowing this, a true professional should be able to recognize good editorial advice and accept it graciously, if not joyfully. But when a deadlock arises about two ways of saying something, or spelling something, and recognized authorities consider both versions acceptable and "correct," the tie goes to the writer.

I hope that Peggy Smith stays loyal to the Author-May-Be-Right school. I like to be known by the company I keep!

Part 3

Handbook

How to Use
the Handbook

This handbook section does not pretend to be complete. It simply explains, in plain language, a few terms, techniques, and usages that working writers need to know. Use it to augment the information contained in Part One.

For convenience, the handbook is arranged in alphabetical order. There are just two exceptions:

Under the heading **grammar—a few elementary principles**, you will find, *not* in alphabetical order, the following items: **nouns, pronouns, number, case, direct object, indirect object, verbs, person and number of verbs, transitive and intransitive verbs, adjectives, conjunctions**, and **prepositions**. Some of this grouping duplicates other material found elsewhere. I have put them all in one unit here because of the interrelationships of the items being discussed.

Similarly, under the heading **sentence—the parts of**, you will find discussions of **subject, predicate, direct object**, and **indirect object**. Again, there is a small amount of intentional duplication, which is in keeping with my belief that individual discussions should be able to stand on their own feet—within reasonable limits!

Readers have a right to ask why I haven't explained other grammatical terms such as *clauses, phrases, complements,* and so on. Perhaps I should have. But we have only so much space, and I have accordingly limited my discussions to items of the most immediate and practical value to most readers. There are dozens of excellent references easily available on all these subjects. Check the bibliography for recommendations.

I would suggest that you read straight through this handbook section. It covers much important material not touched on in Part One.

• Abbreviations and Acronyms

Most administrative writing is riddled with *abbreviations* and *acronyms*. An abbreviation, as you know, is a shortened or contracted word or phrase that is used to represent the whole. An acronym is a word made up by combining the first one or two (and occasionally more) letters from each of a group of words.

To communicate clearly, make sure not to use abbreviations or acronyms without explaining them *unless you are absolutely sure that everyone in your audience will be familiar with them.* Remember that many readers will not have the slightest idea what these shorthand expressions mean.

Play it safe. If there is any doubt in your mind that even a few readers will be unfamiliar with your terms, you should spell out each abbreviation or acronym the first time you use it. Then put the acronym or abbreviation in parentheses. From then on, you can safely use the shortened version. However, if you explain the meaning early in a piece of writing, but do not use the short form again for many pages, don't expect your reader to remember. Spell it out again, or include a *glossary* to aid your reader.

The best and funniest explanation of acronyms I have ever encountered can be found in *The Kidner Report*, a witty and perceptive spoof of bureaucracy. I quote:

. . . Acronymizing is the art of making words by combining the first one or two letters in a group of words. The function is to simplify communications by reducing oft-repeated, complex titles and phrases to a set of initials. However, the acronym is too pedestrian.

The technique is to choose a word to be spelled, then construct the title to yield it. In doing so, remember that the word should be easy to pronounce, and it shouldn't spell anything dirty in any language.

Dirty words sneak up even when merely writing titles and phrases without ever intending to make acronyms out of them. Since I write a lot of government papers, I always keep this rule before me: *Be Absolutely Sure That Acronyms Reflect*

Decency. Indeed, an experienced acronymist converts to an acronym almost unconsciously any time he sees two or more words that are capitalized or appear to have been assembled more for their letters than their meaning.

—*The Kidner Report*, Acropolis Books, pp. 45–46

• Ability/Capacity

Ability is the power to do something; *capacity* is the power to receive something. You can acquire *ability,* but you must be born with *capacity.* Ability can be improved by practice; capacity isn't helped by all the hard work in the world. You can keep the difference straight by picturing the ability of a skilled athlete, on the one hand, versus the capacity of a carton or receptacle, on the other.

• Absolute Construction (Absolute Phrase)

An absolute phrase consists of a *participle* (and sometimes a *complement*) grammatically unconnected with the rest of the sentence, but usually telling when, why, or how something happened.

• Accusative

This term is really taken from Latin grammar, but some teachers of English still use it to indicate the objective case—the direct object of a verb. For example, "John loves Mary."

• Active Voice (See Voice—Active and Passive)

• Adjective

A part of speech that modifies or changes the meaning of a *noun* or *pronoun.*

• Ad Nauseam

Should a writer use foreign-sounding words such as this? Sometimes.

The expression, of course, is Latin, but it's also acceptable English. It means *to a sickening degree,* but expresses the idea more succinctly. It may not be one of your everyday words, but it can be useful on occasion. Indeed, sometimes it's the *mot juste.* (Which, incidentally, is another case in point—an expression that is extremely useful in certain contexts.)

• Adverb

A word that modifies or changes the meaning of a *verb,* an *adjective,* or another *adverb.* Many adverbs—but not all of them—end in the suffix *-ly.* Examples: *quickly, slowly, steadily, belatedly.*

• Almanac

Every writer should have one of these useful one-volume compendiums. (This is another Latin word that's also useful English. A compendium is a brief summary. The plural is as I've used it, not *compendia.*) A good almanac will give you information that's hard or impossible to find anywhere else—items such as the longest rivers, the highest mountains, the biggest cities. Or even what Joe DiMaggio's batting average was when he played with the San Francisco Seals, or what horse won the Kentucky Derby in 1936.

A good almanac is a trivia lover's delight. One of my Army friends used to memorize entire sections of the *World Almanac.* Then he'd go to the nearest bar, make outlandish bets, and win. He raked in a lot of money, but he was also punched in the nose with some regularity.

There are so many excellent almanacs on the market that I won't single one out—go to your nearest bookstore and browse.

• Alphabetical Order

Never underestimate the value of alphabetical order in lining up items so that they will be easy to find and easy to understand. Since the advent of *Sesame Street,* children learn the alphabet even before they start to school. They are comfortable, because they can understand what letter comes before or after some other letter, even if they can't comprehend more complex systems of order. So—don't sell alphabetical listings short. They can be very useful in achieving clear communication.

Alumnus

Like other Latin words, this one gives most of us Americans trouble. Here's everything you need to know in one easy list:

Masculine singular: *alumnus,* pronounced uh-LUM-nus
Masculine plural: *alumni,* pronounced uh-LUM-NYE
Feminine singular: *alumna,* pronounced uh-LUM-nuh
Feminine plural: *alumnae,* pronounced uh-LUM-nee.

The Romans were a bunch of male chauvinist pigs (like some others we won't mention), so when you refer to a mixed group of men and women, you are automatically locked in to using the word used for the masculine plural: *alumni.*

Ambiguity—How to Avoid

Ambiguity is one of the greatest hazards a writer encounters when striving for precision and clarity. If readers can possibly misinterpret, they undoubtedly will. (See *Murphy's Law.*) The fact is that many times the reader will misinterpret even if the writer has taken special care to remove any possibility of ambiguity. Sad, but true.)

Here are some common causes of ambiguity. Notice that each of the following examples can be interpreted in several different ways.

faulty pronoun reference. *John told Jim that he was fired.* Is the "he" John or Jim? The reader can't tell. Rewrite the sentence something like this: *John told Jim, You're fired.* Or, *John had been fired, and told Jim about it.*

misplaced modifiers. Place your modifiers carefully, as close as possible to the words they are intended to modify. Sometimes the results of a misplaced modifier are laughable but harmless. Sometimes they can be downright misleading. One of my favorites is a headline from a news story that appeared in *The Washington Post.* It went like this:

POLICEMAN SHOOTS THIEF WITH KNIFE

dangling modifiers. These are verbal clusters that either (a) have nothing to modify; or (b) give the appearance of modifying a word other than the one intended. Usually they are introductory phrases such as:

Dangling: Walking down the street, a strange sight came into my view.
Corrected: As I was walking down the street, a strange sight came into my view. (This correction is grammatically correct, but stylistically poor, because of an unnecessary shift of subject.)
How about . . . *I saw a strange sight?*

other common causes of ambiguity. There are, of course, many other possible causes of multiple meanings. One of the most common stems from using a word that can be defined in several different ways in a context that makes for confusion or absurdity. For example, *After waiting for a brief period, he changed the comma to a semicolon.*

Another error involves failing to make clear the field of operation of a word or phrase. For example, analyze the adverb *more* in this sentence: *The child needs to be given more nourishing food.* (Greater quantities of food? Or food with improved nutritional qualities?) Here's another example, this time involving a negative: *This report was not submitted because of information received.*

Sometimes you can get rid of an ambiguity by using punctuation, but unless you go to the trouble of correcting the sentence itself, this would-be remedy is often sloppy and ineffective. The late lamented H. W. Fowler once wrote: "It may almost be said that what reads wrongly if the stops are removed is radically bad; stops are not to alter meaning but merely to show it up."

Ambiguity can creep up on us in many guises. Here's a beautiful example of a type that hasn't been illustrated so far. I think I first ran across this gem in *Reader's Digest.*

Sign posted in a cafeteria:

SHOES ARE REQUIRED TO EAT IN THIS CAFETERIA.

Underneath the print on the sign, some wag had penciled:

SOCKS CAN EAT WHEREVER THEY WANT TO.

• Amount/Number

Amount is used to refer to things thought of in bulk (sometimes called *mass nouns*). *Number* is used to refer to things that you count as individual items. Thus, you would say, *The amount of material wasted last week was a scandal.* But you would say, *The number of employees late for work yesterday was higher than at any other time in recent history.*

• Analogy

An *analogy* is a comparison between two objects or concepts. Use the device to show your reader as clearly as you can the ways in which the items you are comparing are similar. For example, you might say, *Rain is to snow as water is to ice.*

Analogies are great for defining terms, explaining processes, or elucidating abstract ideas.

• And/Or

Try to avoid using *and/or* whenever you possibly can. It's a clumsy and awkward way of expressing the idea that either (a) both circumstances are possible, or (b) only one of two circumstances is possible. Use your imagination and you can usually think of a better way of getting the idea across—a way that won't be so confusing to your reader.

• Anecdote

An *anecdote* is an interesting or humorous incident or story indirectly related to the writer's subject. You may have a boss who takes a dim view of using this device in formal writing or correspondence, in which case there may not be much you can do about it. The fact is, however, that many excellent writers use the device frequently, and to good advantage. A well-chosen anecdote can be very useful in developing or clarifying a difficult or obscure point.

• Antecedent

The definition *word, phrase,* or *clause* to which a *relative pronoun* refers. The term *antecedent* literally means "going before." For example, in the sentence *My brother put on his coat,* the word *brother* is the antecedent of *his.*

Don't let the "going before" idea confuse you unduly. There are cases, not necessarily logical, but usually clear, in which the antecedent follows the pronoun. For example, *After her severe fall, Mrs. Jones was never the same again.*

While we're on the subject, let me remind you that a pronoun must agree with its antecedent in *gender, number,* and *person.* Its *case,* however, is determined by its use with other words.

• Anticipatory Constructions
(see **expletives**)

• Anxious/Eager

Careless writers often use these two words more or less interchangeably. They shouldn't. Use *anxious* only when you mean to communicate the idea of real anxiety, as *I am anxious about the lack of safety precautions.* But *eager* is a better choice when you say something such as *I'm eager to see the new Broadway show.*

• Articles, Definite and Indefinite

The word *the* is called the *definite article;* the word *a* or *an* is called the *indefinite article.* In function, articles can be classified with *adjectives.*

• Audience

Find out as much as you can about your intended audience before you begin to write. Perhaps I am exceptionally fussy about this because I spent so many years writing speeches. Even so, in other kinds of writing, the audience is still just as important a consideration.

If you are aiming at, say, a PTA group, you'll use different language, different structure, different illustrations, different almost everything from what you would use for, say, the members of a scientific or technical society.

If you're writing in response to a letter or a memo, you can usually learn quite a bit about your correspondent—just by reading carefully and with understanding. Is the writing formal or informal? How elaborate are the sentence structures? What kind of vocabulary is used? And so forth. Use the original correspondence for your cue; then be as responsive as you possibly can.

To sum up: slant your material to your audience. If you don't have any clues, do this: imagine a reader that is intelligent, but perhaps not well informed on the particular subject you are writing about. Be simple and direct. Avoid complications. And whatever else you do, don't assume a pontifical or preachy tone that insults the reader's dignity or intelligence.

• Avoidance—the Merits of

If a sentence is hopelessly bad, don't spend the day trying to straighten it out. Just fall back and regroup. Rewrite the sentence totally, avoiding the problem of trying to wrestle with it. Using a little flexibility in your thinking can save you much time and heartache. I've used this example elsewhere in this book in another context, but it demonstrates extremely well what we might call the "creative" approach:

Rule 46 of the Oxford Union Society in London reads: *Any member introducing a dog into the Society's premises shall be liable to a fine of one pound. Any animal leading a blind person shall be deemed to be a cat.*

• Bad/Badly

Many otherwise careful writers and speakers apparently don't know the proper distinctions between this pair of words. *Bad* is an adjective; use it to follow such *linking verbs* as *feel* and *look*. For example, you should say, *I felt bad about John's troubles last week.*

Badly is an adverb. Use it to modify a verb, as in *The new equipment performed very badly until the mechanic repaired the control system.*

Saying, "I feel badly" would mean, if you take the expression in its literal meaning, that your sense of touch doesn't work well.

Bi/Semi

These are a couple of terms I wish we could do without—and in many cases we can. Most of the time they confuse the reader unduly.

When you say, "The report comes out biweekly," do you mean it comes out twice a week, or every two weeks?

Well, ordinarily, when used with periods of time, *bi* means "two" or "every two." Thus *biweekly* means "once every two weeks." Unfortunately, many writers don't use it this way.

When *semi* is used, it is supposed to mean "half of" or "occurring twice within the specified period of time." Thus *semimonthly* should mean "twice a month," and *semiweekly,* "twice a week."

In my opinion, to avoid being misunderstood, you'd be a lot better off to say, "twice a week," or "twice a month," or whatever.

If you do ignore my advice and use the terms, remember that they both should normally be joined to the word following them without space or hyphen.

Biannual/Biennial

According to the conventions of English usage, *biannual* means "twice during a single year," and *biennial* means "once every other year." I dislike this usage intensely—it undoubtedly confuses many readers. Why not say *semiannual* to indicate "twice yearly"? (That's the term we used at NASA to title our twice-yearly report to Congress: *The Semiannual Report.* There was still a problem though, when the report fell a year or two behind schedule!)

Brief

A *brief* is a condensed statement of a long document or a series of documents. (In law, a brief is a statement filed by an attorney before arguing a case in court, but we're not concerned with that special meaning here.) Frequently you can help the reader, particularly when you're introducing a long piece of writing, if you give a quick summary of the contents at the beginning. This saves time and aids comprehension by giving a bird's eye view. (Sometimes the words *brief* and *abstract* are used as synonyms, although technically there are differences.)

At times you may find it necessary to furnish a boiled-down version of a report or article. If you're a staff member, you'll be called upon to brief your superiors; that is what most people think of when briefing is mentioned. However, writers can use essentially the same techniques to write a summary or abstract of a report.

The ability to do a good briefing doesn't come naturally. You'll have to work at it. But here are some tips on the most important things you will need to know. They are adapted freely from *Writing Guide for Naval Officers, NAVPERS 10009-A*, no longer in print.

SEVEN STEPS TO EXPEDITE A BRIEF

1. Read the entire report to determine the scope and point of view. If the material is difficult, study it until you are sure of the main ideas.
2. Underline important sentences or phrases in each paragraph. The underlined material should tell what the paragraph is about. Avoid asides and extras, but retain all major thoughts.
3. Write the underlined sentences or phrases in the order in which they appear. As far as possible, keep the author's emphasis and his original plan of organization (In a resume, abstract, or paraphrase, you summarize in your own words and therefore often change the order. In a brief, you follow the author's order of presentation.)
4. Condense by eliminating unessential words and phrases, by substituting one sentence to do the work of two or three, by discarding illustrations and anecdotes, and by making generalizations to cover such data as statistics.
5. Put the author's material in your own words, if this helps the condensation. Use easy words and simple sentence structure. Don't put too many ideas into too tight a package. A style that is too clipped makes for hard reading. Make your sentences complete, and don't leave out verbs.

6. Show relationship of ideas by transitions. Tie the material together so that the reader can progress easily from one idea to the next. A series of short, unrelated statements makes stumbling reading.

7. Judge the length of your summary by the needs of the user. You may have to write and rewrite in order to satisfy the user's requirements and still show the author's intent.

• Can/May

In speech these days, few persons make any real distinction between these two words. Too bad, since the distinction is a useful one. In writing, please observe it if you want to be accurate. *Can* refers to capability, and *may* refers to possibility or permission. For example, you should say, *I can finish this job by this afternoon* to show capability. Say *I may go to town Thursday* to show possibility and *I can go to town Thursday* to show capability. Use *May I go with you to the store?* to ask permission.

• Cause and Effect

(see **organization**)

• Chairman/Chairwoman/Chairperson

Maybe my male chauvinism is apparent here, but I don't really believe so. The word *chairman* serves admirably for both sexes.

If you trace the word back to its roots, the *man* part of the word comes from *Mann,* which encompassed both male and female. It was generic in the true sense. Thus, there is really no need to alter the word. If, however, you find yourself uncomfortable with this usage, why not simply say "Madam Chairman"? That still sounds okay to most ears.

Even *chairwoman* might not be too bad, although far from great. But *chairperson,* it seems to me, sounds terrible—really awful. Go ahead and use it if you feel you must, but not with my blessing.

Many writing books today recommend "chair" when sex is unknown, "chairwoman" for a known female, and "chairman" for a known male. Those books also avoid "chairperson."

Let's consider a few ramifications of this general problem. Back in the time of Amelia Earhart, we used to say *aviatrix*. Nowadays, *aviator* works fine. Elizabeth Barrett Browning, Emily Dickinson, and Christina Rossetti were called *poetesses,* although today we call them *poets*. My point is, many words that once required special feminine endings no longer do, and many once masculine words now encompass both sexes. But—I repeat—such words as *chairman* have always applied to both sexes. So for heaven's sake, let's not overreact! (For further discussion of sexism in language, see **he/she dilemma**)

• Chronological Order
   (see **organization**)

• Collective (Collective Noun)

You compare similar things *with* each other. You compare dissimilar things *to* each other.

Thus, you compare Marlene Dietrich *with* Gloria Swanson, but you compare an orange *to* a baseball.

In my seminars, I often try to explain this by the analogy of a hand in the form of a fist, as singular, or with separate fingers, plural. For example, *The committee is unanimous in its decision* is an obvious case where the collective noun *committee* is working as a single unit. But in the sentence *The membership are divided, with half wanting to secede and the rest wanting to stay,* the plural seems to be in order. The writer is the final judge in making these decisions. However, if you are in doubt, waffle. Write around the problem. You could say, for example, ". . . *The members of the group disagree,*" and the problem disappears. Don't sweat it.

One thing more. Whatever you do, *be consistent.*

• Comma

The punctuation mark we call the *comma* is a tricky little devil, and current newspaper style is making it even trickier. For example, most newspapers do not put a comma before the final *and* in words or phrases in a series. This nefarious practice saves the typesetter from having to whack a lot of extra strokes on the typesetting machine. So who cares if the meaning is obscured in the process?

The question is rhetorical. Many writers care—and care very

much. Strunk and White, for example, and another respected authority, Sheridan Baker (*The Practical Stylist*), are quite firm about this. Indeed, an impressively large and erudite group agrees that the comma before the *and* is important to clarity. Let's consider for a moment an actual example of the "missing comma" usage we're all complaining about: *Write name, address, age, sex and housing requirements.*

For a complete discussion of commas, I must refer you to the authorities I've mentioned, or to many other excellent handbooks. Here I will simply give you four practical rules of thumb that cover most of the everyday problems you're likely to encounter:

1. Use commas between all words in a series, including the last two, unless you are considering the two as an inseparable pair, such as "ham and eggs."
2. Use a comma before conjunctions when joining independent clauses.
3. Enclose parenthetical insertions (see restrictive and nonrestrictive) with a pair of commas. Don't put a comma at one end of the insertion but not at the other.
4. Use a comma after an introductory phrase, to separate it from the rest of the sentence.

• Compare/Contrast

When you *compare* things, you usually point out both the similarities and the differences. When you *contrast,* you point out only the differences.

• Compare to/Compare with

You compare similar things *with* each other. You compare dissimilar things *to* each other.

Thus, you compare Marlene Dietrich *with* Gloria Swanson, but you compare an orange *to* a baseball.

• Compose/Comprise

These are a tricky pair, often confused. Remember that *comprise* contains the idea of "to include." Thus, the whole *comprises* the parts. *Compose,* on the other hand, means "to make up the whole." Thus, the parts *compose* the whole.

• Congenial/Genial

Somewhere along the way you've probably heard someone say, "She's a most congenial hostess." No way. The prefix *con-* means *with; together.* Therefore, the hostess may indeed be marvelous, but she is just one person, so you shouldn't call her *congenial.* If she is kindly, cordial, and all those other good things, call her *genial.* Use *congenial* only when you're talking or writing about two or more individuals who are friendly or get along well together.

• Context—Taking Material Out Of

Lawyers like to put everything including the kitchen sink in one sentence. Most lawyers, that is. They don't really seem to care if the sentence turns out to be several miles long. "If you don't do things that way," they intone piously, "someone will take a statement out of context."

Nonsense! Even the Ten Commandments were written one sentence at a time, and they have held up very well indeed for as long as any legal documents still extant.

My advice to you (and brace yourself, because members of your organization's legal staff may take issue) is: do not worry about being taken out of context. Use the methodology outlined below. If you do, nobody can take anything out of context without being caught with egg on his face. (I used only the masculine form here because we know women would be too clever—and too honest— even to try such a thing.)

So, instead of trying to pack seventeen jillion facts (and ALL the exceptions) into one ridiculously long sentence, do things this way:

1. Say one thing in each sentence. Don't pack in any extra information or thoughts.
2. If the stated idea must be qualified, do so in the very next sentence. It is a mistaken notion to think that all your

qualifications and exceptions must be packaged within one single sentence.

3. Put the most important idea in each sentence at the beginning.

4. Use single words that mean essentially the same thing as phrases whenever you can. For example, instead of saying *persons who are residents of the State of Virginia,* why not say, *residents of Virginia,* or perhaps, *Virginia residents?*

5. Substitute everyday words for difficult words. If you must use technical or legalistic terms, be sure to define them. Give examples if necessary. Don't expect readers to have a lawyer's vocabulary!

6. Don't omit steps or take shortcuts in the belief that the reader will obviously understand.

• Copyright

If you are planning to write a report or a book for publication, and wish to quote material that has been copyrighted, here are a few things you ought to know:

1. Copyrighted material is literary property. If you "borrow" someone else's words, you must give credit where credit is due. This means simply that you will indicate the source of the material—the name of the author, the name of the publication, and usually but not always, the page number. The standard academic way is to put this information in footnotes. To be more informal, you may enclose the information in parentheses.

2. If you're planning to quote more than a few lines, you should formally request permission from the holder of the copyright. What is called "fair use" varies somewhat according to the kind of material. In prose, the standard practice is this: you can use up to about 150 words (in some cases up to about 500, or so I'm told, but I'd play it safe and stick to the lower number) without asking formal permission. Also, if the paper you are writing won't be published or circulated in any way, you don't have to ask permission.

You can use most government documents published by the Government Printing Office (GPO) without having to get copyright permission. The reasoning is that the writing and printing were done at taxpayers' expense, and hence are public property.

In theory, you could borrow such material without even mentioning source or giving formal attribution. But it wouldn't be ethical—and it won't cost you a thing to identify your source. (Some government material is copyrighted. If it is, there will be a standard copyright notice up front.)

You probably already are aware that the works of many great literary figures of the past are now in the public domain. That means simply this: if you want to pick up and use any of this material, you can borrow, quote, or misquote, with no fear of retribution. It still isn't exactly cricket to try to get away with copying a poem such as "How do I love thee, let me count the ways," and taking credit for the composition. (A character in a Peter DeVries novel did just that.) The problem is that there might be some readers around who recognize the language. Perhaps that possibility is all that keeps some writers honest. Who knows?

• Criteria/Criterion

Here is a troublesome pair of words that are frequently confused or misused. *Criteria* is plural. *Criterion* is singular. Pay attention. Don't use them interchangeably, as I have heard many persons do. It's bad enough to use them incorrectly, but to use them incorrectly and inconsistently is even worse!

• Data/Datum

Here is another troublesome pair. In Latin, *data* is plural, *datum* is singular. In English, we find confusion. Some writers use *data* as singular, others use it as plural. The ones who use it as singular probably don't use *datum* at all; they may not even know the word. So, my advice to you is this: be consistent!

According to most good dictionaries, it is considered acceptable to use *data* as either a singular or a plural. Most scientists and engineers prefer the Latin usage. Just about everybody else likes it better the other way. So, take your choice, but stick to it.

• Detail—Need for Attention To

THE CASE OF THE MISSING HYPHEN

When I was working at NASA in the early days of the space program, we had to think up quite a few synonyms for the word "failure." Murphy's Law was, and always is, especially tough on great technological projects at their beginnings. Things went wrong that you wouldn't believe. Jim Aswell and I spent days thinking up new ways to say in our reports that, "although the launch vehicle blew up on the pad, we gained much valuable information from the experiment."

Years later, when the launch record was much, much better, the then NASA Administrator, James E. Webb, asked Jim and me to put together a collection of motion picture film clips. He used this footage to illustrate speeches about the progress of the space program. The film started with 90 seconds of rockets blowing up in all kinds of horrible ways: I can still see it in my dreams.

Mr. Webb was willing to show the failures because eventually our engineers and technicians came as close to achieving perfection as did any organization in all history. Those of us who were there were proud of the accomplishments—and still are.

Still, there were occasional glitches to keep us humble. Once NASA launched a communication satellite that went into orbit, but no one could talk to it. Another time a probe to Mars or Venus (I forget which) didn't do what it was supposed to do because a programmer left out a single hyphen in the programming instructions.

A high NASA official won my undying admiration when he hung prominently in his office a large oil painting: a beautifully white square of canvas with a small, very black hyphen in the middle.

I needn't point out the moral, but I'll do it anyway. When you are dealing with difficult subjects—anything from telling a space probe what to do while on its way to another planet to telling a harassed parent how to assemble a bicycle on Christmas Eve—you can't be too careful about your language.

Most instructions that come with knockdown furniture, kits of various kinds, and similar inventions of the devil appear to be written as if the writer wanted to make sure the reader couldn't possibly understand. If indeed that is the intention, the rate of success is far higher than we ever achieved at NASA in our most halcyon days.

• Diction

This is a word that you may faintly recall having heard your English teacher use. You can doubtless get along quite well without knowing the word, but not without a knowledge of the problem it defines—namely, the choice of words in any type of communication, especially in regard to correctness, clarity, or effectiveness.

Teachers of college courses in composition constantly rail at students with cries of "Faulty diction." That's just their way of saying that a student has used a word improperly, or has used a nonstandard word in a formal paper.

• Direct Object
(see **sentence—the parts of**)

• Draft—Getting Ideas Down on Paper

There are occasions when you don't want to stop and hunt for the exact word you need (what we've called earlier, the "*mot juste.*") One of the most common such occasions is that of writing a first draft.

You have probably discovered it doesn't pay to stop and hunt for a word because you're likely to lose your trend of thought. Your instincts are correct. Just put your idea down on paper fast. Don't hesitate, and don't worry about style, whatever that is. Go ahead and use the wrong word, or a roundabout phrase if you need to—so long as you can keep the idea going. You can come back later for the exact phrase. (I've heard of writers who just put down an illegible scrawl to represent a word they can't think of. Psychologically, that might be a good trick.)

Let me emphasize—don't pause. Get the idea down on paper. Edit it later. You'll be glad, because that way you'll have some copy to edit. That certainly beats staring at a blank sheet of paper.

• Due to/Because of

Back in the olden days, my major professor gave me hell for using *due to* in my thesis when I should have used *because of.* If I had done it today, I might have been able to get away with it, although careful writers should still observe the distinction. *Due to* means "caused by," and can be used properly to follow a linking verb. For example, you could say, *His tired appearance was due to overwork.* Many writers, however, would still consider *due to* unacceptable when used with a non-linking verb to replace *because of.* I suggest that you watch the distinctions, but I have to admit that not too many readers know or care about the difference these days.

• Each Other/One Another

No need to be confused, although many writers are. When you are referring to a relationship between two persons, say *each other.* When you are referring to more than two, say *one another.* Once you understand the difference, it's easy to keep these straight.

• Elegant Variation

Some writers will go to any extreme to avoid repeating a word within some arbitrary measure, usually (but not always) a paragraph. They will substitute far-fetched synonyms, often pretentious ones, instead of simply repeating the word. This amateurish practice is called *elegant variation.* (I believe Fowler coined the term.) A simple word like *letter* becomes an *epistle* the next time it turns up, then perhaps a *missive,* a *note,* or a *written communication.*

Sometimes this practice is annoying but harmless. But it can be not only bad, but dangerous, when you are writing regulations or instructions. If you use something such as *car* in one place, *vehicle* in the next, and *automobile* in the next, you may have demonstrated the breadth of your vocabulary, but you have also probably bewildered the reader. Don't do it. Repeat key words as often as necessary for clarity. Your readers will love you for it.

Sports writers are particularly fond of this device, to the point of frivolity: Ohio *belts* Minnesota; Illinois *buries* Purdue; Pittsburgh *shocks* Indiana; Harvard *thumps* Yale—and so on, *ad nauseam*. Apparently, the writers are having a ball, but a little of this goes a long way. Don't try your readers' patience.

• Emphasis—Word Placement for

If you intend to put particular emphasis on a word or phrase, you have two options: you can put the important information at the very beginning, or at the very end.

Strunk and White say putting important things at the end is better. For literary writing, which is what they're talking about, they're probably right. But for "useful" writing, the advantages of placing the emphatic material at the end may be outweighed by other factors. Your reader needs to know the direction you're taking as soon as possible—otherwise there can be confusion or misinterpretation.

Accordingly—at least in most cases—you'll probably get your emphatic points across more clearly and accurately by putting them up front. That goes—hard to believe—even for conclusions. Granted that conclusions are supposed to conclude. Go ahead and do it that way, but give the reader a preview. Like just about everything else I tell you, this rule isn't a rule, and sometimes it doesn't work. Try the simple trick of writing the information both ways, if you're in doubt. Then you can see which method communicates most clearly and emphatically.

• Expletive

An *expletive* is a word that fills the position or takes the place of another word, phrase, or clause. The ones we use most frequently are *there is* and *there are*. Sometimes such constructions are helpful to avoid awkwardness, but usually they are just fillers, a waste of words. Avoid them if you can. Instead of writing, for example, *There were many members present,* write *Many members were present.*

NOTE: Do not confuse this kind of expletive with the other definition of the term—that is, the "expletive deleted" of Watergate fame.

• Exposition

You hear a great deal in college composition classes about something called "exposition." In the real world, you can probably get through life without ever having to use the term, or certainly, to define it. But just to make sure we are taking advantage of all your previous training in composition, let's pause for a brief reminder.

Exposition is one of four basic forms of communication that you usually bump up against in English Comp I. For workaday writers, including thee and me, exposition is far more important than any of the other three forms. (For the record, the other three are *narration, description*, and *argumentation*, including *persuasion*.)

Probably the most common, efficient, and generally useful pattern of exposition is the example or *analogy*. We use these very naturally in speech; we should try to do the same in writing. Instead of talking in generalities about the qualities of a good football coach, we cite Vince Lombardi or Don Schula or Joe Gibbs. We may build an even stronger and better word picture for our readers by going a step further—we could illustrate our chosen coach's outstanding abilities by giving a specific account of his handling of a crucial situation in the playoffs or the Superbowl or whatever. Elsewhere in this handbook I give you an impassioned dissertation on the advantages of using concrete rather than abstract illustrations. Do that any time you can, for you will automatically increase clarity by so doing. You'll also get increased reader interest at the same time. This is extremely important: *clear writing isn't much help if it puts your reader to sleep.* (I seem to recall having said that before. Oh well, it bears repeating.)

The late Dr. Isaac Asimov, who in my opinion—and his too— was far and away America's best writer when it came to explaining difficult concepts in clear language, was a bearcat at giving *examples* and *analogies*. He often did this so well that I could read one of his explanations and go around thinking, at least for awhile, that I had grasped Einstein's theory and other good stuff like that.

• Familiar Words—Use of

One of the most important rules in useful writing is *Prefer the familiar word to the far-fetched.* Here are a few samples I've collected that show you how *not* to do it:

In order to avoid negative reflections as a result of dysfunctional internal communications, and in order to enhance the possibilities of coordinated balances, I am strongly urging that any item having a direct or indirect affect [sic] on the NW No. 1 Project Area may be made known to me before, rather than after, it's (sic) occurrence, when possible.

—Memo written by an official of the
D.C. Redevelopment Land Agency

(Sign at entrance to a corridor in the Pentagon)

THIS PASSAGEWAY HAS BEEN MADE
NONCONDUCTIVE TO UTILIZATION FOR AN
INDEFINITE PERIOD
—Quoted in *The Kidner Report*, p. 55

• **Files**

Build up files on every subject you might conceivably be writing about. Make them as complete as you can. If you run across an article that might be useful, clip it and stow it in an appropriately labeled folder. (That last is really important. It's no good if you can't find it. Don't put off organizing. Keep on doing it as you go along.)

When I was chief of the ghostwriting group at NASA Headquarters, I was spoiled in this regard. We had secretaries and research assistants to help us keep things organized and sorted out. With their help, we managed to fill half a dozen big file cabinets with material on every conceivable phase of the aeronautics and space program. These beautifully organized files came to our rescue many times when we would get a call at 8:30 a.m. to deliver a finished speech that afternoon.

Nowadays I must do my own clipping and filing. Huge stacks of clippings and papers cover every bit of table and chair space in sight. I know what I am looking for is in there someplace, but I haven't the faintest idea where. Then, by Murphy's Law, I get a short-fuze (**NOTE**: Not short-*fuse*) writing assignment and have to stay up half the night tracking down the items I need.

So, I suggest that you do what I say on this matter, not what I do.

• First Person Singular—The Perpendicular Pronoun

Some organizations and agencies have a rule that nobody but the top boss uses the "perpendicular pronoun." That rule may sound arbitrary, but maybe it's right. Most of us may be writing on behalf of an organization, and very likely are not calling the shots. This doesn't mean you must avoid personal pronouns entirely. Many times, the plural form, *we,* will work just fine. Putting the emphasis on *you* is often even better, but even that can be overdone.

The trick is to place yourself in the background, so that the writing doesn't emerge as a continuing ego trip. As one of my heroes, E. B. White, puts it: "Write in a way that draws the reader's attention to the substance of the writing, rather than to the mood and temper of the author." (*The Elements of Style*, p. 62.)

• Flags (queries)

Many times, when editing, you will encounter sentences that can be interpreted in any of several different ways. You know that you want to edit the sentence so that the correct interpretation is the only one possible. You may believe that you know exactly which interpretation is correct, but you can't always be sure. What do you do?

You can ask the originator to explain the intended meaning, and then rewrite the sentence accordingly. That's easy if the writer is in the next office, or just down the hall. But, suppose the originator is clear across the country. You don't want to waste time and money by making a long-distance call every time you have a question.

Many of the good editors I know use the device called a *flag*— or sometimes, a *query.* It comes as close to being a foolproof way of handling these difficult situations as you are likely to find. Take it in steps, like this:

1. Using all the logic and information you have at your command, make an educated guess. Chances are good you

will come up with the correct intent of the ambiguous sentence.

2. Rewrite the sentence very carefully, the way you think it should be, to reflect the intent you consider correct. Make sure that the rewrite is itself not open to several interpretations.

3. Put in a flag. That is to say, write the word FLAG in big capital letters, underscored, as near as you can to the place on the page where you have made your editorial change. After the word FLAG, query the originator about the problem. Call attention to your change and invite the originator's opinion of your rewrite.

This may sound complicated, but if you leave the sentence as it was with a query in the margin indicating your confusion, there's a good chance the author won't even recognize what your problem is. Since familiarity blinds us to our own words, the author will think the original statement is perfectly clear. But if you rewrite the offending sentence carefully, you will illuminate the problem, even if—as is quite possible—you may choose exactly the opposite meaning from the one intended.

When you rewrite, don't forget the FLAG in the margin. Without it the author, in looking over your rewrite, may not notice the change. But I guarantee you, it will leap off the page of the printed version. And that's when the author will call you on the carpet.

• Footnotes

Footnotes can be very helpful devices for both writer and reader. They enable the writer to keep the narrative going full tilt without having to put in material that would slow things down. But the information is still there, in footnote form, for anyone who wants it.

Readers are happy, because if they are interested primarily in the narrative, they can read straight through. If, on the other hand, they are concerned with minute details, those too are readily and handily available. Writer and reader share the best of all possible worlds.

But footnotes should be used properly, and located properly. One of my pet peeves is the method used by many publishers— the method of putting all the footnotes, bunched together, at the end of a chapter, or worse, clear at the end of the book. This leaves the reader with several choices, all miserable. One choice involves reading through the chapter and then going back and reading the footnotes. This is bad because the reader forgets what the footnotes are referring to. The alternative is just as bad—flip-flopping back and forth between the text and the footnotes—an extremely time-consuming operation.

Incidentally, a properly used footnote can be useful in ways that might not ordinarily occur to you. If you're trying to impress the boss, or your colleagues, don't forget footnotes. Those of you who have written scholarly papers, or a thesis or dissertation, know that footnotes can add an impressively academic-looking appearance to the most ordinary manuscript. Academic illiterates will compose great tangled jungles of jargon, sprinkle in a few *Ibids* and *op. cits.*, and their stupidities take on a protective coloration that makes them much harder to recognize.

Seriously, the footnote device can offer you real benefits. Suppose, for example, that you're writing along, everything is going well, and you have worked up a good head of steam. Then you feel a need to put in material with a degree of detail that some readers will want to know, but others won't care a thing about. Take my advice—put the extra detail in a footnote—and you'll be able to satisfy both groups.

But—I plead with you—don't ever put explanatory footnotes anywhere except on the same page or pages with the material they refer to. (Documentation is a different matter. It's okay to list authors, references, and the like, at the end, if this will be easier for the production staff.)

• Future Tense

Future tense usually is not much of a problem in writing, but upon occasion, some of my seminar students have questioned such constructions as "Tomorrow is Monday." They ask, Shouldn't we say, "Tomorrow will be Monday?"

Well, it is okay to say that if you want to, but it really is not at all necessary. *Tomorrow* expresses all the futurity you need.

If you use the idiom of the American language comfortably, as I hope you do, you shouldn't be bothered at this idiomatic expression. If some literal-minded soul says you should say, "Tomorrow will be Monday," a bit of ear training is in order.

• Fuzzify

I'm putting this term in because I find it irresistible. It was coined by the perceptive and witty James H. Boren. (Dr. Boren is the creator of such slogans as "When in doubt, mumble," and "If you are going to be a phony, be sincere about it.") He defines the term *fuzzify* as "the presentation of a matter in terms that permit adjustive interpretation. Particularly useful when the fuzzifier does not know what he or she is talking about, or when the fuzzifier wants to enunciate a non-position in the form of a position." (The non-Boren word for this is *waffling,* but I don't like it nearly as well.)

• Grammar—A Few Elementary Principles

nouns—Words used to denote persons, places, or things, are called *nouns.* Thus the words *man, woman, child, train,* and *city* are nouns. Nouns are also used as the names of qualities or ideas, such as *patriotism, kindness, happiness, truth,* and *love.*

common nouns name members of a class of persons, places, or things, such as *dog, cat, country,* or *chair.*

proper nouns name particular persons, places, or things (*Bill Clinton, Maryland, Brooklyn Bridge*). Begin a proper noun with a capital letter.

pronouns—In the sentence "The woman saw the little girl but did not speak to her," the word *her* is used instead of *girl.* A word used to take the place of a noun is called a *pronoun.* Pronouns, as well as nouns, are used as *subjects* or *direct objects.*

The word that the pronoun refers to is called its *antecedent.* In the sentence given above, "girl" is the antecedent of "her."

Pronouns are divided into various classes. The pronouns *I, you, he, she, it, we,* and *they* are called personal pronouns.

When *who, which,* and *what* are used to introduce questions, they are called *interrogative pronouns.* When they are used in sentences that are not questions, they are called *relative pronouns.* Thus, in the sentence *Who gave you the money?* the word *who* is an interrogative pronoun. In the sentence, *It was my brother who gave me the money,* the word *who* is a relative pronoun.

number—We have different forms of nouns and pronouns to show whether we are referring to one person or thing or to more than one. Thus *I* refers to one person, and *we* refers to more than one. In the same way, *horse* is in the singular number, and *horses* is in the plural.

case—Such pronouns as *he, she,* and *who* have different forms to show how they are used in sentences. We say *She walks; I see her;* and *I have his tickets.* In these sentences, *she* is a subject, *her* is a direct object, and *his* refers to a person possessing something. Thus we say, *The man walks; I see the man;* and *I have the man's hat.* These different forms and uses of nouns and pronouns in sentences are called—in traditional English grammar—*cases.* The *subject* is in the *nominative case,* the *direct object* is in the *objective case* (sometimes called the *accusative* as a holdover from Latin grammar), and the word referring to the possessor is in the *possessive case* (called the *genitive* in Latin grammar).

direct object—As just explained in the previous entry, a noun or pronoun must be in the *objective* (or *accusative*) *case* when it receives the action of a transitive verb.

indirect object—A *noun* or *pronoun* used to denote the person to whom something is given, said, or shown is termed an *indirect object.* In the sentences, *He gave my brother an apple,* and *My sister told me the news,* the words *brother* and *me* are indirect objects. Instead of saying *I gave John the letter,* we may express the same idea by saying *I gave the letter to John.* In the second version, *to John* takes the place of the indirect object *John* in the first.

verbs—In the sentences *The man sneezed* and *The panther leaped, sneezed* and *leaped* denote actions. Such words are called *verbs.* Some verbs denote mere existence or continuance in place rather than action. In the sentences *Fred is in the kitchen,* and *We shall remain here until noon,* we see examples of this usage.

person and number of verbs—In some tenses, a verb has a different form when its subject is in the *first person* (*I, we*) from what it would have if the subject were in the *third person* (*he, she, it, they*). Thus we say, *I walk,* but *he walks.* The third person plural also differs from the third person singular. Thus, *he walks, she walks, it walks, they walk.* A verb is said to be in the same *person* and *number* as its subject.

transitive and intransitive verbs—A verb that takes a direct object is called a *transitive verb.* In the sentence *William saw the movie,* the verb *saw* is transitive. A verb that does not take a direct object is called an *intransitive verb.* In the sentence, *The prisoner wept,* the verb *wept* is intransitive. However, if the sentence were changed to *The prisoner wept bitter tears,* the verb *wept* would be transitive.

I should mention here, and probably should have mentioned elsewhere, that only *transitive verbs* can have either an *active* or a *passive* form.

adjectives—We often use some other word with a noun to tell about—or to modify—the noun. Thus, in the expressions *tall buildings* and *red paint,* the words *tall* and *red* tell something about the buildings and the paint. Such words are called *adjectives.*

Adjectives that merely indicate what is being referred to without suggesting quality are *this, that, other,* and *same.* The adjectives *the, a,* and *an* also belong in this class, but are called *articles.*

predicate adjectives are used after *linking verbs* (such as *is, was, were,* etc.) and refer back to the subject.

conjunctions—The words *and, but,* and *or* (or *nor*) are used to join words or parts of sentences. In the sentence, *Your brothers and sisters are away from home,* the conjunction *and* is used to join *brothers* and *sisters.*

subordinating conjunctions are such words as *although, after, as, before, because, if, since, than, that, though, unless, when, where* and *whereas.* These join subordinate phrases (or clauses) to the main statement of a sentence, as in *The road is good, although it is narrow.*

prepositions—There is a class of small words such as *by, from, in, of,* and *with,* which are used with nouns or pronouns.

The combination of one of these words and the noun or pronoun it is used with serves to tell something about an act or about a person or thing. These words are called *prepositions.* The noun or pronoun that follows a preposition is called its *object,* or the preposition is said to *govern* the noun or pronoun that follows it. In the phrase, *live in Reston,* the word *Reston* is the *object* of *in.*

• Handles

Indexes are great, but many publications can't or don't use them for one reason or another. How else can you give your readers a "handle" on the material, making it easier for them to track down the specific information they seek? Here are a few suggestions:

Use *titles* and *subtitles, headings* and *subheadings.*
Use *checklists, breakdowns, summaries,* and similar devices.
Use *references* and *cross-references;* use *underscores* or other typographical devices to call attention to important ideas or key words.
Make the *Table of Contents* more than just a chapter listing. Give headings and subheadings as well.
Furnish a *table of figures and illustrations.* Make sure that these illustrations are on the same page as the describing text, or at least on a facing page.
Use *alphabetical* or *numerical* arrangements that readers can easily follow.

• He/She Dilemma (Sexism in Language)

Have you noticed—and I hope you haven't, because if you have I haven't been nearly as slick as I have hoped—throughout this book I have conscientiously strained every nerve to avoid using a single sexist construction. (This may be the first book ever written by a male chauvinist pig to make that claim.) If I've failed it has been through oversight, not design. Mind you, I'm not responsible for quotations from other sources—just my own writing.

Now that I have openly announced my intent, perhaps you can skim through and detect some of the devices I've employed. To help your search, I'll spell out a few:

1. Use a plural subject when the situation permits. This will permit you to use "their" grammatically when you refer to the antecedent.

   Example: Instead of saying, *Any employee who will not reach his or her 40th birthday before* . . . try saying, *Any employees who will not reach their* . . .

2. Refer to the person's job title or organizational position, making no reference to the sex of the individual holding the job.

   Example: Instead of saying, *The girl at the reception desk will give you directions,* say, *The receptionist will give you directions.* (**NOTE**: *The Directory of Occupational Job Titles* is a big help. Sexist titles such as *fireman* or *stewardess* have been changed to *firefighter* and *flight attendant.*)

3. Use your imagination to write around the pronoun.

   Example: Instead of writing *The promotion must come because the employee himself has worked to qualify for it,* try something like, *The promotion must come from the employee's own efforts to qualify* . . .

4. Use a slash between the two gender-related pronouns, if you can't think of any other way to handle it.

   Example: *Each participant must furnish his/her own documentation.* (Even in this case, I think that using the plural *participants* would be better. But, of course, sometimes the plural simply is not accurate or not appropriate—especially in regulatory writing.)

   Above all, bear in mind that with a bit of care and a small amount of ingenuity, writers can almost always write around the problem. This book is intended, among other things, to prove that point. I hope (not *hopefully*) that it has succeeded.

Before we leave this subject, however, one more point needs to be made. (See also the entry under **Chairman/Chairwoman/Chairperson/Chair**.)

Where I truly feel it's necessary to draw the line is at the awkward words and constructions that bend our whole beautiful English language out of shape. Regretfully, I must point out that the indiscriminate use of person is a case in point. A *Washington Post* editorial (September 28, 1977) demonstrates very clearly the problem we're up against here. The editorial stated that the following utterance had appeared in a Presidential Proclamation:

> The United States is a young Nation, but our debt to that courageous *Norseperson,* Leif Ericson, predates 1776 . . . [emphasis added.]
>
> The editorialist went on to say: "Our problem with this bizarre locution is not just that Leif Ericson, God rest his bones, would certainly have hated it. Nor is it merely the fact that Leif Ericson was a Norseman, as distinct, let us say, from a Norsewoman or a Norsechild. No, our concern is with the Big Picture, the pattern and precedent that this usage could easily establish."

The editorialist (incidentally, there's a good example of a non-sexist job title) makes the point that you can carry this person business to ridiculous extremes. (Witness the New England newspaper account of a missing *personhole cover* causing a bad accident during yesterday's snowstorm.)

Surely that's enough to make the point. Hooray for the Women's Movement, but let's not get carried away.

• Hopefully

This word, used correctly, means *with hope.* For example, *The beggar looked hopefully at the well-dressed stranger.*

Some years, ago I attended a convention of the International Platform Association, where I heard some of the best (or at least the highest-paid) speakers in America. Virtually every speaker on the program used the word *hopefully* to mean "I hope" or "It is hoped." So this is probably a lost cause. While hopefully we will stamp out this sloppy usage, there are two chances, as Redd Foxx would say: slim and none.

Nevertheless, it is a slovenly and incorrect usage, and many

careful writers are still concerned with making the appropriate distinction. As Bill Gold wrote in one of his columns: ". . . I hope, one
hopes, it is to be hoped that today's speakers and writers will
avoid misusing the word." (*The District Line, The Washington Post,*
May 5, 1977)

• Hyphen

The *hyphen* (-) is a very tricky punctuation mark. Many otherwise confident writers throw up their hands in dismay when con-
fronted with the choice of using a hyphen or leaving it out.
Fowler, in his *Modern English Usage,* devoted many pages of elaborate discussion to the subject, and then frankly admitted that
many of the policies he prescribed wouldn't always work in actual
practice. If that great expert of experts had so much trouble, what
are the rest of us going to do?

I don't propose to solve all your problems. I'll just give you a
few basic rules of thumb. (Some people would hyphenate that,
rules-of-thumb.) Even those are subject to argument.

My first rule is that two-word (or sometimes three-word or four-
word) modifiers that express a single thought should be hyphenated when they precede a noun. For example, an *out-of-order*
machine, or a *state-of-the-art* component. The trick is to see
whether the individual words can be used to modify the noun, or
whether they must be used all together, as an entity. Thus, it
wouldn't be an *out* or an *of* or an *order* machine—it has to be all
three locked together. If each of the words could modify the noun
without the aid of the other modifying word or words, you should
not use a hyphen. Also, if the first word of the group is an adverb
ending in *-ly,* do not use a hyphen. (**NOTE**: Most *non* prefixes do
not require a hyphen. Indeed, dictionaries mention only a few exceptions when they do require hyphens. Being a crotchety old cur-
mudgeon, I sometimes bravely insert hyphens anyway, when I am
convinced that putting them in will help my readers understand
what I am talking about. If you are not quite so brave, or are in
doubt about using a hyphen with a particular word, by all means
look it up.

The next rule is this: when the modifying words *follow* the noun, do not hyphenate. For example, "Our writing textbooks are hopelessly out of date." (No hyphens.)

• i.e.

The abbreviation *i.e.* stands for the Latin *id est,* meaning "that is." Why not simply say "that is"? In my experience, many readers don't have the faintest idea what *i.e.* means.

NOTE: My friend Allan Lefcowitz (author of *The Writer's Handbook*) disagrees. He believes we should use *i.e.* and give readers a chance to learn something new.

• Indefinite Pronoun

This is a pronoun that does not specify a person—*anyone, each, either, everyone, none, someone.* When such words are used to modify nouns, they are called *indefinite adjectives.* All except *neither* and *none* take a singular verb when followed by the preposition *of* and a plural noun. Example: *Each of the members was consulted.* (**NOTE**: In recent years, many good writers have come to accept the plural verb. In such cases, a plural pronoun must follow. *Each of the members were consulted, and they agreed to have another election.*)

• Indirect Object (See **Sentence—the Parts of**)

• Infinitives—Including the Splitting Thereof

Some years ago I was leading a seminar at a large government agency, and one of the participants asked, "What is a split infinitive? We've been ordered not to split any, but I'm not sure what it is we're not supposed to split!"

Many writers share that problem. For the best discussion I know of on this subject, try Fowler's *Modern English Usage.* You'll find it not only enlightening but entertaining. First, Fowler divides the English-speaking world into five categories, starting with (1) those who don't know what a split infinitive is, and don't care. Then he takes you through other categories, such as (2) those who don't know, but care very much; (3) those who know and approve, going miles out of the way to split infinitives at every opportunity;

(4) those who know and condemn (and this category includes the head of the agency where the question arose); and (5) those who know and distinguish.

I've taken a few liberties with Fowler's language, I'm sure, since I'm playing this back from memory, but this is close enough to give you the idea. Furthermore, I do want you to look up the original.

If you don't however, let me give you a very quick treatment.

An *infinitive* is a form of the verb that is preceded by the *sign of the infinitive,* the preposition *to*. For example, *to go, to walk, to talk, to swim,* etc.

Because the *to* and the rest of the infinitive go together, many writers believe they should not be separated, or "split." A "split infinitive" consists of an infinitive in which a word or words (usually an adverb or an adverbial phrase) has been inserted, thus: *to quickly walk, to loudly talk,* etc. If any of you readers are fellow "Trekkies," you know that "to boldly go" has become firmly entrenched in the language.

In truth, speakers and writers have been splitting infinitives for hundreds of years. The Bard himself split a great many, one time or another. Still, the practice offends many readers, so my advice to you is to avoid splitting whenever you can. (And candidly, that's most of the time, if you practice the art of avoidance, discussed elsewhere.) Sheridan Baker, whom I admire, says you should *never* split an infinitive. Strunk and White, Fowler, and a long list of others will advise you to avoid splitting if you can. They do, however, say that splitting is acceptable if it results in improved clarity. I'll cheerfully go along with that—couldn't ask for better company.

• Inoperative

Ron Ziegler is long gone. Let's send this miserable bit of jargon right along with him (Very few people today remember Ron Ziegler, but his word, "inoperative," seems to keep hanging on like a pit bull.)

• Intensive (or Intensifier)

An *intensifier* is an adverb that emphasizes degree, such as *quite, rather, such, too,* and *very* (last but *very* far from least—emphasis added to make the point). Sometimes a writer really needs and wants an intensifier. Such words can occasionally serve a legitimate and useful function. But they can also sneak up on you.

Most of us use far too many. I'm quite sure I do. (Oops! As I have just demonstrated, I'm not always successful at weeding them out.) So be on your guard. My mentor, Jim Aswell, always said the language would be better off if words such as *very* were wiped right off the map. That pronouncement was severe, but Jim was probably—as he usually was—more right than wrong. Bash out the intensifiers unless they are clearly necessary, and you'll strengthen your writing.

• "-ize" Endings

We've discussed at length the wickedness known as "smothered verbs"—changing verbs into nouns by adding such endings as *-tion, -ization,* and *-ance.* (I haven't put a separate discussion of the subject in this handbook section because of the lengthy treatment in Chapter 3.) But little or nothing has been said so far about another crime that is almost as bad—the reverse situation in which nouns are changed to verbs by adding an *-ize* ending. This practice usually creates long and awkward verbs. Admittedly this device can sometimes be handy, or even useful. But, because it's so easy to do, it's also easy to overdo. These ubiquitous "-ize" endings seem to be a constant source of temptation to many otherwise careful writers.

Let me call once more upon *The Kidner Report*, which gives us a wise and witty discussion on the subject:

> "Ize" is used to add weight to a verb, or to convert a noun to a verb, thereby giving a prod to some pretty slow moving sentences. Bureaucracy never utilizes *use* when *utilize* can be utilized. It also *totalizes,* rarely does it *total.* It *systematizes*; it seldom *arranges.* Programs are *prioritized.*
>
> The approach to ize-ing is uncomplicated. Simply select a word that's been "-ized" already and use it; or pick an "un-ized" word and "ize." The penultimate of the "ize" approach was reached by an Army colonel who, upon finding a project that would get along without many managers, *deproject-*

managerized the whole thing. Logically, then, to undo any result-ing catastrophe, one could easily *non-deproject-managerize* it.

For those of you who are sufficiently entranced to want to read the rest of this brilliant dissertation, you can find it on page 45 of *The Kidner Report*. We can learn a great deal from Mr. Kidner's gentle (and sometimes not so gentle) kidding.

• Jargon

Many editors will tell you to weed out jargon, and most of the time they're right. But not always. As you probably know, *jargon* is the technical language used by persons in the same field to communicate with one another. Over the years, these specialists have developed technical terms that mean precisely what they want them to mean. Thus, by using a single word of jargon, a spe-cialist can often convey information to a colleague that might have required whole sentences, or even paragraphs, to communicate in the less exact language of nonspecialists in the field. So, rather than eliminate *jargon,* the "rule" should be *use jargon only when such language is appropriate to the reader.* After all, you shouldn't really have to care whether a lay reader can understand it if a lay reader isn't going to have to read it.

• Lay/Lie

In 1977, I didn't even think that an entry on the *lay/lie* pair was necessary. Now the constant misuse of the two words has become my *bete noire.* To paraphrase Casey Stengel, doesn't anybody here speak English? I can't think of more than a couple of times lately that I've heard either verb used correctly. Even the news anchors on national TV, who are supposed to know better, habitually get these words backwards. They're driving me crazy.

I think it's my duty to give you an explanation, although you may find better in books devoted specifically to matters of usage, such as Theodore Bernstein's *The Careful Writer.*

Anyway, here goes:

Lay is always a transitive verb (see the entry of **transitive and intransitive verbs**) that means *to put or place.* The past tense is *laid*. [**NOTE**: Well, *almost* always. There are a few exceptions having to do with birds *laying* eggs, or ships *lay-ing* before the wind, but people seldom get these usages wrong. All I want to do is straighten out the mess we've fallen into in the last ten years.]

Lie is always an intransitive verb that means *to recline*. The past tense is *lay,* (which is perhaps responsible for some of the confusion), and the past participle is *lain*.

Don't say, "Tom *laid* down on the floor." Say, "Tom *lay* down on the floor." Don't say, "My notes have been *laying* there for days." Say, "My notes have been *lying* there for days."

• **Layout**

Proper layout of your copy can be a big help to your readers. Use every device you can—headings, subheadings, paragraph in-dentions, and so on. Even white space can be useful—nothing dis-courages a reader more than page after page of solid, close-set type, with nothing to relieve the monotony. Even if the writing it-self is clear, its appearance is formidable.

illustrations—Give your readers the information they need where they need it. If you use an illustration or a table to go with an item in the text, put it on the very same page if you have room.

Put it on a facing page if you don't. Please don't do what so many publishers are doing these days: gathering all the illustra-tions in one bundle and printing them together, usually right in the middle of the book. That way, they make the illustrations essentially useless. Readers either skip them entirely, or look at them all at once without reference to the text they are intended to illustrate.

footnotes—Another evil trick is to put footnotes in a group at the end of the book rather than on the same pages with the mater-ial they document. (**NOTE**: technically, these are called *end notes*, not *footnotes*, but I'm not going to let a technicality stop me from continuing this diatribe!) Any time a reader has to suffer this miser-able flip-flop back and forth from one end of the book to the other, the effectiveness of your communication diminishes accordingly.

forms—You may never be concerned with designing a form. If you are lucky, your organization will have trained professionals to perform this difficult and often thankless task, much better than you are likely to be able to do it. But the time may come when you'll have to do it yourself. Should this catastrophe ever befall you, keep the following guidelines in mind:

Checklist: Forms Design

1. Be careful in designing and laying out the lines. How many forms have you seen lately that don't indicate clearly whether to put the required information above or below the line? The Virginia Driver's License Application is an example of how not to do it. You have to read clear to the bottom before you can figure it out. The only way to put the requested information on the right lines is to start at the end and work backward.
2. Make sure to present the steps in a logical order. If the person using the form needs certain information before answering other questions, follow an appropriate progression.
3. Fill in a sample form yourself, as a test case. If you're tempted to slough this off, just think about how many hours people have been forced to waste in trying to fit required information into the limited spaces of some of the more widely used and well-known government and business forms.

Legalisms

We devoted several pages to this subject in the chapter on how to write regulations. Let's single out a few here that deserve special mention. Weed them out every chance you get: *herein, hereinabove, therein, infra,* and *supra.* Doubtless you can add unfavorites of your own.

Less/Fewer

This word pair gives many people trouble. Careful writers recognize a well-defined difference between *fewer* and *less.* Use *fewer* in cases involving items, persons, etc., that can be counted; use *less* when you refer to matters of quantity or degree. For example, you should write "There are no *fewer* than 50 students in the class." *BUT* "John has *less* capacity for learning than any of the other students."

• Media/Medium

I shouldn't have to remind you, but many writers constantly mix up *media*, which is plural, with *medium*, which is singular. Say, "The news media *are* . . ." not "The news media *is* . . ."

• Murphy's Law

Because I have spent a lot of time with scientists and engineers, I have mistakenly thought that everybody knows about *Murphy's Law*. Several of my readers have told me I am mistaken. That in itself is a demonstration of Murphy's Law, as every engineer knows. For the rest of you, here is the way it goes:

1. Nothing is ever as easy as it looks.
2. Everything will take longer than you think it will.
3. If anything can possibly go wrong, it will.

The third item is the one that is usually quoted, but all three are equally valid and equally troublesome. If you like, you can add Aswell's Adjunct as number four on the list:

4. Even if nothing can possibly go wrong, something will.

. Noun Clusters (Also Known as Noun Adjuncts or Noun Strings)

Administrative writing abounds with *noun clusters*. These are groups of nouns piled end to end; some of them may be used as nouns, others as adjectives, and perhaps still others in oddball permutations and combinations. Careful writers avoid these confusing constructions by using a sprinkling of prepositional phrases. Don't write, for example, *the new car regulation*, or *the expired certificate renewal*. This kind of writing confuses the reader, who must try to figure out whether you are talking about a *new car* or a *new regulation*; an *expired certificate* or an *expired renewal*.

Here is one of the best (read *worst*) examples of noun clusters that I've encountered in all my years. It's the sign on the door of a Montgomery County (Maryland) office:

ROCKVILLE CORRIDOR TRANSPORTATION
IMPROVEMENT ALTERNATIVES FEASIBILITY
STUDY PROJECT OFFICE

• Numerals

According to the *GPO Style Manual*, "Most rules for the use of numerals are based on the general principle that the reader comprehends numerals more readily than numerical word expressions, particularly in technical, scientific, or statistical matter." *GPO* also says that "Arabic numbers are generally preferable to Roman numerals."

Some of the rules are quite complicated. If you are in doubt, by all means check with the *GPO Manual*, if you work for the government, or with the *University of Chicago Manual of Style* if you work for private industry.

Here are a few rough rules of thumb that will get you by most of the time:

- *Spell out* numbers of ten and below: one, two, three, etc.
- *Use figures* for numbers of 11 and higher.
- If you have combinations of numbers above and below ten in a single sentence, be guided by the one that comes first, and make the rest consistent. For example, "Each of 15 major commodities (9 metal and 6 nonmetal) was in short supply." BUT "Although only nine major commodities were in short supply, restrictions were placed on thirteen more."
- Don't begin a sentence with numerals. Spell out, for example, "Twenty-one persons attended." Many times you can rephrase the sentence so that it doesn't start with the number. Instead of saying "One hundred persons or more

passed the test," say "More than 100 persons passed the test."

• Organization—A Checklist For

1. Think before you write.
2. State your purpose and stick to it.
3. Get straight to the point; catch and hold the reader's attention.
4. Answer the questions Who-What-Where-When-Why-How-How Much, not necessarily in that order.
5. Move from the known to the unknown; from the simple to the complex; from the general to the specific.
6. Arrange your material so that one step clearly leads to the next.
7. Pay close attention to format—headings, paragraphing, etc. Give the reader as many "handles" on the material as you possibly can.
8. Use good transitions that clearly show relationships.
9. Keep time sequences in your writing in actual chronological order whenever possible.
10. Sum up! Remind your readers of the important items you want them to remember.

• Organization—Methods of

cause and effect—This is the name of a standard method of development or organization. It is designed to stress the connection between a result and a preceding event. Use it to explain why something happened, or why you predict something is going to happen.

chronological order—Writing things down in the order they occur in real time is usually a good way to help the reader understand. Most people's minds seem to be geared to chronological order; they naturally think that way. By going along with this built-in instinct, you can often avoid many problems.

sequential order—This step-by-step method lends itself naturally to certain types of material, such as explaining a process, or describing a mechanism in operation. It is also the best and most logical method for writing instructions.

The main advantage of the sequential method of development is that it's easy to follow because **the steps lock right in with the elements of the process or the operation being described**.

• Overpunctuation

If you find you're having to use too many commas and parentheses to keep your ideas sorted out, chances are you'd better take a fresh look. Check your sentence constructions and word orders.

Beware of meandering off on side trails, however interesting they may seem at first glance. If you don't stick to the subject, you greatly increase the chances of losing your readers. (I often wish I could follow this advice myself.)

• Please, Thank You, and Other Amenities

Many high officials of government and industry are so accustomed to giving orders that they tend to forget the amenities. Ex-military officers perhaps have some excuse. The services aren't much for saying please. But even ex-officers can be reminded, very politely, that a few *pleases* and *thank you's* won't hurt a thing.

When you are editing, pay special attention in changing passives to actives. Instead of changing, "The report will be submitted" to "Submit the report," how about trying, "Please submit the report." The imperative remains imperative, and you're much more likely to accomplish the desired objective.

• Precipitant/Precipitous

These words are often confused. *Precipitant* is an adjective that means "falling steeply or headlong." (*Precipitate* means essentially the same thing, but can be either a noun or an adjective.) *Precipitous* is an adjective meaning "steep." Thus, you should write that a person made a *precipitant* decision, NOT a *precipitous* decision.

• Precision in Writing—Checklist For

Here's a checklist to help make your writing more precise:

1. Know your audience. Find out as much as you can about your readers, and what they already know, before you write.

2. Aim directly, with a specific purpose, at a central subject.
3. Use exact words. Look them up if you're not sure.
4. Use nouns and verbs that are meaningful to the senses—particularly sight, hearing, and touch.
5. Quantify. Give exact figures when you can, not imprecise generalities.
6. Be as careful with punctuation as you are with words.
7. Check all the facts. Then double-check. Use original sources whenever you possibly can.
8. Avoid ambiguity. Be especially watchful for squinting constructions, improper noun references, and dangling constructions.
9. Omit all extraneous material.
10. Point up the important aspects of the subject. Don't make your readers to detective work.

• Predicate

(see **sentence—the parts of**)

• Preposition—Ending a Sentence With

Somewhere along the way you have probably been cautioned never to end a sentence with a preposition. Nonsense. As some wag once said, "A preposition is often an excellent word to end a sentence with."

There is an even more famous quotation on the subject. This one is ascribed to Winston Churchill. The story goes that an editor corrected one of the great man's manuscripts by marking up a sentence that ended with a preposition. The indignant Winnie responded, "This is the kind of arrant pedantry up with which I shall not put."

• Proofreading

We all know that in manuscript a minor error can slip by even a very careful proofreader. Why is that so? For, ironically, as soon as a mistake appears in cold black type, it seems to be instantly visible to everyone who reads it. And all those readers will take fiendish delight in calling or writing to raise hell.

There is a famous case, perhaps apocryphal, of a 19th-century British publisher who decided to produce the most beautiful book in the history of printing. He signed up the best artists, the best craftsmen, the best printers, the best everything he could find. He spared no expense to ensure perfection. Years went by, as every step was checked and rechecked. But, as the story goes, when the book finally came off the press, it had a typographical error in the title—in 40-point type. Murphy's Law may not have been formulated at that time, but its truth was certainly demonstrated.

Take heed, dear reader. It's not enough to proofread your own copy. You may detect some of the mistakes, but you will certainly miss others. All writers are more or less blind to their own copy because they are too familiar with it. It looks to them the way they think it is supposed to look.

That's why professionals know that proofreading must be done in pairs—with one person holding the original copy while the other reads the final version aloud.

Good proofreaders are hard to find, but with practice on your own copy and that of others, you can sharpen your editorial eye. Work both sides of the street. Sometimes you can be the "copy holder" who reads aloud to the proofreader, noting every paragraph indention, all capital letters and punctuation marks, and any special instructions to the printer that are indicated on the copy. You can even sound as if you know what you are doing by using the special short forms that professional copyreaders use. Say *pos* for *apostrophe*; *bold* for *boldface*; *cap* for *capital*; *cap and low* for *capitals and lower case*; *com* for *comma*; *three points* for *ellipsis*; *bang* for *exclamation point*; *hife* for *hyphen*; *ital* for *italic*; *graf* for *paragraph*; *paren, close paren* for *parenthesis*; *point* for *period*; *query* for *question mark*; *quote, close quote* for *quotation marks*; and *sem* for *semicolon*.

The copyreader must be sure to pronounce every word clearly. Read slowly enough that the proofreader will have time to make any changes or corrections or queries on the galley or proof page.

Don't slough off this important task. The mistakes you prevent may be your own.

NOTE: Even after you have corrected galleys, don't trust the typesetter to correct them properly; look out for other errors made in the process. Always proof corrected proofs!

• Proofreading Ploy (or maybe you'd call it "cop-out")

Here's a technique that some authors and copyreaders have found useful for protecting their flanks. I've constantly admonished you to be *consistent*. This might be a good place to complete my cop-out by quoting Emerson's remark that "consistency is the hobgoblin of little minds."

I assure you readers that, if only software were perfect, my book would undoubtedly be perfect (and consistent) too! (NOT!)

> As a public service, this book contains some errors. People who read books that profess to tell them how to write well dearly love to find misteaks and point them out. Accordingly, dear readers, I remain altruistic to the end.
>
> —Faithfully yours,
> The author

[**NOTE**: I paraphrased and modified this delightful cop-out (anyway, *I* think it's delightful) from a quotation that appeared in *Tailgate Ramblings*, the newsletter of the Potomac River Jazz Club. The editor didn't say where *he* "borrowed" it!]

• Punctuation—The Importance of

Many writer's handbooks begin with a discussion of punctuation, the system of symbols used by writers to help readers understand structural relationships of elements within a sentence. Because so many truly excellent books are available, I have chosen to be skimpy on this subject—particularly since it is far too important to be treated properly in a short space.

Most authorities recognize two schools of punctuation: *open* and *closed*. Observation leads me to believe that most members of my generation prefer the closed system, which employs far more marks (primarily commas) than does the open system espoused by most young people—particularly those in the newspaper business.

Frankly, my elderly colleagues and I are in the minority. Most writers nowadays follow newspaper practice—the fewer punctuation marks, the better.

I'll do my best to stay out of the conflict. Instead, I'll recommend two respected authorities. If you work for private industry, get a copy of *The University of Chicago Manual of Style*.

I'd like to put in a word for another good (and inexpensive) reference: *Punctuate It Right*, by Harry Shaw (published by Barnes and Noble). Shaw is stricter than many other modern authorities. That's probably why I like him so well. His book explains not only what punctuation marks to use, but why Shaw believes you should use them.

The approach is thorough, covering more aspects of punctuation than you'd ordinarily find. Shaw goes into separate discussions for each mark, and gives a glossary of terms often used in grammar. He also furnishes an excellent section on applied punctuation.

Some years ago I ran across a delightful reference on punctuation called *The Well-Tempered Sentence*, by Karen Elizabeth Gordon. (See *Bibliography*.) I love it dearly. It gives excellent definitions, suggestions, and examples, and what's more, it's a delight to read!

So as not to cop out entirely, I've given you a few rules of thumb under appropriate headings, including *commas, hyphens*, and *quotation marks*. These entries will help you solve the more common problems. If they aren't enough, refer to the experts.

• Quotation Marks

Here are a few rules of thumb on quotation marks. First, however, let's bear in mind that there are several widely differing schools of thought on this subject. British practice, in particular, differs quite markedly from what we are setting forth here. My authority for this particular approach is the well-known columnist (now long retired) of *The Washington Post*, Bill Gold. His columns showed him to be deeply concerned about language, and I learned much from his wise and witty comments over the years.

Bill Gold's Rules on Quotation Marks

Commas and periods always go *inside* quotation marks.

Colons and semicolons always go *outside*.

The interrogation point and exclamation point go *inside* quotation marks only when they are part of the quotation. Otherwise they go *outside*.

Examples

"He said, 'Would you like to do as you please?' "

"Does it make sense to tell him, 'Do as you please'?"

"He said, 'If you do it your way, I'll kill you!' "

"Instead of telling me how to handle the crisis, he said, 'Do as you please'!"

　　　　　—"The District Line," (*Washington Post,* November 8, 1976)

• Quotations—Importance of Getting Them Right

When you use quotations in your writing, take special care to make them accurate. Go to the original source if possible; secondary sources can, and often will, mislead you. Many famous quotations are really famous misquotations. For example, does "Water, water everywhere, and not a drop to drink," sound right to you? It isn't.

How about "blood, sweat, and tears"? Wrong again. Actually what Winston Churchill said, when he took office as Prime Minister, was "blood, toil, tears, and sweat."

These examples are from an insufferably scholarly book called *The Dictionary of Misinformation,* by Tom Burnham (Ballantine Books). The book is infuriating, because it demonstrates that so much of what most of us know ain't so. (That, incidentally, is a misquotation from Josh Billings.)

Writing speeches for the space program some years ago, Jim Aswell ran across a Victor Hugo quotation: *Nothing is stronger than an idea whose time has come.* It's a lovely quote, but Hugo didn't say it, or at least not in those words. Research disclosed that the original French was something about *Stronger than the tread of mighty armies is an idea whose time has come.*

One last example. Back in the early '60s, Jim Aswell wrote a stirring speech for NASA Administrator James E. Webb. Jim made up a cute little anecdote with the punchline, "When it's steamboat time, you steam." To give the story an aura of respectability and, as Jim put it, verisimilitude, he ascribed the story to Mark Twain.

Mr. Webb's speech went over big. It was quoted widely in newspapers across the country. I'm told that Mark Twain scholars have been looking for the original steamboat quote ever since. They are not likely to find it. (I hope they read this book and call off the search.)

Readability Formulas

Rudolph Flesch, Robert Gunning, Edgar Dale, John McElroy. Do these names sound at least vaguely familiar to you? If not, it's time you were introduced. These are among the best known of the many writers, psychologists, linguists, and other scholars who have turned their attention to the many problems of making writing more readable. (There is a difference between *readable* and *effective*, although the two usually go together.)

For a long time I thought that Flesch was *the* pioneer in this field. Later, I learned that he had many predecessors; he was, however, the first to popularize the subject of readability; first with his book *The Art of Plain Talk* (1946), then with *The Art of Readable Writing* (1949) I commend them both to you. Flesch, unlike some others in the field, is quite good at practicing what he preaches.

Robert Gunning is another real pro, perhaps even more widely known than Rudolph Flesch. Gunning's approach to measuring readability—called the "Fog Index"—has been widely used by both government and industry in recent years. In truth, Gunning's Fog Index and Flesch's Readability Scale are not all that different. Both are concerned primarily with two factors: (1) the average length of sentences, and (2) the percent of difficult words—that is, words having three or more syllables.

To use the Flesch system, one must employ a chart or—a less well-known but more accurate word—a nomograph. By making a couple of simple counts involving average sentence length and number of syllables per hundred words, you can easily come up with a reading ease score. You simply place a ruler or straight-edge on the appropriate numbers on the two outside columns of his nomograph, and observe where they cross a center line labeled the Reading Ease score. That score can range from zero (for extremely difficult material) to 100 (for very easy material).

Because I am really terrible at arithmetic, I like the Flesch formula, which requires little effort on my part. The trouble is, you must have the nomograph on hand. And, of course, many times when you need it, you simply won't have it available.

Doubtless that explains why Gunning's Fog Index has achieved somewhat wider usage. It is easy to commit the formula to memory, and then you can work out a score any time, anywhere. (If you're good at math!)

As I mentioned earlier, the basic ingredients are essentially the same in these two well-known methods. (Indeed, so far as I know, the sentence lengths and syllable counts are key elements in any of the other going methods designed to quantify readability.)

With both Flesch and Gunning methods, your first step is to pick a 100-word sample and figure the average sentence length. Next, you count the number of difficult words (that is, words having three syllables or more) in the sample. You then add the average number of words per sentence to the number of difficult words per hundred. Then, in the Gunning version, you multiply the result by 0.4. The result, rounded off to the nearest whole number, gives you the *Fog Index*, which Gunning has cleverly designed to be roughly equivalent to the grade level a reader must have completed in order to understand the material. (The Fog Index of that last sentence would be appalling—but remember, you don't go on the basis of single sentences. You go by the *average*. And that is why I now hasten to throw in some short sentences.)

If all this does not seem clear, perhaps an example will help. Suppose that you find the average length of a sentence is 15 words. Then you determine that the percentage of difficult words is 13. Add the 15 and the 13, and you come up with 28. Multiply the 28 by 0.4, and you get a Fog Index of 11.2, which you round off to 11 even. That means a person with an 11th grade education should be able to understand the material. (A score of 6 would mean a 6th grader could handle it. And so on.)

What readability formulas can and can't do—Nobody can

learn to be a writer by using a mathematical formula. Indeed, I have seen many would-be writers mess themselves up by trying to apply the formula while they were actually writing. The result was horrendous. They would lose their flow of words, forget their thought patterns, and end up with nothing worth saving.

The formulas work just fine after the fact, but not before or during. Get the first draft down as fast as possible; don't worry in the least about long sentences and difficult words. You have time enough, when the draft is finished, to check with the formula. Then you can edit, rewrite, or whatever else you need to do to bring the score within a desirable range.

Also remember this: A piece of writing with a bad score is almost undoubtedly unclear, unless the writer was or is a true master of the language.

On the other hand, a good score on the formula does not necessarily guarantee that writing is either good or clear. The formula cannot evaluate the content or information of a message; also, it cannot evaluate the style.

With these provisos in mind, I believe you can use readability scores to excellent advantage, after the fact, as I have said earlier. If you are arguing with a colleague about the readability of a particular item, when all else fails, trot out the formula. You may snatch victory from the jaws of defeat. Of course, if you try this on your boss, the converse could well be true.

The famous simple-minded Bates formula—Perhaps some of you readers are almost as bad at math as I am. If you panic at the thought of doing the arithmetic required to work out the Fog Index, I have a nice surprise for you. We non-mathematicians need a quick-and-dirty system to tell when our sentences are getting too foggy. I won't vouch for the accuracy of the math, but here is the simple-minded system I've been using on my own prose for the last 35 years. Maybe that explains why it remains as foggy as it is.

Rudolph Flesch's famous nomograph tells us that "standard" reading ease (a numerical score of 60 to 70) could theoretically be achieved with an average sentence length of 30 words. To do this, however, you would have to use almost nothing but one-syllable words, and that's not too easy.

To get the desired score with much less trouble, the trick is to cut down to an average sentence length of about 20 words. That way, you can use more long words.

Now let's bring Robert Gunning's Fog Index into the computations. We'll assume a Fog Index of 12 is about equivalent to Flesch's standard reading ease. You can obtain this index by an average of 20 words per sentence with, say, about 10 percent long words—three syllables or more.

Sad to say, a Fog Index of 12 may be too high these days, since reading skills have been deteriorating sharply for the past two decades. A Fog Index of ten would probably be a better goal to shoot for.

Well, here's my simple-minded formula. Any time you can knock two words out of a sentence, you'll reduce the fog index by roughly one point. OR, if you can shorten two long words, you'll get the same effect. If you can eliminate two long words, you'll bring that score down by two whole points—a consummation devoutly to be wished.

So, first of all, keep that average sentence length at 20 or under—if possible, well under. Then, if you find you have sentences that are too long, counterbalance them with some sentences that are very short. And, if that doesn't do the trick, go through the manuscript cutting out excess verbiage until the score comes down.

• Reduce/Lessen

This word pair is confusing to many writers. All you need to remember is that *reduce* refers to a decrease in bulk; *lessen* refers to a decrease in number. Thus, you *reduce* your weight, but *lessen* the number of pounds showing on the scale.

• Reference Materials—Guides To

There are a number of excellent books that tell you where to look up facts on many different subjects. One good one is the *New York Times Guide to Reference Material*, by Mona McCormack. This book has sections on newspapers and magazines, encyclopedias, books and literature, dictionaries, almanacs, atlases, history, poetry, politics, government, current events, science, speeches, sports, and many other items. It's really a who-what-where-when-why, etc. made easy. It's useful not because it gives you the needed information directly, but rather because it tells you where to look. And that is really the key to knowledge.

• Relative Pronouns—That/Which/Who

Much confusion exists concerning the proper usage of these three relative pronouns. It isn't any wonder. Many grammars are quite vague on the subject, or don't bring it up at all. And many topflight writers do not observe the distinctions.

Let's begin with the pronoun *that*. It's the easiest, and accordingly, the least misused. *That* is employed to introduce a statement that is essential to the meaning of a sentence. If the phrase or clause it introduces were left out, the sentence would become meaningless. *That* may refer to persons, animals, things, or ideas.

Which introduces statements that merely describe or explain; accordingly, these statements are not essential to the meaning. *Which* refers only to animals, things, or ideas. It is not used to refer to persons.

Who (like *which*) introduces statements that merely describe or explain; again, statements that are not essential to the meaning of the sentence. *Who* refers only to persons—not to animals, things, or ideas.

Now let's look at some examples:

Example One: essential to the meaning *My car was the only one that wasn't wrecked in the accident.*

(Obviously, the sentence would have no meaning at all if it read *My car was the only one in the accident.* Therefore *that was not wrecked* is essential to the meaning.

Example Two: not essential to the meaning *My car was not wrecked, which is fortunate.*

(*My car was not wrecked* is a complete and understandable sentence. The rest of the statement, *which is fortunate*, is not essential to the meaning—it merely adds a nonessential expression of gratitude that my car wasn't wrecked.)

Example Three: not essential to the meaning *My father, who is a former college professor, is retired.*

(The essential fact is contained in the statement *My father is retired.* The explanation *who is a former college professor* is nonessential. But let's suppose, instead, that I had written *My father, who is a former college professor, is the one member of our family that enjoys smoking,* the contrast should be clear. This version plainly calls for that instead of who, for without the essential *that enjoys smoking,* the sentence would lose its meaning.)

Research—Getting to the Bottom of Things

Be curious—and suspicious. Don't take *anything* on faith. Mazie Worcester, one of the best technical editors I know, used to caution me, "Don't believe a word they say until they prove it. Add up all the numbers. Check out *all* the facts."

Also, if you run across a technical term and you're not sure exactly what it means, find out—even though the word may be a standard part of the vocabulary of the subject under discussion.

Experience shows—although it seems strange if not impossible—that a good editor can improve the writing in an abstruse scientific or technical report without comprehending all the information it contains. But to do this, the editor must check closely with an expert at every stage and all along the line. Editor Barbara Hart says, "I usually use my lack of expertise in the field in a subtle way to get the 'techie' to explain to me in plainer English—then we use those words."

Here's a reminder to paste over your word processor. Look at it often:

One of the worst crimes an editor can commit is to introduce errors of fact into a report under the guise of making it easier to read and understand.

Finally, none of this gives you an excuse NOT to understand the material, if all that stands in your way is the need for doing a bit of homework. Any report will be much improved if the editor doesn't cop out and give in to sloth. Even if you are not technically trained in the field, you might try Li'l Abner's system: "Any fool kin unnerstan' this. Ah unnerstan's it."

- **Research Methods (see Bibliography Cards, Note Cards, Files)**

- **Restrictive and Nonrestrictive**

You probably learned these terms in school. Or instead, you may have been taught to say essential and nonessential, or limiting and nonlimiting. No matter—they all mean the same thing.

A restrictive phrase or clause limits, or restricts, the meaning of what it modifies. If you take it out of the sentence, the essential meaning of that sentence will be changed or destroyed. Here's a simple punctuation rule to remember. NEVER set off a restrictive construction by commas. Examples: "All members desiring to attend the game should be at the bus stop before noon." (*desiring to attend the game* is restrictive.) "The dog that barked all night belongs to my neighbor." (. . . *that barked all night* is restrictive.)

A *nonrestrictive* phrase or clause gives additional information about what it modifies, but you can get along without that information. It does not limit or restrict the meaning of the sentence. In effect, it's a parenthetical element. Your punctuation rule for nonrestrictives is this:

ALWAYS set off nonrestrictive elements with commas—one comma at the beginning, the other at the end.

Examples: "The book, *which was on the bestseller list for months*, was banned in Boston."

"The instrument, *called a thermometer*, is used to measure temperature." (The italicized phrases in both these examples are *nonrestrictive*.)

- **Sentence—The Parts of**

subject—When we make a statement or ask a question, there is some word that indicates the person or thing we are talking or asking about. Thus, in the sentences "The airplane flies," and "The book is thick," we say something about the airplane and the book. In the question, "When did the mail arrive?", we ask something about the mail. A word that is used in this way in a sentence is said to be the *subject* of the sentence.

In the sentences given above, *airplane, book*, and *mail* are the subjects.

predicate—What we say or ask about the subject is called the *predicate*. In the sentences that have been given, *flies, is*, and *did arrive* are the predicates.

A **noun** or **adjective** that is joined to the subject by a form of *to be* is called a **predicate noun** (or **predicate nominative** and **predicate adjective**, respectively.)

In the sentence "My father is a lawyer," the word *lawyer* is a **predicate noun**. In the sentence, "Your cousin is sleepy," the word *sleepy* is a **predicate adjective**.

direct object—Frequently the subject of a sentence is said to do something that directly affects a person or thing. In the sentence "The dog chased the rabbit," the act that the subject performs directly affects the rabbit. A word used to denote a person or thing directly affected by an act is said to be the *direct object*. In like manner, in the sentences "My uncle climbed Mount Everest," and "The flame burned the carpet," the words *Mount Everest* and *carpet* are direct objects.

indirect object—An *indirect object* is a noun or pronoun used to denote the person to whom something is given, said, or shown. In the sentence "I gave my dog a bone," the word *dog* is an indirect object. (The *bone* is the direct object.)

• Since/Because

Many writers habitually use the word *since* as a synonym for *because*. Sometimes I do it myself, but that doesn't make it right. Remember that in its primary meaning, the word *since* denotes the passing of time. Use it to mean from then until now or from some particular past time to the present. James J. Kilpatrick, a columnist who cares very much about language, wrote, "When *since* is used in place of the honest *because*, the eye flickers and the mind stumbles." (*Washington Star*, July 6, 1976.)

- ## Subject
  (see **sentence—the parts of**)

- ## Sloppy Constructions

  "Language skills prevent our young people from performing their studies." No. *Lack of* language skills.

  "Reduced speed ahead." (Sign frequently seen along Virginia highways.) No. *Reduce* speed ahead.

  "This road only leads to higher prices." (Sign in front of motel in Fairfax, Virginia.) No. This road *leads only* . . .

- ## Talking Down (or Writing Down)

  This is a dreadful but prevalent sin. Like many other sins that are far more enjoyable, it can sneak up on any of us if we don't exercise constant vigilance. The best defense is to keep an imaginary reader constantly in mind—a bright and perceptive imaginary reader.

  You certainly don't want to insult the intelligence of that paragon of readers, so you make an assumption—he or she may not know some of the facts you are explaining. That's probably why you are writing in the first place. But follow the golden rule of writing, and just tell your story. Your attitude alone can make all the difference.

- ## Tantalizing/Enticing

  The advertising agencies have just about done us in on the distinction between these two words. *Tantalizing* is not by any means the same thing as *enticing*. To *tantalize* carries the connotation of *torment* or *torture* by arousing an intense desire for something that is forever withheld. Most of the time, *enticing* will be the word you want. If you don't like it, you might try *appetizing, provocative, savory,* or *tempting*. Remember that coffee does not have a tantalizing aroma unless you are forever denied the drinking of the glorious beverage.

- ## Teaching Machine Logic

  Dr. B. F. Skinner, in setting forth his gospel of programmed learning, said of the programmer: His goal must be to keep refining his program until the point is reached at which the answers of the average child will almost always be right.

That's a good principle for writers to remember. Think about it the next time you try to explain a difficult or unfamiliar concept to your readers.

• Title

The *title* of your writing enterprise is the first thing your reader sees. It is therefore the most important single handle to lead your reader to your project in the first place.

Accordingly, your title should perform at least these three important functions:

1. It should clearly indicate the specific subject or topic of the project.
2. It should suggest the project's scope and objectives.
3. It should grab the reader's attention.

Don't make your title too short or too vague. If you do, your reader may never be able to find your project or report in the first place, and all your work will have gone for nothing.

Put as many *key words* as possible in your title. That way, when your report is catalogued in publications guides, indexes, and computerized data systems, your reader will be able to track it down, even when coming at it from several different directions.

• Transition

A *transition* is a guidepost or road sign for your readers. Sometimes the guidepost can be read in either direction—just as in the small town where I lived as a child. Opposite sides of the same sign read "Entering Warrenton" and "Leaving Warrenton."

The writer should strive to lead the reader as easily and painlessly as possible from one idea to the next. To do this is not really difficult, but it does require thoughtful attention.

Transition can be achieved by a word, a phrase, a sentence, or even a paragraph.

Certain words are particularly useful to show transition. Here are some suggestions:

To express *addition*, use *also, besides, furthermore, moreover,* or *too.*
To express *comparison,* use *likewise* or *similarly.*
To express *example,* use *as an illustration, for example, for instance,* or *specifically.*
To express *result,* say *as a result, consequently, hence,* or *therefore.*

Besides using transitional words and phrases such as those just listed, you can also achieve effective transition by (a) repeating key words or phrases from preceding sentences; (b) using pronouns that refer clearly to antecedents in previous sentences; and/or (c) using parallel structure.

• Unnecessary Repetition

As we have explained many times, a careful writer must always strive not to waste words—particularly by unnecessary repetition. Here's an example, out of a real document, that shows how NOT to write:

It has been noted that not all persons who received training during the time frame have been noted. It has also been noted that the listing for some directorates reflect that none of its employees have received training.

• Variety and Style in Writing

After you've mastered all the skills we've talked about up to now, and have practiced them until they become second nature, you're ready to start working on some of the refinements of the writing craft.

Of these, one of the most important is variety of sentence structure—the rhythms and cadences that, taken to the ultimate, will give you a recognizable writing style of your own.

Many professional writers will tell you the best way to acquire a good style is to study carefully the work of writers whose craft you respect. Read, and read some more. But learn to read critically, not simply for entertainment. If you happen to run across a piece of writing you think is particularly well done, try to figure out how the writer achieved the effects you admire.

In the olden days, many writers—Robert Louis Stevenson is an example who comes immediately to mind—deliberately copied the works of the masters. In the process, writers can learn as Stevenson did—not simply to imitate, but to create new and original effects.

When I was growing up, every aspiring young jazz trumpet player wanted to play the way Louis Armstrong did. Roy Eldridge learned how to do that extremely well before he found out that he could play like Roy Eldridge. Later came Dizzy Gillespie, who could sound more like Eldridge than Eldridge himself, until Diz developed his own distinctive and revolutionary style.

MORAL: It's a good idea to learn the traditions and follow the rules set forth by the recognized craftsmen of the writing trade before you try too hard to do your own thing.

But, you might ask, are there any exercises an aspiring writer can practice, the way that an ambitious young pianist might tackle Hanon and Czerny and the Bach two-part inventions?

Frankly, I don't know of very many. But here is a sampling of some simple two-handed studies you might try working on:

1. Make a conscious effort to vary the length of your sentences. If you tend toward long sentences, throw in some short ones— you might deliberately make them very short indeed, perhaps just a few words. Maybe just one. See? That not only varies the monotony, but also helps bring down your fog count.

2. Mix in a few *periodic sentences*. (A *periodic sentence* is one in which the meaning of the main clause is not completed until the end of the sentence. It is the opposite of a *loose sentence*, which is one in which various details are added after the meaning of the main clause is complete. Short sentences are often periodic; long sentences tend to be loose.) A famous example of a periodic sentence comes to mind—a parody of the style affected in

Time magazine during the years Henry Luce was in charge. The sentence went something like this: "Backward ran the sentences of *Time* until reeled the mind."

3. Strive to master the use of *parallel construction*. Study the beautifully balanced cadences of the Old Testament Psalms and the New Testament Beatitudes. Read—or better still, listen to—the "I Have a Dream" speech of the late Dr. Martin Luther King. Observe how he built that speech to greater and greater dramatic effects with every repetition, every cadence.

4. Experiment with sentence arrangements, particularly by altering the way you handle modifying phrases and parenthetical expressions. That is, try them at various locations within the sentence. Always make sure, of course, that you haven't created any ambiguities, or confused your readers with squinting constructions. (*Squinting constructions*—usually squinting modifiers—are words so placed in a sentence that they can be interpreted in two or more ways, according to whether they "look" at the words they precede or the words they follow.)

• Voice—Active and Passive

The term *voice* is used in English grammar to indicate, by a change in the verb form, whether the subject *acts* (active voice) or is *acted upon* (passive voice).

Writers should strive to use the active voice whenever possible. By doing this, they will make their writing stronger, clearer, shorter, and more emphatic. For example:

Active: I rang the bell. Theodore submitted the report. The
cow jumped over the moon.
Passive: The bell was rung by me. The report was submitted
by Theodore. The moon was jumped over by the cow.

As you can see, to form the passive versions, you take what was formerly the *direct object*, or *complement*, of the *transitive* verb and transform that word into the subject. You follow this by a verb phrase made up of some form of *to be* plus the past participle.

The passive voice is used far too much in most administrative writing. If you are alert, you have noticed that I appear to have broken my own "rule" by using a passive here. But insofar as the point of my discussion is concerned, the passive version is preferable here. Does this confuse you? I don't blame you if it does. There are exceptions to almost every rule, and this is a case in point. When you are writing about a particular subject at some length, as I am here, you logically should make the subject of your topic sentence the same as the subject of your essay. To start with "Most administrative writers" would put the emphasis in the wrong place. The paragraph is concerned primarily with the passive voice, not with administrative writers.

Another exception: when the doer of the action is unknown or unimportant, use the passive voice. Or if you deliberately want to be obscure, or to keep a low profile, or to avoid responsibility, by all means use the passive. You can't beat it!

• -"wise" as a Suffix

The worlds of government and business seem to have gone wild about -wise as a suffix, as in policy-wise. Let's consign the whole kit and caboodle of them to Gehenna. Here's an illustration that should help convince you of the wisdom of this suggestion. I can't remember the source, but it purports to be a question asked of a wise old owl:

"Hey, owl, how are you doing wise-wise?"
The owl's answer: "Otherwise."

• Writer's Block

Just about everyone who's even faintly interested in writing has heard of "writer's block." Pray that you never suffer from it—the malady professional writers fear most.

Some writers I know are superstitious about it. They say one should never even mention the subject, or even think about it. That attitude seems ostrich-like, to say the least. If you find you are being called upon to write more and more, take this advice: start forming the kinds of habits and attitudes most likely to protect you against having the well run dry.

The first important step you must take is to find out—assuming that you don't already know—what time of day you function best.

Are you a morning person or a night person? When my son Bill was in college, he couldn't even get his motor running until the rest of us were ready to give up and go to bed. Some of his friends seemed to be on the same schedule, so perhaps his pattern was not so unusual as I once thought. Unquestionably, differing biological rhythms among individuals means that we can't expect all people to do their best work at the same time of day. By trial and error, you should be able to get your best time zeroed in.

Here, then, are a few tips:

1. Find out when your best creative time is, and try never to undertake any really demanding writing jobs except during your good hours. (It's hard enough to get started at best; we need to have everything going for us that we can manage.)
2. Set a regular pattern and routine. (Sometimes this can be carried to ridiculous lengths, or so it would appear. But don't knock it.)
3. [I am going to make you wait for this one. Have to tell you a couple of anecdotes first.]

A very famous writer of western stories, Zane Grey, was popular during my youth. Somewhere I've read that when he was getting started as a writer, he worked in a beat-up old Morris chair. It was so dilapidated that the stuffing was coming out, but it was all he could afford. Using an old pine board that he had cut to fit across the chair arms, he'd park his old Remington portable typewriter there, lean back in his chair, and start blazing away.

The system worked. He became successful and the money started to roll in. Then his wife, as wives will, decided to surprise him on his birthday. She donated his old chair and typewriter to the Salvation Army, and bought him a fancy new chair and a fancy new typewriter. There was just one problem: poor old Zane could no longer write a word. He just couldn't get cranked up to write under those posh but unfamiliar conditions.

He had to rush down to the Salvation Army and buy back his old chair and typewriter. (I understand that they threw in the board at no extra charge.) The whole story may or may not be true, but if it isn't it ought to be. It has the ring of verisimilitude. (That's a nice long word that seems particularly appropriate in this context, so to hell with the rule about preferring simple words.)

Another good example of a writer with bizarre habits was Thomas Wolfe, the late novelist from North Carolina, not to be confused with the still-living journalist Tom Wolfe. Thomas Wolfe was about six foot six, and he wasn't at all comfortable sitting at desks designed for persons of average size. He discovered that he could write best standing up, using the top of a refrigerator for his desk. It was just about the right height.

Whenever he ran out of ideas he'd pace up and down the kitchen and then come back and write some more. He was so enormously productive that sometimes he'd write for 16 or 18 hours at a stretch when things were going well.

I understand that Wolfe never had any trouble with writer's block except for once or twice when he was in Europe and couldn't find a refrigerator the right height. Apocryphal? Probably not.

Another stand-up (I use the term literally) writer was the man who may well have been the greatest master of the English language since James Joyce. I refer to Vladimir Nabokov, who died some years ago. (What is most depressing to me is that English was Nabokov's *second* language. He is reputed to have written even better in Russian.) Nabokov always wrote standing up, and he always wrote his initial drafts on index cards. We can wonder what happened if he ran out of cards.

The famous German poet, Schiller, had some kind of Freudian quirk whose significance I don't pretend to understand. Apparently he wrote most creatively only when he had a basket of half-rotten apples on his desk. The smell apparently stimulated his imagination. Don't ask me why.

Here's one final tip. Many professional writers use it and say it works for them. Maybe it will work for you as well.

3. When you get to the end of your day's production, stop right in the middle of a sentence that is going well.

The psychology is this: When you return to work the next day, you can start getting up to speed by completing that unfinished sentence. The rest of the sentence should come easily, and if you're lucky, it will stimulate you to continue.

I leave you with this good advice, and with the heartfelt hope that writer's block will never happen to you. Although you may not yet be a professional writer in the sense that you are writing for a living, you can at least approach your writing tasks in a professional way. "May the force be with you," as the *Star Wars* fans say, or—in the language of the olden days, "Hail and farewell!"

Part 4

Exercises

Exercise 1: Passive Constructions

Rewrite the following sentences, changing passives to actives whenever you believe the change is appropriate. You may keep the passive construction if you can explain why you consider it preferable.

1. It has been pointed out that American influence abroad is weakened by dissent at home.
2. It was suggested by the committee that the construction schedules be revised by the project manager.
3. Compilation of the financial data should be completed by branch managers no later than July 1st.
4. Room reservations should be scheduled by the attenders.
5. Local issues, it was reported by newscasters, are the prime causes for the strike.
6. Daniel J. McGower was named vice president, manufacturing and development, for the Hamilton, Ontario, branch of IBM.
7. It was decided by the commissioner that more decisions should be made by the regional offices.
8. A reduction in job-related accidents was achieved by an incentive program.
9. Delivery of all items must be achieved by the carrier within five work days.
10. The regulations specify that research must be conducted by technically qualified personnel.
11. Permission must be received from the commanding officer before new projects may be started.
12. Under the new policy, sales goals will be established by the national office.
13. A progress report should be submitted weekly.

14. It is expected that this basic plan will be supported by the salespersons as well as the sales managers.
15. Feedback would be hampered by the complicated forms.

Exercise 2: Smothered Verbs

Get rid of the smothered verbs in the following sentences. Make any other editorial changes you believe will improve clarity.

1. To effect a proper utilization of time, ensure that preparation of an agenda has been accomplished before the meeting.
2. Mr. Lynn will need reissuance of his credentials with a reflection of his new title.
3. The improvement in the return on the overall investment is a result of an increase in the average yield on the mortgage portfolio.
4. The Nuclear Regulatory Commission was accused of a failure to force compliance on nuclear powered plants by the GAO.
5. There is little guarantee that the bill would lead to improvements in the agency's efficiency, accountability, and effectiveness.
6. Assessment of the situation should precede implementation of the program.
7. Although a significant reduction in the budget was achieved by the standardization of the reporting system, the business still succumbed to failure.
8. An announcement was made by the President that a revision would be made in the government's fast breeder reactor program.
9. Implementation of these guidelines should be accomplished immediately.
10. After your completion of the registration process, proceed directly to the Alexander Hamilton Room.
11. Individualization of learning programs should be a more frequent occurrence in the public schools.
12. The candidate sought the discreditation and defeat of his opponent.

13. Institutionalization of the patient cannot be achieved without the procurement of a court order.
14. The committee reached a decision to cancel the project after extensive deliberation.
15. Rejection of the applicant without specific cause may result in the institution of grievance proceedings by the applicant.

Exercise 3: Conciseness

Delete the deadwood from the following sentences; make them as concise as possible without altering shades of meaning.

1. Almost without exception, policy papers should be written to provide alternatives, although there are exceptions to this.
2. This point is not included in the sample papers that go to make up the enclosure.
3. The purpose of this memo is to provide a reference for the staff of the formats of various papers which go forward to the Commission.
4. There is a particular need for the agency to centralize assigning the change numbers for the various guides. At times, several individuals may be working on assigning change numbers in the same guide at the same time and are not aware of the change numbers assigned to other revisions.
5. Enclosed is a copy of last year's annual report for the fiscal year 1989.
6. The new manuals will be available for sales agents at a cost of $10.89 per each copy.
7. You will receive payment faster if we mail your checks rather than waiting for your agent to pick them up, since mail in the District of Columbia is usually delivered on a next-day basis.
8. It is my opinion that the cooperation shown by the employees and the cooperation shown by management were responsible for last year's increase in sales.
9. I currently work as the administrative officer for IPX's midwestern division and I administer all of IPX's programs in that division.

10. At some point in time we must decide on whether or not we are going to build the new addition.
11. Will Rogers was a man who liked informality.
12. A strong economy will benefit each and every one of us.
13. We have received your deposit in the amount of $30.00, which we will hold pending receipt of the remaining $30.00.
14. Due to the fact that all the information was not available, we will withhold making a decision until such time as all the information is accessible.
15. The health care program offered by the company is a health care program which provides the greatest number of health benefits for an equivalent premium.

Exercise 4: Concrete vs. Abstract

Substitute concrete, specific terms for the more abstract and general ones. Use your imagination to change dull, vague statements into sentences that will build word pictures in the reader's mind.

1. The mayor graduated a few years ago from a large midwestern institution of higher learning.
2. A college professor has set a government form to classical music, according to a report in a prominent newspaper.
3. Certain steel discounts will be eliminated because of increased company costs, a midwestern steel producer announced.
4. The sailboat won the second race by a narrow margin.
5. The large electrical manufacturer advertised two job openings in the field of communications.
6. A small book by two authors is considered to be an outstanding text on writing.
7. A significant amount of budgeted money remains unspent by the federal government.
8. The professional speaker gave an interesting talk about his business.
9. A recent issue of one of our city's newspapers described the resignation of a government official.

10. Tips on writing and a lot of other stuff are described in the book.
11. The youth got into the car quickly and drove off rapidly.
12. The man moved painfully down the sidewalk without noticing things around him.
13. Some people think one thing about the candidate, others think something else.

Exercise 5-A: Misplaced Modifiers

Reorder the following sentences to place modifiers as close as possible to the words they are intended to modify.

1. The program provides additional services to participants running a wide gamut from transportation to advice.
2. The public affairs officer described satellite programs which are launched on boosters.
3. Based on a recent inspection of the plant, the safety director decided to revise the safety procedures.
4. Based on extensive testing, the physician recommended immediate surgery.
5. The new product was developed in two weeks that doubled the company's gross sales.
6. The announcer said, "I'll be back to tell you how to spend a month in Austria in a minute."
7. The director spoke to the intern with a harsh voice.

Exercise 5-B: Dangling Modifiers

Edit these sentences to eliminate dangling modifiers.

1. Having been well coached by his campaign manager, the candidate's speech gathered support for the candidate.
2. Blinded by the approaching car's headlights, John's car swerved off road into a ditch.
3. To learn the technique thoroughly, the first three exercises must be completed.

4. To receive full retirement benefits, the pension plan must be participated in for twenty years.

5. By reducing each situation to its simplest elements, the answer was discovered by the analyst.

6. Sitting at her desk, the secretary brought the mail to the director.

7. By substituting blue for black ink, the brochure gained greater visual impact.

8. After being rejected by three companies, my employment counselor suggested I rewrite my resume.

9. After researching the topic for five months, my supervisor canceled the project.

10. By using less water for showers and washing, the water authority will be able to meet the demand for water throughout the summer.

11. While waiting for a client to return from lunch, the parking meter expired and a police officer ticketed my car.

12. To increase their sales, computers are being used by salesman to place at least 12 additional telephone calls each hour.

13. After waiting six days for the jury to return a verdict, concern grew that the trial might end in a hung jury.

14. While on the floor, a page summoned the Senator to meet with a group of constituents.

15. While mowing the lawn, a new idea popped into the writer's head.

Exercise 6: Unnecessary Shifts

Rewrite the following sentences to eliminate all unnecessary shifts.

1. In order for Sunshine Act procedures to be followed, include a statement in the Scheduling block.

2. I certainly appreciate the opportunity to have met with you and introduce you to our staff during your visit.

3. We have reviewed your draft and the following comments are submitted.

4. Mr. Cochran criticizes the loan department and has even asked for a new loan officer.
5. Forest fires destroyed thousands of acres of timber as it roared through the valley.
6. The director believes it would be in the best interest of the manufacturer to report on the initial list all the chemicals they can.
7. Metro trains were delayed by a malfunctioning signal, causing many to be thirty to forty minutes late to work.
8. Although I was satisfied, the job seemed to require less imagination than expected.
9. Release the safety catch and the operator then turns the valve.
10. A frequent source of complaints were the difficulties encountered in registration.
11. Before starting your own business, you should decide how much money they require.
12. The possibility of additional federal regulations on airline operations cause concern among airline industry officials.
13. The best way to use the note pads is to check off cards as they become known and using the initials of the player showing the card is an additional aid.

Exercise 7: The Simple Word

Rewrite these sentences, improving them by using simple words and phrases and making other changes that clarify their meaning.

1. Pursuant to the rules being promulgated as of this date by the publications division, endeavor to employ uncomplicated words in writing.
2. The maintenance of simplicity and the avoidance of circumlocution will enable your readers to achieve improved comprehension.
3. The federal bureaucracy is presently predominantly comprised of hardworking individuals.
4. Subsequent to next Wednesday's meeting, implement the revised guidelines.

5. After a thorough consideration of the proposal, the president was convinced the agency should adopt a negative posture toward it.
6. Providing meaningful jobs for the unemployed will ameliorate a difficult situation and will help reduce the unemployed worker's sense of impuissance.
7. Inclusion of your ZIP code will expedite the order.
8. The chairman's espousal of the tax bill was unexpected in view of his earlier opposition to it.
9. The lack of jobs forced John McKay, who holds a Ph.D. in English, to take a job that was not commensurate with his skills.
10. Initiate a savings program at your earliest possible convenience.
11. Wrecking crews leveled the edifice to clear a location for a shopping center.
12. The police surmise that the local drug purveyor was the recipient of shipments weekly from out of state.
13. The turf, psychologically speaking, tends to have the appearance of being more verdant beyond the barrier prohibiting one's access thereto.
14. The occurrence of the accident took place on the circumferential highway that surrounds the city.
15. Textilewise, early repairs are estimated to be nine times more efficacious than when remedial measures are significantly delayed.

Exercise 8-A: Unnecessary Repetition

Rewrite the following sentences to eliminate unnecessary repetition.

1. One of the clerk's responsibilities is the compiling of time and attendance reports. These time and attendance reports go to the branch chief, who verifies that the information on each time and attendance report is accurate and complete.
2. Next year's proposed budget needs to be revised before being

released to the public. Otherwise the budget may draw sharp criticism, because it is not a zero-based budget.

3. Mr. Jensen received 21 excellent ratings, five good ratings, and no poor ratings.

4. The information obtained from the study should be reported to the committee by June 23. All information should be complete; and information that is not complete should be clearly marked "incomplete."

5. Although industry officials view the proposed regulations as unnecessary, they are less opposed to these regulations than to the regulations proposed last year.

Exercise 8-B: Elegant Variation

Rewrite the following paragraph to eliminate elegant variation.

Each owner of an automobile is required to register the car within 30 days of the time of the purchase of the vehicle. The driver must report the car's serial number, engine number, make, and model. The owner must also indicate whether the vehicle is used for business purposes. Finally, the owner must indicate whether he bought the automotive conveyance at a recognized automotive vehicle dealer's establishment. No unlicensed personal car will be permitted to operate.

Exercise 9: Parallel Construction

Rewrite the following sentences, following the principle of parallel structure.

1. Save gasoline by avoiding jack-rabbit starts, maintaining an even speed, and look ahead to anticipate signal changes.

2. I would like to learn the following from this book:
   1) How to start writing,
   2) Punctuation,
   3) How to develop style.

3. See immediate returns from the course through greater filing efficiency, quicker insurance claims processing, and collecting overdue accounts.
4. Four methods of providing company training are:
   . three-day seminars
   . correspondence courses
   . hiring a consultant
   . in-house sessions.
5. Please observe the following regulations:
   . Equipment must be reserved two weeks ahead;
   . Removing equipment without signing out is not approved;
   . Equipment must be returned within 48 hours of use.
6. I have nothing to offer but blood, toil, crying, and sweating.
7. The manager described the department's problems succinctly, clearly, and with candor.
8. Reviewing the records daily is as important as to collect accurate information.
9. Charles Jarvis is an excellent lecturer, personable conversationalist, and he writes well also.
10. Please observe the following regulations:
    . Equipment must be reserved two weeks ahead;
    . Removing equipment without signing out is not approved;
    . Equipment must be returned within 48 hours of use.

Exercise 10-A: Orderly Arrangement

Rewrite the following memo, using a more logical arrangement. Don't forget to apply all the other principles you have learned.

In accordance with your instructions, which you transmitted to me telephonically during the prior week, a search of the literature has been made and the undersigned has arrived at the determination that any one of the following copying machines should be entirely satisfying in fulfilling the needs of your department.

The Whizbang Model OD-227 has a selling price of $1,985. It has demonstrated the capability of making 20 copies per minute. The maximum size of paper it is capable of handling is fairly large-up to eleven inches in one dimension and seventeen in the other. It will make reasonably good, but not excellent, copies on both sides of a sheet, if you so desire that feature. A service contract can be arranged for $400 per annum.

The Tolable Model 3-D will make copies anywhere from postcard size up to legal size. It is very fast—40 copies a minute. It is probably the best machine in its price range for making two-sided copies. The service contract is $600 per year. Cost of the machine itself is $2,495.

The Copycat Model 1347 is reported to have a demonstrated capability of making one copy every five seconds. It will make enlargements and reductions, and can handle copies up to double the size of a standard 8-1/2 by eleven inch page. It is not recommended for making copies on both sides of a sheet of paper. Its selling price is just $1,995, and a service contract is only $275 for a period of 12 months.

Exercise 10-B: Orderly Arrangement— Correct Order

Here is a description, in the wrong order, of the easy way to outline. Rearrange the items in a more logical progression.

1. The idea should be easy to grasp with a quick glance.
2. Spread out the cards on a table.
3. Check each pile to be sure the ideas are related.
4. Use 3 x 5, 4 x 6, or 5 x 8 cards.
5. Make a topic card for each pile.
6. Write only one idea on each card.
7. Rearrange topic cards to try many sequences until you are satisfied with one particular sequence.
8. In writing down the idea, use as few words as possible.
9. Put related ideas together in piles.
10. Here is the procedure for organizing an easy outline.
11. Discard ideas that, on re-examination, do not seem to fit the topic.
12. With the cards in order, you have completed your "easy outline."

13. Write down on the top of the cards the ideas that must be included in the report.
14. Using abbreviations will help.
15. Decide on a sequence to present your ideas.
16. One idea per card allows flexibility of thought.
17. Study the cards carefully.
18. Make cards for new ideas that come to mind.

Exercise 10-C:

The following information is given in steps, as any good instructions should be. But the steps as shown are not arranged in the proper order. Rearrange them for the best logic, so that the reader is led properly from one step to the next.

Step 1. Check to see that language and nomenclatures in the illustrations are consistent with those of the text.

Step 2. Present each step in its normal order.

Step 3. Divide the process into distinct steps.

Step 4. Go through all the steps to see if they're in the right order, if they tell the reader all necessary information, and they really work.

Step 5. Write an opening paragraph to set the stage. Explain the purpose of the entire operation. Give the reader a clear view of what is expected. (Find out what the reader already knows before you start!)

Step 6. Rewrite, rewrite, rewrite as many times as necessary to achieve clarity.

Step 7. Check for, and eliminate uncommon words and complicated phrasing. Define technical terms, if necessary.

Step 8. If necessary, divide the text with appropriate headings and subheadings.

Step 9. SHOW the reader. Use working drawings, charts, illustrations, schematics, etc.

Exercise 11: "Report to Stockholders"

Some years ago (mid-80s), a company that had just gone public asked me to edit their first *Annual Report to Stockholders*. (Their staff had never done such a report before.)

The original draft was reasonably literate. It contained no misspelled words or obvious grammatical errors. Most of the problems could be boiled down to—

- too many unnecessarily long sentences;
- wordiness; and
- fuzziness—a lack of focus.

Moral of the story: sometimes it is harder to edit fairly good copy than it is to edit really bad copy.

The following is the introductory section of the original draft; only the name of the corporation has been changed. Your task is the same that mine was—to edit, and, if necessary, rewrite—the copy for brevity, clarity, coherence, and appeal to the stockholder audience.

(ORIGINAL DRAFT)

*Profile: The Evolution and Growth
of Professional Services
(Introduction to the First Annual Report to Stockholders
of XYZ Corporation.)*

From the very earliest days of the republic, and continuing virtually unchecked throughout the first half of the 20th century, the strength of the American economy has always had its roots growing out of the basic areas of tangible physical capital—agriculture, mining, and the conversion of raw materials through the manufacturing process.

But in the period following the end of World War II, thoughtful observers have observed that the situation has been changing dramatically, with that former strength shifting at an ever-faster rate to the intangible commodities of clerical, managerial, professional and technical services.

The change started evidencing itself almost immediately after the close of World War II, when service industries began to move steadily to the economic forefront. Today, they have arrived at a point where these industries currently represent two-thirds of the Gross National Product.

As a Nation, we have now entered into a new stage of economic developments, and modern growth industries are increasingly being focused on human capital in place of physical capital and replacing new materials with the resources of the human mind.

The professional services industry has now started evolving within the service sector as a specialized subgroup whose knowledge and intensive skills represent a relatively new industrial entity. Its services are being used to address critical defense, economic, social, and environmental issues brought on by the complexities of modern times. In essence, the professional services industry is an industry of problem solvers. At XYZ Corporation, we are proud of our role in this rapidly growing and important segment of the American economy.

I'll give you a few suggestions below.

A Few Tips on Attacking the Problems

I suggest that before you tackle the actual rewriting process, you—

1. Identify the purpose, by asking the following questions:
   a. What main point is this introduction trying to make?
   b. Is the point stated clearly?
2. Study the organization and relationship of ideas in the text:
   a. Does the introduction prepare the readers (stockholders) for what follows?
   b. Is there a clear relationship among main ideas?
   c. Are the transitions from one topic or idea to another clear and logical?

3. Analyze the content:
   a. Can the reader easily follow the main ideas?
   b. Are enough details furnished to develop main ideas or topics?
   c. Are examples used to illustrate and support general statements?
4. Sharpen the style:
   a. Are the sentences too long?
   b. Is sentence structure varied and smooth?
   c. Is the tone appropriate to the purpose and subject?
   d. Does the theme grab and hold the readers' attention?

Now you should be ready to try your own rewrite. When you finish, if you like, you may compare your final version with mine on page (299).

Exercise 12: Gobbledygook Rewriting Contest

The paragraph that follows is taken from an actual document, written by a government official of my home state, the Commonwealth of Virginia. The irrepressible James Boren—whom I have mentioned several times earlier in this book—singled out the paragraph some years ago and published it in his newsletter, *Mumblepeg*, as an example of gobbledygook.

Some time later, *The Editorial Eye*,[1] an excellent newsletter for professional writers and editors, picked up the document from Mr. Boren's newsletter and used it as the subject of a rewriting contest for the *Eye*'s subscribers. After reviewing all the entries, the *Eye* published the winning rewrite, with comments by chief judge Peggy Smith, who was at that time editor of the *Eye*.

Try your own hand at rewriting. You'll observe the passage to be edited consists of a single sentence more than 100 words long. Give

[1]This material is used with the permission of *The Editorial Eye* and its publisher, Editorial Experts, Inc. (EEI), 60 Canal Center Plaza, Suite 200, Alexandria, VA 22314-1538.

it your best shot, then compare your rewrite with the winning entry,
which you'll find on page 300.

With the prospect of the probable necessity of substantial increased expenditures of fiscal resources and the probable necessity of fiscal resources and the probable necessity for optimal
natural resources development and use which transcend political
boundaries it is believed wise to consider a more assertive role in
water resources development of the part of the state, which role
might undertake the provision of financial aid to the local political
subdivisions to facilitate needed development, or the actual construction and operation of such facilities by the state under auspices of a statewide water authority with revenue-production
mechanisms and potential foresight to provide the additional in-
crement of water projected to be needed.

Answers to Exercises

Exercise 1: Passive Constructions—Suggested Answers[1]

1. Dissent at home weakens American influence abroad.
2. The committee suggested that the project manager revise the construction schedule.
3. Branch managers should compile finance data by July 1.
4. Attendees should make room reservations.[2]
5. (*In view of the fact that the local issues are probably more important in this sentence than the newscasters, leave the sentence in the passive.*)
6. (*Here again, the name of the person being appointed is more*

---

[1]As explained earlier, the suggested answers in this section, as well as the parenthetical comments and explanations, were furnished by my two former partners in Speak/Write Systems, Inc. In a few cases, however, I haven't been able to resist the temptation of putting in a comment or two of my own. Each of these comments is clearly identified—COMMENT BY JDB.

[2]COMMENT BY JDB: If this were my sentence, I'd probably take even more pains to avoid possible misunderstanding. I think I'd write something such as "Attendees are responsible for making their own room reservations." OR "Attendees are responsible for reserving their own rooms."

important than that of the one doing the appointing; leave this sentence in the passive.)

7. The commissioner decided that the regional offices should make more decisions.
8. An incentive program reduced job-related accidents.
9. The carrier must deliver all items within five work days.
10. The regulations specify that technically qualified personnel must conduct the research. (If you want extra emphasis on the *research*, leave the sentence in the passive.)
11. The commanding officer must approve new projects before they may be started. (*Notice that the second part of the sentence remains in the passive because we don't know who would be starting the projects.*)
12. Under the new policy, the national office will establish sales goals.
13. Submit a progress report weekly. (Note use of imperative.)
14. Sales clerks as well as sales managers will, we expect, support this basic plan.
15. Complicated forms would hamper feedback.[3]

Exercise 2: Smothered Verbs—Suggested Answers

1. Use time properly, prepare an agenda before the meeting. (*Why not "utilize"? Isn't that the verb form of "utilization"? Yes, it is. But "use" is shorter and less stuffy.*)
2. Mr. Lynn will need revised credentials reflecting his new title.
3. The return on the overall investment improved because the average yield on the mortgage portfolio increased.
4. GAO accused the Nuclear Regulatory Commission of failing to force compliance on nuclear power plants. (*Perhaps you put, ". . . to force nuclear powered plants to comply." That might be fine for most of us lay persons, but it would upset the regulators to whom "compliance" has a specific meaning. They have pages of regulations defining "compliance." So be careful not to*

---

[3]COMMENT BY JDB: Many writers take a dim view of "feedback." I think it's a useful word here.

change words that have special connotations to specific groups of readers.)

5. There is little guarantee that the bill would improve the agency's efficiency, accountability, and effectiveness.
6. Assess the situation before implementing the program.[4] (*Or more simply: "Look before you leap."*)
7. Although standardizing the reporting system significantly reduced the budget, the business still failed.
8. The President announced that the government's fast breeder reactor program would be revised. (*Note the appropriate use of the passive. Since we don't know who will revise the program, we must keep the second part of the sentence in the passive. Another suggested answer. "The President announced a revision of the government's fast breeder reactor program" avoids the passive, but distorts the meaning. The program has not yet been revised. It is going to be revised.*)
9. Implement these guidelines immediately.
10. After you register, proceed (go) to the Alexander Hamilton Room.
11. Individualized learning programs should occur more frequently in the public schools.[5] (*Or better, "Public schools should individualize learning programs more frequently."*)
12. The candidate sought to discredit and defeat his opponent.
13. The patient cannot be institutionalized without a court order. (*Many editors would object to "institutionalize." If we knew the specific institution, we could get rid of the word easily; for example, ". . . cannot be placed in a mental hospital," or ". . . in a detention home," etc. Even without knowing, many editors*

[4]COMMENT BY JDB: Many writers abhor the verb "implement." If you are one of them, you could say ". . . before putting the program into effect." Good for you. But as a one-time—and long-time—bureaucrat, I must reluctantly admit that "implement" in this sense no longer offends me. And it is one word instead of the two or more required in the other versions. Let your conscience be your guide!

[5]COMMENT BY JDB: I think it would be still better to say something like "Public schools should fit more learning programs to the ability of the individual." The word **individualize** is educator's jargon, and doesn't communicate very clearly to the average reader.

would probably change this to read, "cannot be placed in an institution.")

14. After deliberating extensively, the committee decided to cancel the project.

15. An applicant rejected without specific cause may institute (begin) grievance proceedings.

Exercise 3: Conciseness—Suggested Answers

1. Almost without exception, policy papers should provide alternatives.

2. This point is not included in the samples.

3. This memo gives examples of the formats for papers that go to the Commission.

4. The agency needs to centralize assigning the change numbers for the various guides. At times, several individuals may be assigning numbers in the same guide, unaware of numbers assigned to other revisions. (*Or: "The agency needs to centralize assigning the change numbers for the various guides to avoid duplication."*)[6]

5. Enclosed is the report for fiscal 1989. (*"Copy" is an over-used word; it is rarely necessary in most writing. The difference between a **Cezanne** and a copy of a Cezanne is significant. The distinction between the **annual** report and a **copy of the annual report** is difficult to determine and certainly not worth the effort.*)

6. Sales agents may purchase the new manuals for $14.89 each.

7. You will receive payment faster if we mail your checks, because mail in the District of Columbia is usually delivered the next day.

8. I believe that the cooperation of management and employees was responsible for increasing sales last year.

9. I am the administrative officer for IPX's Midwestern division and am responsible for all its programs.

---

[6]COMMENT BY JDB: I think we can make this sentence much clearer by shifting the emphasis: "*To avoid* duplicating change numbers, the agency should make one office responsible for assigning all numbers."

10. Sometime we must decide whether to build the new addition.
11. Will Rogers liked informality.
12. A strong economy will benefit each of us.
13. We have received your $30.00 deposit, which we will hold until we receive the remaining $30.00.
14. We will decide after receiving all the data.
15. The health care program offered by the company provides the greatest number of benefits for the price.

Exercise 4: Concrete vs. Abstract—Suggested Answers

1. Mayor Thomas Walker earned a B.A. degree in journalism from Ohio State University in 1989.
2. Edwin Avril, music professor at Glassboro State College, has set the 1040 tax form to the music of Bach's Easter Cantata, according to a report in the *Wall Street Journal*.
3. "Foreign fighter" price discounts will be eliminated because of increased wage costs, Armco Steel Corporation announced.
4. *Courageous* won the second race of the America's Cup by one minute and three seconds.
5. General Electric advertised two openings for technical writers.
6. *The Elements of Style*, by William Strunk and E. B. White, is considered to be an outstanding text on writing.
7. More than $22 billion budgeted for use by the federal government remains unspent.[7]
8. Steven Thomlin explained how he started a mail-order business in his home and made a million dollars in 12 months.
9. The September 23, 1977 issue of *The Washington Post* described the resignation of Bert Lance.
10. Tips on the easy way to make an outline, avoid writer's block, and improve clarity are included in *Writing with Precision*.
11. Jim Moynihan, the star quarterback of the Silver Creek Silver Streaks, hopped into the front seat of his Buick convertible without even opening the door, and flooring the accelerator, rocketed out of the driveway.

[7]COMMENT BY JDB: If you believe that, stand on your head!

12. The 90-year-old man limped painfully down the street without even a glance at the squealing preschoolers playing hopscotch.
13. Young voters consider the Coalition's candidate, Betty Markham, to be perfect for the Silver Creek school board vacancy, while old-timers doubt she has the maturity to handle the teachers' demands for more authority in the classroom.

Exercise 5-A: Misplaced Modifiers—Suggested Answers

1. The program furnishes participants with additional services, running a wide gamut from advice to transportation.
2. The public affairs officer described satellite programs that involve the use of booster rockets.
3. The safety director's decision to revise the safety procedures was based on a recent inspection of the plant.
4. After extensive testing, the physician recommended immediate surgery.
5. The new product, which was developed in two weeks, doubled the company's gross sales.
6. The announcer said, "I'll be back in a minute to tell you how to spend a month in Austria."
7. The director spoke in a harsh voice to the intern. (*Or perhaps better: "The director spoke harshly to the intern."*)

Exercise 5-B: Dangling Modifiers—Suggested Answers

1. After extensive coaching from his campaign manager, the candidate gave a speech that gained him support.
2. Blinded by the approaching car's headlights, John swerved his car off the road into a ditch. (*Is "his car" necessary? Judgment call.*)
3. To learn the technique thoroughly, you must (*or "one must"*) complete the first three exercises.
4. To receive full retirement benefits, employees must participate in the pension plan for 20 years.
5. By reducing each situation to its simplest elements, the analyst discovered the answer.

6. The secretary brought the mail to the director who was sitting at her desk. (*No comma would imply that there is more than one director. A comma after the word "director" would imply the one and only director.*)

7. By substituting blue for black ink, the printer increased the brochure's visual impact.[8] (*Or: "Changing from black to blue ink gave the brochure greater visual impact."*)

8. My employment counselor suggested I rewrite my resume after I was rejected by three companies. (*Or, perhaps better, "After my rejection by three companies, my employment counselor suggested I rewrite my resume.*)

9. My supervisor canceled the project after I had researched it for five months. (*Or: "My supervisor canceled the project after I had spent five months researching it."*)

10. If customers use less water showering and washing, the water authority will be able to meet the demand for water throughout the summer.

11. While I was waiting for a client to return from lunch, the parking meter expired and a police officer ticketed my car.[9]

12. To increase sales, sales clerks are using computers to place 12 extra phone calls an hour.[10]

13. After waiting six days for the jury to return a verdict, observers became concerned that the trial might end in a hung jury.

14. While on the floor, the Senator was summoned by a page to meet with a group of constituents. (*For those of you unfamiliar with the workings of government, "on the floor" in this case means being present on the floor of the Senate. This sentence is a good example of the passive voice used correctly; presumably,*

---

[8]COMMENT BY JDB: If this were my sentence, I'd say "Changing the color of ink from black to blue gave the brochure greater visual impact." But I realize I'm probably being overly fussy.)

[9]COMMENT BY JDB: I can't resist this, because I can picture that meter dying before my very eyes. I'd say, "the time on the parking meter ran out . . ."

[10]COMMENT BY JDB: This sentence sounds ugly to me because "sales" and "sales clerks" repeat their sounds right next to each other. How about trying, instead, "Sales clerks, to increase their sales, are using computers to place—or that can place—12 extra phone calls an hour."

the senator and the constituents are more important than the page.)

15. While the writer was mowing the lawn, a new idea popped into her head.

Exercise 6: Unnecessary Shifts—Suggested Answers

1. In order to follow Sunshine Act procedures, include a statement in the Scheduling block.[11]
2. I certainly appreciated the opportunity of meeting with you and of introducing you to our staff during your visit.
3. We have reviewed your draft and are submitting the following comments.
4. Mr. Cochran criticized the loan department and even asked for a new loan officer.
5. Forest fires destroyed thousands of acres of timber as the flames roared through the valley. (*Did you put "they" where I've used "the flames"? Fine, except someone is going to say, They refers to "thousands of acres" not to "forest fires."*)
6. The director believes it would be in the manufacturer's best interest to report as many chemicals as possible on the initial list.
7. Metro trains were delayed by a malfunctioning signal, causing many commuters to be 30 to 40 minutes late for work.
8. Although I was satisfied, I had expected the job to require more imagination. (*Or: "Although the job satisfied me, it seemed to require less imagination than I had expected."*)
9. (*If the instructions are intended for one person*) Release the safety catch and then turn the valve.

   (*If the operator is another person not being directly addressed:*)

   Release the safety catch; then the operator will turn the valve.

---

[11]COMMENT BY JDB: If you believe that "in order" is redundant, your instincts are basically sound. But to my ear, taking out the phrase changes the meaning slightly. I would suggest that, if you decide to take it out, you could preserve the original shade of meaning by saying something like, "To comply with Sunshine Act procedures . . ."

10. A frequent source of complaints was the difficulties encountered in registration. (*If this sounds awkward, reverse the order: Difficulties in registration were a frequent source of complaints.*)

11. Before starting your own business, you should decide how much money the business requires. (*The sentence would be stronger if it were more specific. Does the writer mean the money needed to open the business? Or the amount needed not only to open the business but to pay personal expenses until the business makes a profit?*)

12. The possibility of additional federal regulation of airline operations causes concern among airline industry officials.

13. The best way to use the note pads is to check off the cards as they become known. (*Or: "The best way to use the note pads is to check off the cards as they become known. As an additional aid when checking off each card, use the initials of the player who shows it."*)

Exercise 7: The Simple Word—Suggested Answers and Tips

1. Follow the publications division's new rules (being put into effect today) and use simple words. (*The phrase shown in parentheses is a "judgment call" here; use it if you think it's needed for precision.*)

2. Simple, straightforward writing will help your readers to understand.

3. The federal bureaucracy now chiefly consists of hardworking individuals.

4. After next Wednesday's meeting, use the revised guidelines.

5. The President thoroughly examined the proposal and decided the agency should not adopt it.

6. Providing an unemployed worker with a meaningful job will ease a difficult situation and help reduce that person's sense of impotence.

7. Including your ZIP code will speed up your order.

8. The chairman's support of the tax bill was unexpected because he had opposed it earlier.

9. To take a job for which he was overqualified.
10. Start a savings plan as soon as possible. (*ASAP?*)
11. Wrecking crews leveled the building.
12. The police think the local drug pusher receives weekly shipments from out of state.
13. Grass is greener.
14. The accident occurred on the Beltway.
15. A stitch in time.

Exercise 8-A: Unnecessary Repetition

1. One of the clerk's responsibilities is the compiling of time and attendance reports. These time and attendance reports go to the branch chief, who verifies that the information on each time and attendance report is accurate and complete.
2. Next year's proposed budget needs to be revised before being released to the public. Otherwise, the budget may draw sharp criticism, because it is not a zero-based budget.
3. Mr. Jensen received 21 excellent ratings, 5 good ratings, and no poor ratings.
4. The information obtained from the study should be reported to the committee by June 23. All information should be complete; and information that is not complete should be clearly marked incomplete.
5. Although industry officials view the proposed regulations as unnecessary, they are less opposed to those regulations than to the regulations proposed last year.

Exercise 8-B: Elegant Variation—Suggested Answer

Owners must register their cards within 30 days of purchase by reporting the car's serial number, engine number, make, and model. An owner must state whether the car is used for business and whether it was bought from a recognized dealer. An unlicensed personal car may not be operated.

Exercise 9: Parallel Construction—Suggested Answers

1. Save gasoline by avoiding jack-rabbit starts, maintaining an even speed, and looking ahead to anticipate signal changes.
2. I would like to learn the following from this book:
   1) How to start writing,
   2) How to punctuate, and
   3) How to develop style.
3. See immediate returns from the course through greater filing efficiency, quicker insurance claims processing, and improved account collections.
4. Four methods of providing company training are—
   • three-day seminars
   • correspondence courses
   • private consultants
   • in-house seminars
5. Please observe the following regulations—
   • Equipment must be reserved two weeks ahead;
   • Equipment may not be removed without being signed out;
   • Equipment must be returned within 48 hours of use.
   (*Or why not strengthen the whole construction by putting the regulations in the **active voice—imperative mood**.*)
   • Reserve equipment two weeks ahead;
   • Sign out equipment before removing it from the storage room;
   • Return equipment within 48 hours.
6. "I have nothing to offer but blood, toil, tears, and sweat."
7. The manager described the department's problems succinctly, clearly, and candidly.
8. Reviewing the records daily is as important as collecting accurate information.
9. Charles Jarvis is an excellent lecturer, personable conversationalist, and fine writer.
10. "With malice toward none; with charity for all; with firmness in the right . . . let us strive on to finish the work we are in: to bind up the nation's wounds; to care for him who shall have borne the battle; . . . ourselves, and with all nations." (*Sound*

familiar? It's from Lincoln's second Inaugural Address. Notice how effectively the parallel structure moves the message along.)

Exercise 10-A: Orderly Arrangement—Hints and Tips

There are probably at least a dozen different ways to rewrite this exercise. Accordingly, we aren't going to give you a "suggested answer" here; instead, we'll give you a few hints and tips that will help you tell whether your own version is a good one, and perhaps enable you to make it even better.

Make use of all the principles you've learned so far. (If you are alert, you may be wondering right now why we didn't simply say "use" instead of "make use." Think about it, please. Our word choice here is deliberate, and we made it because there is a shade of difference we feel it's important to express. Precision!)

Read all the way through before you start to edit or rewrite. Be systematic. Look for passive voice (. . . has been made . . .), smothered verbs (. . . arrived at the determination . . .), and deadwood (. . . in accordance with . . .). Remedy these faults if you can; while you're doing that, you'll probably find yourself gaining additional insights on how to improve the arrangement of facts.

Is the information presented in parallel fashion? Is the order logical? (Make sure you don't express copying speed in terms of "number per minute" for one machine and "a copy every X seconds" for another.)

Is exactly the same information presented for each machine? If not, readers may become uncomfortable about the omissions, even if they aren't consciously aware of them.

Is the order logical? That is, have you chosen a scheme of presentation based on, say, alphabetical order? Or price? Or speed of operation?

Would the material be easier to understand if it were presented in tabular form? Maybe you'd like to try it both ways. (And, since some readers are "word-oriented" and some are "engineering-oriented," you might even consider using both a narrative and an illustrative tabular chart.)

If you still feel the need for more help, we suggest you go back and carefully re-read pages 57 and 58.

Once you've done all this, you're ready for the final test. Put yourself in the reader's shoes. Try to read the rewritten version as if you had never seen it before. Does it answer all your questions? Would it make it easy for you to make a decision if you were buying a copying machine? We devoutly hope so.

Exercise 10-B: Orderly Arrangement—Correct Order

10, 4, 13, 6, 16, 8, 14, 1, 2, 176, 11, 18, 9, 3, 5, 15, 7, 12

Exercise 10-C: Writing Instructions—Suggested Answer

If your answer came out approximately like this, you're on the right track. There may be some minor variations; some of the choices are strictly judgment calls.

Step 1. Write an opening paragraph . . .
Step 2. Divide the process into distinct steps.
Step 3. Present each step in its normal order.
Step 4. Check for and eliminate uncommon words . . . *(judgment call)*
Step 5. SHOW the reader . . . *(judgment call)*
Step 6. Check to see that language and nomenclatures . . .
Step 7. If necessary, divide the text . . .
Step 8. Go through all the steps to see . . .
Step 9. Rewrite, rewrite, rewrite . . .

Exercise 11: "Report to Stockholders"—Suggested Rewrite

PROFILE: The growth of the Special Services Industry

World War II marked the end of an old economic era and the beginning of a new one.

Before the war, America's economic strength stemmed primarily from raw materials and physical capital—the tangible assets of agriculture, mining, and manufacturing.

But at war's end, that strength began to shift dramatically. Physical capital was still important, of course; indeed, it always will be. But it had relinquished its place as America's economic cornerstone. Our nation began building its new postwar economy largely on the intangible commodities of the human mind—in the form of clerical, managerial, professional, and technical services.

Nowhere has the change been more evident than in the advance of professional services to the economic forefront. Today, service industries represent 60 percent of the American labor force and two-thirds of the Gross National Product.

Much of this growth evolved in direct response to the complexities of high technology in the age of space exploration, computers, and nuclear industry. Within the service sector, a specialized "knowledge-intensive" group of problem solvers known as the professional services industry has taken the lead. This group frequently offers the best—and sometimes the only—solutions to our nation's most critical defense, economic, social, and environmental problems. Here at XYZ Corporation, we are proud of our role in this rapidly growing and increasingly important segment of the American economy.

Exercise 12: Gobbledygook Contest—Suggested Answer

The text of the winning entry follows. My incredible modesty forbids me from confiding to you the name of the person who won the contest.

Virginia's need for water and the cost of obtaining it are both expected to continue rising; accordingly, prudence dictates that the state take strong measures to—use present water resources to best advantage; and develop new ones without regard to political boundaries. We should consider establishing a statewide water authority to determine future needs well in advance, and ensure that these needs are wisely met. Such an authority, empowered to produce revenue, could guide political subdivisions and aid them financially. Or, at option, the water authority could actually construct and operate water development facilities for the state.

In comparing your own rewrite with the one shown on the previous page, you might find it helpful to read Peggy Smith's explanation of why she found certain rewrites and rewordings unacceptable.

The following submissions don't quality: Two entries use the word or idea of taxes—not the same as *revenue-producing mechanisms* (water can be sold); one says "the state believes it wise"—not the same as a recommendation from the Water Control Board. Two misinterpret political boundaries, a geographical designation, as politics. One says, "the burden of these expenditures should transcend political undaries"—when the original says "development and use" are what should transcend. One misstates the WHY and says "the states should play a more assertive role" since the development and use of natural resources transcend political boundaries. One says political units and one says local agencies—not the same as political subdivisions (the Republican party is a political unit and a homeowner's association is a local agency). One mentions only municipalities—when local subdivision could include counties. One says a state authority can "provide local funds"—local funds? One mentions "a more active role on the part of states"—when we're talking abort only one state.

About the Contributors

The exercises in Part Four—and the suggested answers—were designed in part by my former partners, Lou Hampton and the late Charles E. "Chuck" Waterman. It was my privilege to work with them in Speak/Write Systems, Inc., where we shared in the seminar and consulting work of the company. (Lou Hampton left Speak/Write in 1983 to become president of his own firm.)

I greatly miss my long-time partner, Chuck Waterman, who received numerous awards both for his speaking abilities and for his management skills. In 1987, when I retired from Speak/Write Systems, Inc.—and from active seminar leadership—Chuck took over as president of the company. He served as the prime instructor and speech coach in all of the company's oral communication programs until his untimely death from cancer in 1995.

Recommended Reading

Amis, Kingsley. *The King's English: A Guide to Modern Usage.* New York: St. Martin's Press, 1998.

Crystal, David. *Encyclopedia of the English Language.* New York: Cambridge University Press, 1995.

Deimling, Paula, et al. *The Writer's Essential Desk Reference* (2d Ed.). Cincinnati: The Writer's Digest, 1996.

DK Illustrated Oxford Dictionary. New York: Oxford University Press and DK Publishing Company, 1998.

Fiske, Robert Hartwell. *Dictionary of Concise Writing.* Cincinnati: The Writer's Digest, 1996.

Flexner, Stuart Berg, and Ann H. Soukhanov. *Speaking Freely: A Guided Tour of American English.* New York: Oxford University Press, 1997.

Lunsford, Andrea, and Robert Connors. *The St. Martin's Handbook.* New York: St. Martin's Press, 1989.

McArthur, Tom, ed. *The Oxford Companion to the English Language,* New York: Oxford University Press, 1992.

O'Connor, Patricia T. *Woe Is I.* New York: G. P. Putnam Sons, 1996.

Rees Cheney, Theodore A. *Getting the Words Right: How to Revise, Edit & Rewrite.* Cincinnati: Writer's Digest Books, 1983.

Bibliography

STYLE MANUALS

For private industry, corporate executives, publishers, etc., the most respected style manual is undoubtedly—

The Chicago Manual of Style (14th Edition, Revised and Expanded), Chicago: University of Chicago Press, 1993.

For government employees, your usage "Bible" is—
GPO Style Manual, U.S. Government Printing Office, Washington, DC, 1984.
For journalists, there are several choices. Some of the most respected and widely used are—
The Associated Press Stylebook and Libel Manual (Revised Edition), Reading, MA: The Persian Press, 1998.
The *New York Times* and *Washington Post* stylebooks are listed below in the regular bibliography.
Writers in the U.S. armed services should also be familiar with the *GPO Manual*. In addition, I would recommend (for all services)—
Guide for Air Force Writing (AAF Pamphlet 13-2), Department of the Air Force, Headquarters, U.S. Air Force, Washington, DC, 1 November 1973. (This is the edition I still have from the olden days. There is

probably a later edition, but I suspect it may not be readily available to the general public.)

For students, it would be a good idea for you to have a look at all of the above, plus this very valuable and inexpensive guide—

Turabian, Kate L. *A Manual for Writers of Term Papers, Theses, and Dissertations*. Chicago: University of Chicago Press, 1996.

Now that these basic references are taken care of, the rest of the bibliography is in straight alphabetical order. The books listed are those I referred to in writing earlier editions of *WWP*. I have updated references, publishers, and dates, as thoroughly as I can.

Many of the referenced works are no longer in print, but you may be able to find them in your public library. (Wherever possible, I have indicated here whether they are still in print. I determined this by searching *Amazon.com* on the Internet. That company and others on the Net, may be willing to search them out for you on special order.)

Baker, Sheridan, and Robert Yarber. *The Practical Stylist: With Readings*. New York: Harper and Row, 1985. (Latest Edition: Addison-Wesley, 1997.)

Barzun, Jacques. *Simple and Direct*. New York: Harper and Row, 1975. (Latest edition: University of Chicago, 1994.)

———. *On Writing, Editing, and Publishing*. Chicago: The University of Chicago Press, 1986.

Bernstein, Theodore M. *The Careful Writer: A Modern Guide to English Usage*. New York: Macmillan, 1965. (Latest Edition, 1977, out of print)

———. *Miss Thistlebottom's Hobgoblins*. New York: Simon & Schuster, 1984. (out of print)

———. *Reverse Dictionary*. 2nd ed. New York: Times Books, 1988. (out of print)

———. *Watch Your Language*. New York: Macmillan, 1965. (out of print)

Birk, Newman P. and Genevieve B. Birk. *Understanding and Using English*. 5th ed. with Readings. New York: The Odyssey Press, Inc., 1972. (out of print)

Brady, John. *The Craft of Interviewing*. New York: Random House, 1977.

Brusaw, Charles T., Gerald J. Alred, and Walter E. Olin. *The Business Writer's Handbook*. New York: St. Martin's Press, 1975. (Latest edition, 1997)

Burnam, Tom. *The Dictionary of Misinformation*. New York: Ballantine Books, 1975. (out of print)

Buzan, Tony. *Use Both Sides of Your Brain*. New York: E. P. Dutton, Inc., 1983. (3rd Edition, 1991)

Chomsky, Noam. *Reflections on Language*. New York: Pantheon Books, 1975. (out of print)

Copperud, Roy H. *American Usage and Style: The Consensus*. New York: Van Nostrand, Reinhold Co., 1980. (out of print)

Cottam, Keith M., and Robert W. Pelton. *Writer's Research Handbook*. South Brunswick and New York: A. S. Barnes and Company, 1977. (out of print)

Cottle, Basil. *The Plight of English*. New Rochelle, NY: Arlington House, 1975. (out of print)

Crawford, Tad. *The Writer's Legal Guide*. New York: Hawthorn Books, Inc., 1977. (Latest edition, 1996)

Dean, Leonard F., Walker Gibson, and Kenneth D. Wilson. *The Play of Language*. New York: Oxford University Press, 1971. (out of print)

DeBono, Edward. *Wordpower*. New York: Harper Colophon Books, 1977.

Ehrlich, Eugene, and Daniel Murphy. *Basic Grammar for Writing*. McGraw Hill Book Company, 1967. (out of print)

Elbow, Peter. *Writing Without Teachers*. London, New York: Oxford University Press, 1973. (Latest edition, 1998)

Eschholz, Paul A., Alfred F. Rosa, and Virginia P. Park (edited by). *Language Awareness*. New York: St. Martin's Press, 1974. (Latest edition, 1998)

Evans, Bergen and Cornelia Evans. *A Dictionary of Contemporary American Usage*. New York: Delacorte Press, 1968. (out of print)

Flesch, Rudolph. *The Art of Plain Talk*. New York: Macmillan, 1985. (out of print)

———. *The Art of Readable Writing*. New York: Macmillan, 1986. (out of print)

———. *Say What You Mean*. New York: Harper and Row Publishers, Inc., 1972. (out of print)

Fleugelman, Andrew, and Jeremy Joan Hewes. *Writing in the Computer Age*. Garden City, NY: Anchor Books, 1983. (out of print)

Follett, Wilson. *Modern American Usage*. New York: Hill and Wang, 1966.

Fowler, H.W. *A Dictionary of Modern English Usage*. London: Oxford University Press, 1987. (Latest edition, 1997)

Fowler, H.W. and F.G. Fowler. *The King's English*. 3rd ed. London: Oxford University Press, 1985.

Fries, Charles Carpenter. *The Structure of English*. New York: Harcourt Brace & Co., 1952. (out of print)

Funk, Charles Earle. *Heavens to Betsy!* New York: Warner Paperback Library, 1972. (out of print)

Gordon, Karen Elizabeth. *The Well-Tempered Sentence*. New Haven: Ticknor & Fields, 1983. (Latest edition, 1993)

Gowers, Sir Ernest. *Plain Words*. New York: Alfred A. Knopf, 1954. (out of print)

Graves, Robert, and Alan Hodge. *The Reader Over Your Shoulder*. New York: The MacMillan Co., 1961. (Latest edition, 1979, out of print)

Gunning, Robert. *The Technique of Clear Writing*. New York: McGraw Hill, 1952. (out of print)

Guthrie, L.O. *Factual Communication*. New York: The Macmillan Company, 1948. (out of print)

Hall, Donald. *Writing Well*. 3rd ed. Boston: Little, Brown, 1979. (Latest edition, Addison-Wesley, 1997)

Henderson, Bruce. *How to Bullet-Proof Your Manuscript*. Cincinnati: Writer's Digest Books, 1986.

Hersey, John, ed. *The Writer's Craft*. New York: McGraw-Hill, 1973. (out of print)

Hicks, Tyler G. *Writing for Engineering and Science*. New York: McGraw-Hill, 1961. (out of print)

Hodges, John C., and Mary E. Whitten. *Harbrace College Handbook*. 7th ed. New York: Harcourt Brace Jovanovich, Inc., 1970.

Hogan, Robert, and Herbert Bogart. *The Plain Style*. New York: American Book Co., 1967.

Irmscher, William F. *The Holt Guide to English*. New York: Holt, Rinehart and Winston, Inc., 1972.

Jones, Virgil Carrington. *Gray Ghosts and Rebel Raiders*. New York: Holt, 1956.

Jones, W. Paul. *Writing Scientific and Technical Reports*. Dubuque, Iowa: Wm. C. Brown Company Publishers, 1971.

Jordan, Lewis. *New York Times Manual of Style and Usage*. New York: Times Books, 1982.

Kane, Thomas S. *The New Oxford Guide to Writing*. New York: Oxford University Press, 1988.

Kenin, Richard, and Justin Wintle. *The Dictionary of Biographical Quotations*. New York: Alfred A. Knopf, 1978.

Kidner, John. *The Kidner Report*. Rev. ed. Washington, DC: Acropolis Books Ltd., 1975. (out of print)

Kierzek, John M., and Walter Gibson. *The MacMillan Handbook of English*. 4th ed. New York: The MacMillan Company, 1960.

Kilpatrick, James J. *The Writer's Art*. Kansas City: Andrews, McMeel & Parker Inc., 1984.

Kredenser, Gail. *Write It Right*. New York: Barnes & Noble Books, Division of Harper & Row, Publishers, 1968.

Lefcowitz, Allan B. *The Writer's Handbook*. Englewood Cliffs, NJ: Prentice-Hall, Inc., 1976. (out of print)

Linton, Calvin D. *Effective Revenue Writing 2*. Training No. 129 (rev. 7–62), Washington DC: U.S. Government Printing Office, 1962. (out of print)

MacCampbell, Donald. *The Writing Business*. New York: Crown Publishers, Inc., 1978. (out of print)

Mack, Karin, and Eric Skjei. *Overcoming Writing Blocks*. Los Angeles: J. P. Taracher, Inc. (distributed by St. Martin's Press, NY), 1979. (out of print)

Martin, Phyllis. *Word Watcher's Handbook*. New York: David McKay Company, Inc., 1977. (out of print)

McCarthy, Colman. *Inner Companions*. Washington, DC: Acropolis Books Ltd., 1975. (out of print)

McCullo, Marion. *Proofreader's Manual*. New York: Richards Rosens Press Inc., 1969. (out of print)

McWilliams, Peter A. *The Word Processing Book*. Los Angeles: Prelude Press, 1983. (out of print)

Menning, J. H., and C. W. Wilkinson. *Communicating Through Letters and Reports*. 4th ed. Homewood, IL: Richard D. Irwin, Inc., 1967. (out of print)

Mitchell, John H. *Writing for Technical and Professional Journals*. New York: John Wiley & Sons, Inc., 1968. (out of print)

Mitchell, Richard (The Underground Grammarian). *Less Than Words Can Say*. Boston: Little, Brown & Co., 1979. (out of print)

Moore, Robert Hamilton. *Handbook of Effective Writing*. New York: Holt, Rinehart and Winston, 1966. (out of print)

Morris, William and Mary Morris. *Harper Dictionary of Contemporary Usage*. New York: Harper & Row, 1985. (out of print)

Morsberger, Robert E. *Commonsense Grammar and Style*. 2nd ed. New York: Thomas Y. Crowell Company, 1975. (out of print)

Mueller, Robert Kirk. *Buzzwords*. New York: Van Nostrand Reinhold Co., 1974. (out of print)

Munson, Gorham. *The Written Word: How to Write for Readers*. New York: Collier Books, 1949. (1st Collier Book edition, 1976)

Newman, Edwin. *A Civil Tongue*. New York: Warner Books, 1977. (out of print)

———. *Strictly Speaking*. New York: Warner Books, 1974. (out of print)

Nicholson, Margaret. *A Dictionary of Modern English Usage*, based on Fowler's *Modern English Usage*. New York: Signet Books (by arrangement with Oxford University Press, Inc.), 1959. (out of print)

Nuenberg, Maxwell. *Questions you always wanted to ask about grammar but were afraid to raise your hand*. Old Tappan, NJ: Washington Square Press, 1982.

O'Brien, Robert, and Joanne Soderman. *The Basic Guide to Research Sources.* New York: A Mentor Book—New American Library, 1975.

Opdycke, John B. *Harper's English Grammar.* New York: Warner Books, 1983.

Payton, Geoffrey (compiled by). *The Merriam-Webster Pocket Dictionary of Proper Names.* New York: Pocket Books, 1972.

Pei, Mario. *Doublespeak in America.* New York: Hawthorn Books, Inc., 1973.

Perlmutter, Jerome H. *A Practical Guide to Effective Writing.* New York: Delta Books, Dell Publishing Company, 1965. (out of print)

Peter, Dr. Lawrence J. *Peter's Quotations: Ideas for Our Time.* New York: Bantam Books, 1979. (out of print)

Pirsig, Robert M. *Zen and the Art of Motorcycle Maintenance.* New York: Bantam Books, 1976.

Pitkin, Walter B. *The Art of Useful Writing.* New York: Whittlesey House, McGraw Hill Book Co., Inc., 1940. (out of print)

Reader's Digest. Success With Words: A Guide To The American Language. Pleasantville, NY: The Reader's Digest Association, Inc., 1983. (out of print)

Rivers, William L. *Finding Facts.* Englewood Cliffs, NJ: Prentice-Hall, Inc., 1975.

———. *Writing: Craft and Art.* Englewood Cliffs, NJ: Prentice-Hall, Inc., 1975. (out of print)

Roberts, Paul. *English Sentences.* New York: Harcourt, Brace & World, 1962. (out of print)

Shaw, Harry. *Punctuate It Right!* New York: Harper and Row Perennial Library, 1986.

Sheehan, Paul D. *Reportorial Writing.* Radnor, PA: Chilton Book Co., 1972. (out of print)

Sheppard, Mona. *Plain Letters.* Washington, DC: U.S. Government Printing Office, 1955.

Shostak, Jerome. *Concise Dictionary of Current American Usage.* New York: Washington Square Press, Inc., 1968. (out of print)

Sisson, A. F. *Sisson's Word and Expression Locator.* West Nyack, NY: Prentice-Hall, 1966. (out of print)

Strunk, William, Jr., and E. B. White. *The Elements of Style.* 2nd ed. New York: MacMillan Publishing Co., Inc., 1972.

Turner, David R. *English Grammar and Usage for Test-Takers.* New York: Arco Publishing Company, 1976.

Venolia, Jan. *Write Right!* Berkeley, CA: Ten Speed Press, 1988. (Latest edition, 1995)

Webb, Robert A. (compiled and edited by). *The Washington Post Desk-*

book on Style. New York: McGraw-Hill Book Company, 1978. (out of print)

Wermuth, Paul C. *Modern Essays on Writing and Style*. New York: Holt, Rinehart & Winston, Inc., 1964, 1969.

Willis, Hulon. *Structure, Style, Usage: A Guide to Expository Writing*. New York: Holt, Rinehart and Winston, 1964. (out of print)

Wincor, Richard. *Contracts in Plain English*. New York: McGraw Hill, Inc., 1976. (out of print)

Wykoff, George S., and Harry Shaw. *The Harper Handbook*. 4th ed. New York: Harper & Row, Publishers, 1975. (out of print)

Ziegler, Isabelle. *The Creative Writer's Handbook* 2nd ed. New York: Barnes & Noble Books, a Division of Harper & Row, Publishers, 1975.

Zinsser, William. *On Writing Well: An Informal Guide to Writing Nonfiction*. New York: Harper & Row, 1985. (6th ed., 1998)

———. *Writing To Learn*. New York: Harper and Row, 1987. (out of print)

———. *Writing with a Word Processor*. New York: Harper and Row, 1983. (out of print)

Index